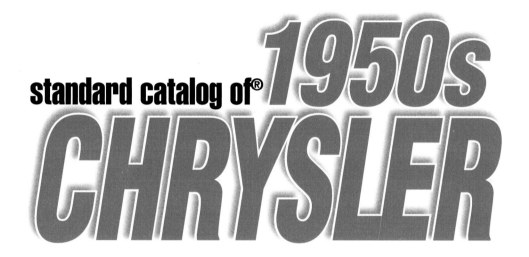

standard catalog of® **1950s CHRYSLER**

Jon G. Robinson

©2006 Krause Publications

Published by

krause publications

An Imprint of F+W Publications

700 East State Street • Iola, WI 54990-0001
715-445-2214 • 888-457-2873

Our toll-free number to place an order or obtain
a free catalog is (800) 258-0929.

Library of Congress Catalog Number: 2006932613

ISBN 13-digit: 978-0-89689-249-1
ISBN 10-digit: 0-89689-249-2

Designed by Kara Grundman
Edited by Tom Collins

Printed in the United States of America

CONTENTS

INTRODUCTION

POWER FOR SAFETY!

One of the classic looks of the era, the 1958 De Soto's three taillights and fin.

Welcome to the *Standard Catalog of® 1950s Chrysler!* Chet Krause founded his publishing company in 1952 for the enthusiast, collector, and investor, beginning with *Numismatic News.* Chet is an avid car enthusiast and, by the early-1970s, his weekly newspaper *Old Cars* was a hit among other car enthusiasts.

The *Standard Catalog of® American Cars, 1946-1975* made a splash when it came out in 1984. Krause Publications followed it quickly with the *Standard Catalog of® American Cars, 1805-1942,* and *Standard Catalogs* covering the period from 1975 and later have been constantly updated over the years. By 1990, Krause produced specialized, brand-specific versions beginning with the *Standard Catalog of® Chevrolet, 1912-1990.*

In the 21st century, F+W Publications has added Krause Publications to its stable of existing publishers. F+W believes in the *Standard Catalogs* and is taking these books to the next level by enhancing their informative, encyclopedic qualities with color photography, detailed shots, more informational tables and all-new feature articles. The year-by-year encyclopedia has expanded some with more detailed descriptions of the cars' features, personalities, and how they fit their times.

Most encyclopedic books attempt to present the absolute facts, but in the swirling world of automobile production, the facts can be hard to come by, leaving the encyclopedia to confirm the unconfirmable. A car company invested millions of dollars into producing a line of automobiles, and decades later, there are few or no records that the company even built the car. Previous editions in the *Standard Catalog* series deserve huge credit for the monumental task of establishing the first database of bare-bones information. The information has been added to, corrected, and confirmed over the years.

Is every production figure perfect? Is every shipping weight perfect? No, but the proportions are there.

Did a Chrysler leave the factory with an option that wasn't on the options list? It wasn't uncommon. Did a Chrysler from one year have a trim piece that didn't exist until the following year? It was quite possible, especially if the car was built at the end of the model-year run. And Chrysler Corporation also made variations in cars they introduced as "Spring Specials."

Did cars come with accessories that didn't belong on them? Yes, most often because dealers wound up with more accessories than cars, and would use them to enhance a sale. So a base model Plymouth was seen with full wheel covers that didn't belong on it.

The *Standard Catalogs* are not perfect, but they serve as reliable guides. They may not always hit the bull's-eye, but they always hit the target.

The memorable toothy grille of the 1950 De Soto.

The large fin and abbreviated taillight of the 1959 Chrysler.

The 1950s

1950 Chrysler on the road.

The 1950s began in the Jet Age and ended in the Space Age, with all of it reflected in the cars. American cars entered the 1950s with round taillights that imitated jet engines, and they left the 1950s with push-button dashboards and slanted radio antennas that imitated Sputnik. They entered the 1950s with aviation influences and left the 1950s with rocket streamlining. They began the 1950s with elegant, neutral-colored cloth interiors, and they ended the 1950s with bright, fashionable interiors influenced by the popular colors and fabrics of Paris fashion shows.

The 1950s had a downside. Nothing was more important socially than conforming and being modern. The throwaway car culture set in and the words "planned obsolescence" entered the American vocabulary.

Between 1900 and 1940, cars improved quickly and if a person traded in an older car for a newer one, he or she really got a better one. There really were good reasons for buying a new car from time to time. By the 1950s, having an older car just became a fashion-based embarrassment for many people. Cars were changing superficially and buyers flocked to the latest styling fad. They threw away good cars quickly.

On the other hand, a compilation of automotive reliability statistics from 1957 shows something interesting. The statistics report that automotive reliability increased tremendously from 1930 to 1940, but between 1946 and 1953, automotive reliability decreased terribly with engines and electrical systems being the biggest car-killers. All economy-class cars in the early 1950s still had engines from the 1930s, but they were challenged to keep up on America's growing freeway system. The improving roads were forcing early-1950s cars with 1930s engines and low-geared rear axle ratios to travel at 65 mph.

Chrysler's early 1950 six-cylinder and straight eight-cylinder engines had taken their final form in 1935. Chrysler's box-frame chassis construction had appeared in 1936 on their big cars and had been refined in 1940. This basic chassis served the corporation through 1956. The truth is that, under the skin, a 1956 Chrysler Corporation car is mostly 1937, even with the Forward Look, Flightsweep-inspired body.

The good news is that the components were technologically advanced enough to still serve the public well in the early 1950s. There were no dip-oiled engines as there were at Chevrolet, and there were no chronic problems like Ford's overheating.

Still, economy Dodges and Plymouths soon were up against freeway driving. Overdrive finally made a return at Dodge and Plymouth in 1952. The big cars got the hemi V-8s one by one through 1954. It wasn't until 1957 and the second wave of the "Forward Look," with Torsion-Aire front suspension and cars designed to handle freeway speeds approaching 75 to 80 mph, that Chrysler Corporation finally had a chassis that matched the engine, capable of the speed and endurance needed for the improving highway system. Chrysler had cars that matched the times.

The 1950s were optimistic, and the cars were optimistic. The teenagers of that time grew up through the tumult of the 1960s, the gas crunch of the 1970s, and the sad shadows of American cars in the 1980s. Often, they missed the cars of their youth.

The era was not perfect, with segregation, the H-bomb, McCarthyism, and a growing youth delinquency, but in spite of those problems, the times were really good and life seemed to be getting better for the average American family.

There were good reasons to think the problems would get better, too. Cars from the 1950s reminded Americans of their country at its best. The cars were not just transportation. They were color television, chrome kitchens, and hi-fi. They were Dave Brubeck, Truman Capote, and *Playhouse 90*. They showed the world that free Americans, who grew up in the Depression and won the war, could now have new home, often in growing suburbs, and even two cars on one family income.

Plymouth was in reach for the low-income family—while Dodge, De Soto, Chrysler and Imperial each reflected a step on the ladder of economic achievement.

The *Standard Catalog* series puts authoritative automotive information and history within the reach of the low-income person, too. Hopefully, the information and history in the *Standard Catalog of 1950s Chrysler* will help someone who wants to preserve a Chrysler product in its original condition decide which car to get and what part it played in the Jet Age, the Space Age—and now in the 21st century.

The late Forward Look front end of the 1959 Dodge.

CHRYSLER

*Clockwise: The 1950 New Yorker dash has colors keyed to the car's
exterior and is brightly finished with chrome.*

*The chrome strips were used on the three-piece back windows on
some Chryslers and Imperials in 1950 and 1951.*

Chrysler featured a stylized hood ornament on its 1950 models.

Chrysler's logo symbolized excellence in the 1950 automotive world.

1950-1959

Chrysler entered 1949 with high, square bodies that flew in the face of the Jet Age. The good news was that Chrysler's interiors were larger. They retained "chair-high" seats Chrysler's intrepid engineering team had developed with the Airflow design of the 1930s. Walter P. Chrysler himself had dictated that a large man should be able to ride comfortably in his car with his hat on.

The flashy 1950
Chrysler New
Yorker sedan.

Kaufman Thuma (K. T.) Keller mentioned the hat-wearing public in a speech at the Stanford University School of Business in the summer of 1948.

"Many of you Californians have outgrown the habit, but there are parts of the country, containing millions of people, where both the men and the ladies are in the habit of getting behind the wheel, or in the back seat, wearing hats," author Beverly Rae Kimes recalled in a 1968 *Automobile Quarterly* article.

"Company executives used to stand in dread of Mr. Keller's knocking off his hat while entering a Chrysler-built car," observed writer Jeffrery Godshall in a later *A. Q.* article about the Dodge Wayfarer.

Given his proclivity for sitting in for hours with designers, as recalled by Bill Miller, a retired Senior Modeler at the Chrysler Design Office, it's no wonder the height of the postwar Chrysler models grew an inch. "He wanted his way and usually got it," observed Miller. Keller even dismissed some competitive styling, calling some postwar designs the "Jell-O school of design."

So Chrysler's 1949 design theme was not in keeping with the lower, sleeker, fa hardtop bodies from General Motors,* but from behind the wheel, a Chrysler was easily the most comfortable car on the road, and Chrysler steering and braking were second to none.

*Ironically, Chrysler may have pioneered the two-door hardtop had the corporation decided to put them into production in 1946 or 1947. Seven 1946 Town and Country hardtop pilot models were produced. But the classic wood-bodied Chrysler T & C convertibles and lesser numbers of production sedan versions overshadowed the two-door hardtop concept. When the General Motors two-door hardtops arrived with the 1949 model year, GM all but ignored Chrysler's earlier hardtop efforts. Chrysler Corporation then built one more prototype Town and Country two-door hardtop in 1949. That one became their 1950 production models.

A minor facelift of the 1949 models centered around a bolder, heavier-looking egg-crate grille treatment and blade-like front and rear bumpers. License plate location changed from the deck lid to the center of the rear bumper, and the multi-purpose device that combined the license plate housing, brake light, backup light, license plate light, and trunk handle disappeared from all of Chrysler Corporation's cars. These large, obtrusive units had been in good stead with the ornate Art Deco era, but Chrysler was wise to clean up the styling for 1950. Chrysler's taillights flared flush into the rear fenders, and the backup lights did not protrude very far from the surface between the rear fender and the trunk lid. All Chrysler Corporation cars enlarged their rear windows in 1950, but the Chrysler had two chrome strips down the outer edges to create a three-piece back window that appeared to be a deliberate shot at Cadillac.

Chrysler continued its model names from the 1940s. Chrysler divided its cars into two series—six-cylinder and eight-cylinder. The Royal was the low-priced six, and the Windsor was the high-priced six. The Saratoga was the low-priced eight, and the New Yorker was the high-priced eight. The difference between the high-priced and low-priced cars was mostly noticeable inside where the high-priced cars had upholstery, and dashboards were color-coordinated with the exterior colors. The low-priced cars were comfortable, but the interiors were less fancy and not color-coordinated. Chrysler's dashboard was the only place the Jet Age showed on the car. The Chrysler dash put an aircraft-inspired instrument pod in front of the driver, sitting on top of the steering column, something like a similar pod in Nash's "Airflyte."

Chryslers and De Sotos continued the Feather-Light steering from 1949. With it, the steering gear sat on its side on the frame and the pitman arm swung front-to-back instead of side-to-side. The pitman arm's series of connections to the tie rods added leverage and eased steering effort.

The Chryslers compared better to competition within their own price range than they did with sleeker, more streamlined and less expensive cars. The Chrysler looked square and high compared to GM's fastback cars, but when compared to a 1950 Cadillac sedan, Chrysler models compared well.

The 1950 Chrysler Windsor club coupe was a high-end six-cylinder car that shared its flashy, color-coordinated interior with the New Yorker.

ROYAL SERIES — (6-CYLINDER): This was the last year for the Royal nameplate. Royal nameplates were found on the front fender, behind the wheelhouse opening and below the horizontal trim molding.

The "Town & Country" station wagon was not a part of the wood-trimmed Town & Country hardtop and convertible series, which was built on the New Yorker chassis. This wagon came on the six-cylinder chassis carried over 1949 styling except for offering a different configuration for the rear spare tire embossed tailgate. No longer was the emboss visible from the exterior. Also continued was ash paneled trim, bolted onto the steel body. Later, a new all-steel station wagon body was introduced as a running addition.

CHRYSLER I.D. NUMBERS: Serial numbers were located, as in previous models, on the left door hinge post. Engine numbers were found on the left side of the block below the cylinder head between the first and second cylinders. [Royal] Detroit-built serial numbers ran 70058001 to 70079351. Los Angeles-built Royals used serial number 65004001 to 65063318. Engine numbers ran from C48-1001 to C48-133824. [Windsor] Detroit production numbers ran from 70794001 to 70889370. Los Angeles serial numbers ran from 67011001 to 67024682. Engine numbers for all six-cylinder cars started at C48-1001 and ended with C48-133824. [Saratoga] Saratogas were built only in Detroit. Serial numbers were 6774501 to 6775800. Engine numbers on the eights ranged upward from C49-1001 to C49-43041. [New Yorker] Serial numbers ranged from 7119001 to 7159341. Town & Country numbers ran from 7411501 to 7412201. Engine numbers were C49-1001 to C49-43041.

The six-cylinder 1950 Chryslers had a painted panel with a rectangular parking light.

Royal Series

Model Number	Body/Style Number	Body Type & Seating	Factory Price	Shipping Weight	Production Total
Standard Wheelbase					
C48S	N/A	2-dr Club Coupe-6P	$2,114	3,540 lbs.	5,900
C48S	N/A	4-dr Sedan-6P	$2,154	3,610 lbs.	17,713
Long Wheelbase					
C48S	N/A	4-dr Sedan-8P	$2,855	4,190 lbs.	375
C48S	N/A	4-dr T&C Station Wagon	$2,735	3,964 lbs.	599
C48S	N/A	4-dr Station Wagon-6P	$3,163	4,055 lbs.	100

Chrysler was fast becoming a leader in all-steel station wagons and the woodie era was ending quickly. Still, the Chrysler Royal station wagon was a handsome package.

WINDSOR SERIES — (6-CYLINDER): Traditionally an upgraded Royal, the Windsor line now had a different selection of body styles to offer. No station wagon was available. A Traveler sedan melded sedan styling with the utility of a station wagon. The floor extended from rear deck lid to the back of the front seat when the rear seat was folded forward. The Traveler, while not popular, included a Town & Country-style roof rack. Big news this year was the Newport two-door hardtop, which featured a new roofline and wraparound three-piece rear window. Windsors were available in more colors than Royals, and the interior was color-coordinated with the exterior.

Windsor Series

Model Number	Body/Style Number	Body Type & Seating	Factory Price	Shipping Weight	Production Total
Standard Wheelbase					
C48W	N/A	2-dr Club Coupe-6P	$2,306	3,670 lbs.	20,050
C48W	N/A	4-dr Sedan-6P	$2,329	3,765 lbs.	78,199
C48W	N/A	2-dr Convertible-6P	$2,741	3,905 lbs.	2,201
C48W	N/A	2-dr Newport-6P	$2,637	3,875 lbs.	9,925
C48W	N/A	4-dr Traveler-6P	$2,560	3,830 lbs.	900
Long Wheelbase					
C48W	N/A	4-dr Sedan-8P	$3,050	4,295 lbs.	763
C48W	N/A	4-dr Limousine-8P	$3,176	4,400 lbs.	174

SARATOGA SERIES — (8-CYLINDER): The Saratoga was the eight-cylinder equivalent of a Royal, but it had a longer hood and front fenders, necessitated by the longer eight-cylinder engine and stainless steel facia surrounding the parking lamps beside the grille. Only two body styles were offered in this low-line eight series.

Saratoga Series

Model Number	Body/Style Number	Body Type & Seating	Factory Price	Shipping Weight	Production Total
C49K	N/A	2-dr Club Coupe-6P	$2,616	4,110 lbs.	300
C49K	N/A	4-dr Sedan-6P	$2,642	4,170 lbs.	1,000

NEW YORKER SERIES — (8-CYLINDER): This became the last year for the Chrysler inline eight that began production on the 1931 Series CD-8. The high-line New Yorker used all wool carpeting and offered a larger selection of interior fabrics and colors than the comparable Saratoga. The Newport two-door hardtop was another first for Chrysler, although, seven hardtops had been manufactured as Town & Country semi-customs in 1946. Newport shared body shells with the convertible.

The Town & Country was now produced as a Newport only and 1950 was to be the last year for wood-trimmed cars from Chrysler. Bodies were all-steel with wood trim added as in 1949. Tail lamps were unlike other 1950 series Chryslers, but were more closely akin to the 1949 Town & Country. The rear bumper no longer wrapped around the rear fender as in 1949. The back-up light was now placed on Town & Country's rear deck and the license plate frame was now mounted to the rear bumper as on other 1950 Chryslers. Rear fender trim was also mounted in a higher position than on other 1950 Chryslers. Panels between the ash-wood structure were painted body color.

New Yorker Series

Model Number	Body/Style Number	Body Type & Seating	Factory Price	Shipping Weight	Production Total
C49N	N/A	2-dr Club Coupe-6P	$2,732	4,110 lbs.	3,000
C49N	N/A	4-dr Sedan-6P	$2,756	4,190 lbs.	22,633
C49N	N/A	2-dr Convertible-6P	$3,236	4,360 lbs.	899
C49N	N/A	2-dr Newport-6P	$3,133	4,370 lbs.	2,800
C49N	N/A	4-dr Wood Wagon	—	—	1
C49N	N/A	Chassis	—	—	2
C49N	N/A	2-dr Town & Country Newport	$4,003	4,670 lbs.	700

ROYAL/WINDSOR ENGINE: L-head six-cylinder. Cast iron block. Displacement: 250.6 cid. Bore and stroke: 3.438 x 4.50 inches. Compression ratio: 7.0:1. Brake hp: 116 at 3600 rpm. Five main bearings.

SARATOGA/NEW YORKER ENGINE: L-head eight-cylinder. Cast iron block. Displacement: 323.5 cid. Bore and stroke: 3.25 x 4.875 inches. Compression ratio: 7.25:1. Five main bearings. Brake hp: 135 at 3200 rpm.

CHASSIS FEATURES: Wheelbase: (New Yorker/Saratoga) 131.5 inches; (Royal/Windsor) 125.5 inches; (long wheelbase models) 139.5 inches. Overall length: (New Yorker/Saratoga) 214-⅛ inches; (station wagons) 214-⅛ inches; (long wheelbase models) 222-¼ inches; (standard Royal/Windsor) 208-½ inches. Tires: (station wagons and long wheelbase models) 8.20 x 15-inch; (all other models) 7.60 x 15-inch.

CONVENIENCE OPTIONS: White sidewall tires. Wing vent wind deflectors. Exhaust deflector. Radio. Heater. Locking gas cap. Weatherproof ignition. Mopar Auto Compass. Windshield washer. Spare tire valve extension. A brand new option, for eights only, was electrically operated power window lifts.

HISTORICAL FOOTNOTES: Dealer introduction for 1950 Chrysler was Jan. 5, 1950. The Town & Country Newport hardtop was added to the line May 23, 1950.

The beautiful 1950 Chrysler Town & Country Newport

Chrysler still resisted Jet Age styling, but a flatter hood and disappearance of the egg-crate grille helped the car look a little more modern. The Chrysler really didn't have a true grille in 1951 but, rather, only had two long, large slots divided in the middle by a center-piece with a Chrysler blue-ribbon logo. Parking lights were now located directly below the headlights within the top grille molding. The top grille molding also wrapped completely around the front end and ran rearward to the middle of the front door. The three-piece rear window now wrapped around the rear roof area, emulating the style and theme of the 1950 Newport hardtop. Rear styling essentially duplicated the 1950 Chrysler, with the exception of a new bumper design. Windsor nameplates were located on the front fenders, above the trim moldings.

Chrysler used the same instrument cluster but mounted it flatter against the dash so the cluster no longer sat atop the steering column.

Production of this series ran for two model years (18 months). Production figures for 1951 and 1952 are combined as a two-year total.

The big news was the introduction of the hemispherical V-8 and Fluid Torque. The "hemi" was a born legend, and its performance quickly rivaled the Oldsmobile Rocket V-8s and Cadillac's worthy overhead-valve V-8.

Chrysler still did not have a fully automatic transmission to hook to the hemi, but Chrysler did introduce Fluid Torque transmission. It was a modern torque converter which transmitted power much more efficiently than the original Fluid Drive that still lurked behind the six-cylinder engines that operated on centrifugal force alone.

WINDSOR SERIES — (6-CYLINDER): The Royal line was dropped from the Chrysler fold and the Windsor became the low-priced series with both the characteristics of the previous Royal and Windsor. It was more sparely styled on the interior than the New Yorker. This was the last year the corporation used the 251 cubic-inch six-cylinder engine in a Chrysler, but it would live on three more years in De Sotos.

Town & Country station wagons were a part of the Windsor series. The Windsor did not trim the grille openings or grille divider and only had two big bars above and below the openings. The Windsor front treatment was very plain even for the lowest-priced model of a relatively expensive marque.

While the Chrysler Saratoga carried the same new V-8, it was on the shorter chassis than this New Yorker, one shared by De Soto and six-cylinder Chryslers.

Dick Romm

CHRYSLER I.D. NUMBERS: Serial numbers were located on the left front door hinge post. Engine numbers were located on the left side of the block below the cylinder head, between the first and second cylinders. Only serial numbers were used for identification purposes. [Windsor] Detroit-built cars used numbers 70081001 to 70094148. Los Angeles-built cars used numbers 65007001 to 65008808. Engine numbers ranged from C51-1001 to C51-84487. [Windsor Deluxe] Detroit-built cars were numbered 70891001 to 70952163. Los Angeles-built cars were numbered 67026001 to 67033209. Engine numbers used the same prefix as on Windsors. [Saratoga] Detroit-built cars had numbers 76500001 to 76511983. Los Angeles-built cars had numbers 66500001 to 66501672. Engine numbers began with C51-8-1001 and up. [New Yorker] Serial numbers for the New Yorkers ranged from 7165001 to 7199806. Engine numbers used the C51-8 prefix. New Yorkers were manufactured in Detroit only.

Windsor Series

Model Number	Body/Style Number	Body Type & Seating	Factory Price	Shipping Weight	Production Total
Standard Wheelbase					
C51	N/A	2-dr Club Coupe-6P	$2,368	3,570 lbs.	Note 1
C51	N/A	4-dr Sedan-6P	$2,390	3,627 lbs.	Note 1
C51	N/A	4-dr Station Wagon	$3,063	3,965 lbs.	Note 1
C51	N/A	4-dr Ambulance	—	—	(153)
Long Wheelbase					
C51	N/A	4-dr Sedan-8P	$3,197	4,145 lbs.	Note 1

The large three-piece back window, unique to Imperials and hardtops in the 1950 Chrysler Corporation lines, spread to all 1951 Chrysler sedans and club coupes.

Dick Romm

NOTE 1: *Production totals are for 1951 1952 combined. See the 1952 chart.*

WINDSOR DELUXE SERIES — (6-CYLINDER): This top-of-the-line six was identified externally by the use of a Windsor Deluxe nameplate on the front fender, above the wheelhouse opening. Presto-matic transmission was standard on this model. The Traveler model continued in this series with the same features as the 1950 Traveler, but the luggage rack became an optional feature. Windsor Deluxes seemed to have more color-coordination on the interiors than the Windsor had in the previous years.

Windsor Deluxe Series

Model Number	Body/Style Number	Body Type & Seating	Factory Price	Shipping Weight	Production Total
Standard Wheelbase					
C51-2	N/A	2-dr Club Coupe-6P	$2,585	3,700 lbs.	(8,365)
C51-2	N/A	4-dr Sedan-6P	$2,608	3,775 lbs.	Note 1
C51-2	N/A	4-dr Traveler-6P	$2,867	3,890 lbs.	(850)
C51-2	N/A	2-dr Convertible-6P	$3,071	3,845 lbs.	Note 1
C51-2	N/A	2-dr Newport-6P	$2,953	3,855 lbs.	Note 1
Long Wheelbase					
C51-2	N/A	4-dr Sedan-8P	$3,416	4,295 lbs.	(720)
C51-2	N/A	4-dr Limousine-8P	$3,537	4,415 lbs.	(152)

NOTE 1: *Production totals are for 1951-1952 combined. See the 1952 chart.*

The eight-cylinder 1951 Chryslers had a large band of bright metal around the front corners of the car with a large rectangular parking light inside.

An updated 1940s Chrysler tradition was available in the 1951 Chrysler New Yorker. It was the plaid Highlander trim. Dick Romm

SARATOGA SERIES — (8-CYLINDER): The Saratoga combined the New Yorker hemi V-8 with the lighter, smaller, six-cylinder Windsor chassis. The big-engine/small chassis concept harked back to the prewar Buick Century that dropped the big Roadmaster straight-eight into the small Special body. The Saratoga's wheelbase was a full six inches shorter than the Hemi-engined New Yorker, while weight was about 250 pounds less than the longer series, and this, of course, was the car that Chrysler took to Daytona. The Saratoga was a late addition to the line and was introduced to the public more than three months after other 1951 Chryslers. Saratoga nameplates were located on the front fenders and a new "V" ornament graced the hood and deck lid. Presto-matic semi-automatic transmission was standard equipment. A Town & Country station wagon was a part of this series and was the first Chrysler wagon with a V-8.

The eight-cylinder Chryslers also trimmed the grille openings with solid plates of chrome, which gave the front treatment of the car a much more finished look than the six-cylinder models.

The 1951 Chrysler hood ornament was a unique circle that appeared almost like a handle.

Saratoga Series

Model Number	Body/Style Number	Body Type & Seating	Factory Price	Shipping Weight	Production Total
Standard Wheelbase					
C55	N/A	2-dr Club Coupe-6P	$2,989	3,948 lbs.	Note 1
C55	N/A	4-dr Sedan-8P	$3,016	4,018 lbs.	Note 1
C55	N/A	Town & Country Wagon-6P	$3,681	4,310 lbs.	Note 1
Long Wheelbase					
C55	N/A	4-dr Sedan-8P	$3,912	4,465 lbs.	Note 1
C55	N/A	4-dr Limousine-8P	$4,240	—	Note 2

NOTE 1: *Production totals for 1951-1952 combined; see 1952 chart.*

NOTE 2: *Special order.*

NEW YORKER SERIES — (8-CYLINDER): With the Saratoga being a late-arrival, the New Yorker really was the first V-8 Chrysler. Many Chrysler enthusiasts think of the New Yorker as the top-of-the-line Chrysler while the Imperial is thought of as above-top-of-the-line. The New Yorker wheelbase was longer than the Windsor or Saratoga models by six inches. Cars with V-8 power

In 1951, the Chrysler taillight was small, square and practical.

in the Chrysler lines were identified by large "V" ornaments on the hood and deck lid. New Yorker nameplates were placed on the front fenders. Power steering was an industry first and Oriflow shock absorbers were now available. Styling changes were basically limited to the area in front of the cowl. Grille changes consisted of a heavily chromed look with a chromed centerpiece. There was a new location for the parking lights below the headlamps, and a chrome panel separated the two grille bars on each fender. Side trim on the rear fender began above the stone shield, then dipped abruptly before continuing horizontally to the rear. Town & Country rear fenders matched those of the Windsor and Saratoga in design. The dash panel continued its padded design and remained similar to the 1949 type.

There was a stately look to the front of the 1951 Chrysler line.

New Yorker Series

Model Number	Body/Style Number	Body Type & Seating	Factory Price	Shipping Weight	Production Total
C52	N/A	2-dr Club Coupe-6P	$3,348	4,145 lbs.	(3,533)
C52	N/A	4-dr Sedan-6P	$3,378	4,260 lbs.	Note 1
C52	N/A	2-dr Convertible-6P	$3,916	4,460 lbs.	Note 1
C52	N/A	2-dr Newport-6P	$3,798	4,330 lbs.	Note 1
C52	N/A	Town & Country Wagon-6P	$4,026	4,455 lbs.	(251)

NOTE 1: *Production totals for 1951 and 1952 models were recorded as a single total, with no model year breakout available except as shown for some 1951 models.*

SIX-CYLINDER ENGINES: L-head. Cast iron block. Displacement: 250.6 cid. Bore and stroke: 3.438 x 4.50 inches. Compression ratio: 7.0:1. Brake hp: 116 at 3600 rpm. Five main bearings. Solid lifters. Carburetor: B-B E9A1 with Fluid Drive and M-6 transmission.

HEMI V-8 ENGINE: Overhead valve. Displacement: 331.1 cid. Bore and stroke: 3.81 x 3.63 inches. Brake hp: 180 at 4000 rpm. Five main bearings. Hydraulic valve lifters. Compression ratio: 7.5:1. Carburetors: Early cars used Carter WCD 830S, 830SA, 830SB or 931 SC. Later cars used Carter WCD 931 S, 931 SA, 931 SB or 931 SC.

CHASSIS FEATURES: Wheelbase: (New Yorker) 131.5 inches; (Windsor/Windsor Deluxe/Saratoga) 125.5 inches. Long wheelbase models measured 139.5 inches. Tire size: 7.60 x 15-inch for Windsor and Windsor Deluxe short wheelbase and 8.20 x 15-inch for long wheelbase. Saratoga used 8.00 x 15-inch and 8.20 x 15-inch tires for long wheelbase. New Yorkers used size 8.20 x 15-inch tires. Windsor and Windsor Deluxe were 202.5 inches overall. Saratogas were 207.8 inches in overall length.

CONVENIENCE OPTIONS: White sidewall tires. Electric window lifts. Sun visor. Radio. Heater. Power steering. Fluid-Torque Drive. Exhaust deflector. Locking gas cap. Windshield washer. Fog lamps. Outside rearview mirror. Vanity mirror.

HISTORICAL FOOTNOTES: Dealer introduction of 1951 Chryslers was scheduled for Feb. 9, 1951. On a calendar year basis, total 1951 production was 165,000 units of which 78,000 were six-cylinder powered and 87,000 had the new Firepower V-8 installed. Also on a calendar year basis for 1951, Chrysler manufactured approximately 4,000 convertibles, 14,460 two-door hardtops and 1,950 station wagons. (Note: It should be pointed out that calendar and model years were nearly concurrent at this time, as opposed to the system in use today).

Chrysler was voted *Motor Trend* "Car of the Year" in 1951 and was the Indianapolis 500 Pace Car that year. The Chrysler also was awarded first place among cars tested by *Consumer Reports* late in 1951. In a test among a Chrysler New Yorker and a Cadillac 62, an Olds 98, a Hudson Hornet and a Packard 200, the Chrysler finished first in a nine-percent grade climb while averaging 17.5 mpg.

Ready to enjoy a sunny day is this 1952 Chrysler Windsor Deluxe convertible.

The 1952 Chrysler was a rerun of the 1951 models so completely that their serial numbers and production totals are combined into a single two-model-year-long series. One of the only distinctions between the two years is that the backup lights were no longer separate units and were combined into the taillight.

WINDSOR SERIES — (6-CYLINDER): A continuation of the 1951 Windsor series carried forward with only a minor change in tail lamp design. The six-cylinder engine was given a longer stroke for more torque and horsepower.

CHRYSLER I.D. NUMBERS: Serial numbers were located on the left front door hinge post. Engine numbers were located on the left side of the block below the cylinder head, between the first and second cylinders. Only serial numbers were used for identification purposes. [Windsor] Detroit-built cars had numbers from 70094301 to 70103232. Los Angeles-built cars had numbers 65008901 to 65009895. Engine numbers continued with the C52 prefix. [Windsor Deluxe] Detroit-built cars used numbers 70952301 to 70936308 and Los Angeles-built cars used numbers 67033301 to 67036059. [Saratoga] Detroit-built cars used numbers 76512101 to 76593089 and Los Angeles-built cars used 66501801 to 66505363. Engine number prefix was C52-8. [New Yorker] 1952 production runs began with car number 7199901 and ended with car number 7217301. Engine number prefix was C52-8.

Windsor Series

Model Number	Body/Style Number	Body Type & Seating	Factory Price	Shipping Weight	Production Total
Standard Wheelbase					
C51-1	N/A	2-dr Club Coupe-6P	$2,475	3,550 lbs.	6,735
C51-1	N/A	4-dr Sedan-6P	$2,498	3,640 lbs.	16,112
C51-1	N/A	Town & Country Wagon-6P	$3,200	4,015 lbs.	1,967
Long Wheelbase					
C51-1	N/A	4-dr Sedan-8P	$3,342	4,145 lbs.	633

NOTE 1: *Production totals are combined 1951-1952 output, with no breakouts, except as shown in 1951 Windsor section.*

A period photo shows the 1952 Chrysler New Yorker convertible

WINDSOR DELUXE SERIES — (6-CYLINDER): For the 1952 model year, the club coupe was dropped, as well as the Traveler and eight-passenger sedans in this series. Interior appointments were slightly upgraded over the Windsor series.

Windsor Deluxe Series

Model Number	Body/Style Number	Body Type & Seating	Factory Price	Shipping Weight	Production Total
C51-2	N/A	4-dr Sedan-6P	$2,727	3,775 lbs.	75,513
C51-2	N/A	2-dr Coupe-6P	$3,210	3,990 lbs.	4,200
C51-2	N/A	2-dr Newport-6P	$3,087	3,855 lbs.	10,200
C51-2	N/A	2-dr Convertible-6P	$3,230	3,945 lbs.	4,200

NOTE 1: *Production totals are combined 1951-1952 output, with no breakouts, except as shown in 1951 Windsor Deluxe section.*

SARATOGA SERIES — (8-CYLINDER): This series continued with virtually no changes from the 1951 model. The tail lamp design with integral back-up lamp was the major styling change.

Saratoga Series

Model Number	Body/Style Number	Body Type & Seating	Factory Price	Shipping Weight	Production Total
Standard Wheelbase					
C55	N/A	2-dr Club Coupe-6P	$3,187	3,948 lbs.	8,501
C55	N/A	4-dr Sedan-6P	$3,215	4,010 lbs.	35,516
C55	N/A	Town & Country Wagon-6P	$3,925	4,345 lbs.	1,299
C55	N/A	4-dr Ambulance	—	—	1
Long Wheelbase					
C55	N/A	4-dr Sedan-6P	$4,172	4,570 lbs.	183

NOTE 1: *Production totals are combined 1951-1952 output, with no breakouts, except as shown in 1951 Saratoga section.*

NOTE 2: *One hardtop with New Yorker body is included in the total for Club Coupe.*

> "There are few American cars on the road today that can match the punch of the Chrysler Saratoga."
>
> *Walt Moron, Motor Trend, October 1952*

NEW YORKER SERIES — (8-CYLINDER): New Yorker design was a continuation of the 1951 model with the only styling change paralleling other 1951 and 1952 changes in the tail lamps. The Club Coupe and Town & Country bodies were dropped with the onset of 1952 production.

New Yorker Series

Model Number	Body/Style Number	Body Type & Seating	Factory Price	Shipping Weight	Production Total
C52	N/A	4-dr Sedan-6P	$3,530	4,260 lbs.	40,415
C52	N/A	2-dr Convertible-6P	$4,033	4,460 lbs.	2,200
C52	N/A	2-dr Newport-6P	$3,969	4,325 lbs.	5,800
C52	N/A	Chassis	—	—	1

NOTE 1: *Production totals are combined 1951-1952 output, with no breakouts, except as shown in 1951 New Yorker section.*

SIX-CYLINDER ENGINE: L-head. Cast iron block. Displacement: 264.5 cid. Bore and stroke: 3.438 x 4.75 inches. Compression ratio: 7.0:1. Brake hp: 119 at 3600 rpm. Five main bearings. Carburetors: (with Fluid Drive and M-6 transmission) B-B E9A1 Carter or Stromberg 380349.

HEMI V-8 ENGINE: Overhead valve with hemispherical combustion chamber. Displacement: 331.1 cid. Bore and stroke: 3.81 x 3.63 inches. Brake hp: 180 at 4000 rpm. Five main bearings. Hydraulic valve lifters. Compression ratio: 7.5:1. Carburetors: Carter WCD 931 S, 931 SA, 931 SB or 931 SC.

CHASSIS FEATURES: Wheelbase: (New Yorker) 131.5 inches; (Windsor/Windsor Deluxe/Saratoga standard wheelbase) 125.5 inches, (long wheelbase models) 139.5 inches. Tire size: (Windsor/Windsor Deluxe) 7.60 x 15-inch and 8.20 x 15-inch tires for long wheelbase; (Saratoga) 8.00 x 15-inch on the standard wheelbase and 8.20 x 15-inch tires for the long wheelbase while New Yorker used 8.20 x 15-inch tires.

CONVENIENCE OPTIONS: White sidewall tires. Electric window lifts. Sun visor. Radio. Heater. Power steering. Fluid-Torque Drive. Exhaust deflector. Spare tire valve extension. Locking gas cap. Windshield washer. Fog lamps. Outside rearview mirror. Vanity mirror. Solex glass (1952 only). Power brakes.

HISTORICAL FOOTNOTES: The 1952 Chrysler line was introduced in dealer showrooms on Dec. 14, 1951. Chrysler received OPS (Office of Price Stability) permission to raise prices on Feb. 11, 1952, as was necessary in the Korean War era. Calendar year production was registered at 120,678 units. Model year production or sales totals for 1952 Chryslers were not reported as single year figures, but only as a combined total with cars sold as 1951 models. On a calendar year basis, Chrysler was estimated to have turned out 8,337 two-door hardtops; 2,793 convertibles; and 1,942 station wagons built to 1952 model specifications. (Note: Model years and calendar years were nearly concurrent at this time). On a calendar year basis, Chrysler manufactured approximately 46,491 six-cylinder 1952 models and 70,206 cars carrying the new Firepower V-8 engine. (All figures above include Imperials, which are covered in the Imperial section of this catalog). Power steering was available on sixes this year.

Chrysler introduced a much more stylistically modern car in 1953. Its design competed much better with those from General Motors. In silhouette, the '53 Chrysler looked very much like a Buick. Chrysler president K.T. Keller had insisted that a Chrysler remained comfortable regardless of popular styling themes. The '53 Chryslers and De Sotos accomplished this goal well. The sloping roofline proportions were such that the roof appeared lower, while interior head room remained cavernous and allowed the continuation of Chrysler's comfortable chair-high seats. The one-piece curved windshield was the first since the Chrysler model CW Imperial Airflow of 1934-1937. The rear fenders were higher and carried the taillights optimistically high. The four-door sedan doors were longer. While the rear fenders still carried the bulge that was the ghost of the pre-war era when rear fenders were bolted on, the front part of that bulge opened with the rear doors in a more modern way. The three-piece rear window of 1951 and 1952 was cleverly fitted into the new roofline.

1953 Chrysler New Yorker sedan

Curiously, Chrysler did not give this new car a new grille. It still had the two long, open slots, and the Windsor still had no trim in the grille, leaving the space between the upper and lower grille bars empty with an ungainly vacancy. The car also retained the pretty but aging 1949 dash, although, it was flattened like the 1951 models.

The Club Coupe now became more sedan-like in style while all station wagons and eight-passenger cars continued to use the 1951 and 1952 rear fenders including trim and tail lamps. The gas filler was now located below the deck lid on the left side, except on those models using the earlier style fender. PowerFlite, a fully automatic two-speed transmission, debuted near the end of the model year. Chromed wire wheels made their debut after a hiatus of 20 years. The Windsor remained the low-price Chrysler offering.

Some think of Chrysler as having downsized in 1953, but all the company really did was eliminate the extra-long New Yorker wheelbase. The Windsors and New Yorkers all road on the same 125-inch wheelbase that the six-cylinder cars used from 1949 on. This wheelbase still made Chryslers and De Sotos longer than much of their competition, and their ride was very comfortable.

WINDSOR SERIES — (6-CYLINDER): Other than the one-piece windshield, the Windsor looked much as it had in 1951 and '52 when looked at straight on from the front. There was still no trim around the two slot-like grille openings, leaving the front of the car looking unfinished.

CHRYSLER I.D. NUMBERS: The serial number was found on the left door hinge post and the six-cylinder engine number was on the left side of the block below the head between the first and second cylinders. Engine numbers on the V-8 were positioned on top of the engine block between the heads and under the water outlet elbow. [Windsor] Detroit-built cars had numbers 70110001 to 70140156. Los Angeles-built cars had numbers 65011001 to 6013020. Engine numbers ranged from C53-1001 to C53-82918. [Windsor Deluxe] Detroit-built cars used serial numbers 71005001 to 71050372 and Los Angeles-built cars used numbers 67040001 to 67043434. Engine numbers used the C53 prefix. [New Yorker] Serial numbers for Detroit-built cars were from 76540001 to 76585872. Serial numbers for Los Angeles-built cars were 66506001 to 66509462. Engine numbers were from C53-8-1001 to C53-8-86292. [New Yorker Deluxe] Detroit numbers were 7222001 to 72245465. Los Angeles numbers were 69001001 to 69003868. Engine numbers used the C53-8 prefix as on the New Yorker.

Windsor Series

Model Number	Body/Style Number	Body Type & Seating	Factory Price	Shipping Weight	Production Total
Standard Wheelbase					
C60-1	N/A	2-dr Club Coupe-6P	$2,555	3,595 lbs.	11,646
C60-1	N/A	4-dr Sedan-6P	$2,577	3,655 lbs.	18,879
C60-1	N/A	Town & Country Wagon-6P	$3,279	3,955 lbs.	1,242
Long Wheelbase					
C60-1	N/A	4-dr Sedan-8P	$3,279	3,955 lbs.	425

WINDSOR DELUXE SERIES — (6-CYLINDER): An upgraded version of the Windsor featured only three body styles. Styling was identical to the Windsor series. Windsor rear fender stone shields were noted for their stylized horizontal bumps.

Windsor Deluxe Series

Model Number	Body/Style Number	Body Type & Seating	Factory Price	Shipping Weight	Production Total
C60-2	N/A	4-dr Sedan-6P	$2,806	3,770 lbs.	45,385
C60-2	N/A	2-dr Convertible-6P	$3,290	4,000 lbs.	1,250
C60-2	N/A	2-dr Newport-6P	$3,166	3,770 lbs.	5,642

NEW YORKER SERIES — (8-CYLINDER): The Saratoga series was dropped and replaced by the New Yorker on the Windsor wheelbase of 125.5 inches. The third year for the Hemi engine continued with the same configuration of 331.1 cid and 180 bhp. Even the Buick surpassed the mighty Chrysler in the horsepower department. Major styling changes paralleled the Windsor changes, and the New Yorker added a much-needed third bar to the grille. With the reduction in wheelbase, Chrysler accomplished a 5 percent weight reduction on its V-8 cars. A common option was two-tone paint. The "V" insignia was affixed to the hood and rear deck lid and denoted the Hemi engine. The eight-passenger and Town & Country models used the 1951-1952 style rear fenders and trim.

New Yorker Series

Model Number	Body/Style Number	Body Type & Seating	Factory Price	Shipping Weight	Production Total
Standard Wheelbase					
C56-1	N/A	2-dr Club Coupe-6P	$3,336	3,920 lbs.	7,749
C56-1	N/A	4-dr Sedan-6P	$3,365	4,000 lbs.	37,540
C56-1	N/A	2-dr Newport-6P	$3,782	4,015 lbs.	2,252
C56-1	N/A	Town & Country Wagon-6P	$4,077	4,260 lbs.	1,399
Long Wheelbase					
C56-1	N/A	4-dr Sedan-8P	$4,363	4,510 lbs.	100

NEW YORKER DELUXE SERIES — (8-CYLINDER): The top-of-the-line Chrysler used the same wheelbase as all other Chrysler series in 1953. The Deluxe offered an additional body style, the convertible coupe and deleted the eight-passenger sedan and Town & Country station wagon. The upholstery was upgraded notably. Air conditioning and wire wheels were the big option news in 1953. The modern, fully automatic PowerFlite transmission became standard equipment late in the model year, replacing Fluid Drive or Fluid-Torque Drive transmissions. Nameplates were located on the front fender above the wheelhouse opening.

New Yorker Deluxe Series

Model Number	Body/Style Number	Body Type & Seating	Factory Price	Shipping Weight	Production Total
C56-2	N/A	2-dr Club Coupe-6P	$3,470	3,920 lbs.	1,934
C56-2	N/A	4-dr Sedan-6P	$3,526	4,020 lbs.	20,585
C56-2	N/A	2-dr Convertible-6P	$4,025	4,290 lbs.	950
C56-2	N/A	2-dr Newport-6P	$3,493	4,020 lbs.	3,715
C56-2	N/A	Chassis	—	—	1

WINDSOR SERIES ENGINES: L-head six-cylinder. Cast iron block. Displacement: 264.5 cid. Bore and stroke: 3.438 x 4.75 inches. Compression ratio: 7.0:1. Brake hp: 119 at 3600 rpm. Five main bearings. Carburetors: (Fluid Drive and M-6 transmission) Carter Ball and Ball E9A1; (standard transmission) B-B E9C, E9C1.

NEW YORKER ENGINE: V-8. Overhead valve with hemispherical combustion chamber. Displacement: 331.1 cid. Bore and stroke: 3.81 x 3.63 inches. Brake hp: 180 at 4000 rpm. Five main bearings. Hydraulic valve lifters. Compression ratio: 7.5:1. Carburetors: Carter WCD 935 S, 935 SA.

CHASSIS FEATURES: All standard wheelbase cars used a 125.5-inch wheelbase. Long wheelbase cars used the 139.5-inch wheelbase. Six-cylinder cars used 7.60 x 15 tires. New Yorker V-8s used 8.00 x 15 tires. The long wheelbase cars used 8.20 x 15 tires. Overall length for standard wheelbase cars was 211 inches.

CONVENIENCE OPTIONS: Air conditioning. Power steering. Power brakes. Power windows. Radio. Heater. Outside rearview mirrors. Two-tone paint. Wire wheels. Continental wheel kit. Locking gas cap. Fog lamps. Fluid-Torque Drive. PowerFlite (late in model year). Windshield washer. Solex glass. Exhaust deflector. Spare tire valve extension. Sun visor.

HISTORICAL FOOTNOTES: The 1953 Chrysler line was introduced in dealer showrooms on Oct. 30, 1952. A new Chrysler Custom Imperial Newport was added to the line March 18, 1953. Prices on most Chrysler models were lowered on March 25, 1953, by $27 to $274. Model year production was counted at 182,187 cars. Calendar year production totals included 78,814 sixes and 83,373 V-8s. PowerFlite transmission was introduced in June and over 35,000 had been installed in Chryslers by the end of the model year.

1953 Chrysler Windsor Deluxe sedan

1954

Chrysler finally had a grille for 1954. The Windsor and New Yorker grilles were nearly identical with only a plastic center piece being different between the two, and even the Windsor looked ritzier than it had looked since 1950. The parking lights became part of the grille instead of being additions. The three-piece rear window was gone, replaced by a one-piece window of the same shape.

The Chrysler body was the same one used in 1953 with fancier side trim and more elaborate taillights. The dash got its first update since 1949, and the instruments were housed in two circular dials instead of the single pod.

The PowerFlite became the transmission of choice on all V-8 Chryslers, De Sotos, and Dodges, but the semi-automatic was still serving the six-cylinder cars well, if in an old-fashioned way.

The strategy that had worked for Chrysler in 1953 backfired in 1954. The public wanted the long-looking, gliding cars from General Motors, and while Chrysler had to suffer through 1954 with really good but unpopular cars, good things were on the boards for 1955, and by 1957, GM would be running to catch up to Chrysler's styling.

WINDSOR DELUXE SERIES — (6-CYLINDER): The Windsor was gone, leaving only the Windsor Deluxe. The flathead six-cylinder engine was in its last year in a Chrysler, and the club coupe was also in its last year as a Chrysler body style.

CHRYSLER I.D. NUMBERS: Serial numbers were found on the left front hinge post. Engine numbers were located on the block behind the water pump. Only serial numbers were meant to be used for identification purposes. Cars built in Detroit were numbered 70141001 to 70181908. Los Angeles-built cars were numbered from 65014001 to 65015185. Engine numbers used a C54 prefix. [New Yorker] Cars built in Detroit used numbers 76591001 to 76610490. Los Angeles-built cars used numbers 66510001 to 66510937. Engine numbers began with C541-8-1001 and up. [New Yorker Deluxe] Cars built in Detroit were numbered 7249001 to 7279807. Los Angeles-built cars used numbers 69005001 to 69007248. Engine numbers began with C542-8-1001 and up.

Windsor Deluxe Series

Model Number	Body/Style Number	Body Type & Seating	Factory Price	Shipping Weight	Production Total
Standard Wheelbase					
C62	Note 1	2-dr Club Coupe-6P	$2,541	3,565 lbs.	5,659
C62	Note 1	4-dr Sedan-6P	$2,562	3,655 lbs.	33,563
C62	Note 1	2-dr Convertible-6P	$3,046	3,915 lbs.	500
C62	Note 1	2-dr Newport-6P	$2,831	3,685 lbs.	3,655
C62	Note 1	Town & Country Wagon-6P	$3,321	3,955 lbs.	650
Long Wheelbase					
C62	Note 1	4-dr Sedan-8P	$3,492	4,186 lbs.	500

NOTE 1: *Code numbers identifying body style were not used.*

NEW YORKER SERIES — (8-CYLINDER): A slight face-lift of the 1953 model paralleled the changes in the Windsor Deluxe series as far as body and trim. Only New Yorker nameplates were seen on the rear fenders and the "V" insignia on the hood and deck lid were means of outwardly identifying this Hemi-engined model It was the last year for the long wheelbase 139.5-inch chassis.

New Yorker Series

Model Number	Body/Style Number	Body Type & Seating	Factory Price	Shipping Weight	Production Total
Standard Wheelbase					
C63-1	Note 1	2-dr Club Coupe-6P	$3,202	3,910 lbs.	2,079
C63-1	Note 1	4-dr Sedan-6P	$3,229	3,970 lbs.	15,788
C63-1	Note 1	2-dr Newport-6P	$3,503	4,005 lbs.	1,312
C63-1	Note 1	Town & Country Wagon-6P	$4,023	4,245 lbs.	1,100
Long Wheelbase					
C63-1	Note 1	4-dr Sedan-8P	$4,368	4,450 lbs.	140

NOTE 1: *Code numbers identifying body style were not used.*

NEW YORKER DELUXE — (8-CYLINDER): This top-of-the-line Chrysler used more trim than other series in 1954. The grille center bar was bow shaped and dipped at both ends to parallel the upper grille design. The front fender stone shield was unique to the New Yorker Deluxe. The rear fender stone shield had a horizontal trim piece in the middle, matching the trim on the front fender shield. Hubcap design was unique to the New Yorker Deluxe and consisted of a flat spinner-like design in gold color that matched the exterior insignia. The big news this year was the beginning of the horsepower race, as Chrysler raised the ante with new heads, four-barrel carburetors and dual exhaust. The division capped the top spot in the performance race with a rating of 235 hp. The 1954 Chrysler was advertised as "Anything less ... Yesterday's Car!" Styling, however, was essentially six years old and sales plummeted more than 40 percent on all Chryslers, although the New Yorker Deluxe outsold its 1953 counterpart by nearly 25 percent. Performance, it seems, did sell cars in 1954.

New Yorker Deluxe Series

Model Number	Body/Style Number	Body Type & Seating	Factory Price	Shipping Weight	Production Total
C63-2	Note 1	2-dr Club Coupe-6P	$3,406	4,005 lbs.	1,816
C63-2	Note 1	4-dr Sedan-6P	$3,433	4,065 lbs.	26,907
C63-2	Note 1	2-dr Convertible-6P	$3,938	4,265 lbs.	724
C63-2	Note 1	2-dr Newport-6P	$3,707	4,095 lbs.	4,814
C63-2	Note 1	Chassis	—	—	17

NOTE 1: *Code numbers identifying body style were not used.*

WINDSOR DELUXE ENGINE: L-head six cylinder. Cast iron block. Displacement: 264.5 cid. Bore and stroke: 3.438 x 4.75 inches. Compression ratio: 7.0:1. Brake hp: 119 at 3600 rpm. Five main bearings. Carburetors: (PowerFlite transmission) Carter, Ball and Ball, Model B-B E9B1; (standard transmission) B-B E9C, E9C1.

NEW YORKER ENGINE: V-8. Overhead valve with hemispherical-segment combustion chambers. Displacement: 331.1 cid. Compression ratio: 7.5:1. Bore and stroke: 3.81 x 3.63 inches. Brake hp: 195 at 4400 rpm. Five main bearings. Hydraulic valve lifters. Carburetor: Carter WCD 2039S, 2039SA.

NEW YORKER DELUXE ENGINE: V-8. Overhead valve with hemispherical combustion chamber. Displacement: 331.1 cid. Compression ratio: 7.5:1. Bore and stroke: 3.81 x 3.63 inches. Brake hp: 235 at 4400 rpm. Five main bearings. Hydraulic valve lifters. Dual exhaust system. Carburetor: WCFB Carter 2041S.

CHASSIS FEATURES: A 125.5-inch wheelbase was used with all models, except for eight-passenger sedans. Tire size: 7.60 x 15-inch on Windsor Deluxe; 8.00 x 15-inch on New Yorker and New Yorker Deluxe; 8.20 x 15-inch on long wheelbase cars. Coil springs, front; leaf springs, rear. Length: 215.5 inches for New Yorker and New Yorker Deluxe.

OPTIONS: PowerFlite on Windsor ($175). Power steering ($130). White sidewall tires. Power brakes. Radio ($101). Heater ($79). Air Temp air conditioning ($595). Solex tinted glass ($20). Fog lights. Wire wheels ($260). Continental kit. Rear seat radio speaker. Windshield washers. Spot lamps. Outside rearview mirror. Two-tone paint. Highlander trim ($63). New Yorker leather trim ($121). Power windows ($125).

HISTORICAL FOOTNOTES: Chrysler opened its Chelsea Proving Grounds in 1954 and Chrysler test drivers teamed with Tony Bettenhausen to complete a 24-hour endurance run of 2,836 miles averaging 118.18 mph.

A nice-looking survivor is this 1954 Chrysler Windsor Deluxe club coupe.

John Gunnell

Famed Chrysler designer Virgil Exner had more and more control at Chrysler, and his influence on the 1955 Chryslers and De Sotos was nearly total. He brought Chrysler fans a new car from stem to stern dripping with the "100 Million Dollar Look." The car was longer, lower-looking, completely out of the 1940s, and completely into the 1950s.

The Exner trend had begun in the early 1950s with show cars including the K-310 and a pair of Imperial show cars. Before Exner, according to former Chrysler Engineer Cliff Noss, stylists at Chrysler weren't allowed in the company's clay rooms. Under Exner, Chrysler Corporation headed into a new era of style.

"We wanted to give the 'Forward Look' cars an appearance of fleetness," Exner said explaining the styling was "...the eager, poised-for-action look we feel is the natural and functional shape of automobiles."

"He had an intuitive sense of body form," said Bill Brownlee, a member of Exner's Chrysler design team in an *Automobile Quarterly* interview in 1991. "He was concerned primarily with the side, the silhouette, the proportion and the mass."

Chrysler was all V-8s, and there wasn't a six-cylinder engine to be seen anywhere near a Chrysler or De Soto in 1955.

The Imperial officially became a separate Chrysler Corporation division, and the Windsor, 300, and New Yorker were the only true "Chryslers."

The Windsor and New Yorker grilles had a curious half-imitation of the 1955 Imperial grille. The Imperial and 300 grille had a two-piece egg-crate design, but the Windsors and New Yorkers had only the top halves of these grilles, as if they were hiding and peeking out from behind the lower grille bars. The tall, narrow "Twin-Tower" taillights were housed under large, fancy, chrome fender extensions.

The dashboard was a work of art. Under its padded top, the dash was deeply recessed and curved outward and back in again as it progressed downward. All the switches were arranged in a row in the middle of the dash above the radio, and the instruments were in two large dials in front of the driver. The dash came in a wide variety of colors that were coordinated with the exterior, and the panel in front of the driver was usually of a mildly or heavily contrasting color to the rest of the dash.

The stately 1955 Chrysler New Yorker St. Regis

John Lee

A look from behind the 1955 Chrysler New Yorker St. Regis

John Lee

WINDSOR DELUXE SERIES — (8-CYLINDER): The Windsor went V-8, and the new power plant was a 301-cubic-inch polyhead engine, which was interesting. The poly-head combustion chambers had essentially a hemi design, but the valves were operated by only one rocker shaft per head instead of the hemi's two. The result was the poly engine had nearly the breathing characteristics of the hemi, but with fewer moving parts.

The Windsor only had a single chrome spear down each side of the car, and the taillight lenses had no little chrome trim pieces over their ribs. The parking lights were round and attached right to the painted body panel below the headlights. The lower grille opening had nothing in it. Windshields were now of the wraparound style, as were the rear windows on the hardtop and sedan. Back-up lamps were affixed to the panel beneath the deck lid. A new, highly touted feature was the dash-mounted shift lever for the PowerFlite automatic transmission.

A pair of two-door hardtops were offered in the Windsor series. The low-line version was named the Nassau and the high-line was named the Newport. Later in the model year another Newport was offered, with slightly modified trim borrowed from the New Yorker St. Regis. Depending upon the color ordered, the late versions were named "Green Falcon" or "Blue Heron." In addition, the sedan used the same trim package as the later Newports.

CHRYSLER I.D. NUMBERS: Serial numbers were found on the left front hinge post. Engine numbers were located on the block behind the water pump. [Windsor Deluxe] Detroit-built cars were numbered W55-1001 to W55-99194. Los Angeles-built cars were numbered WSSL-1001 to WSSL-4777. Engine numbers were WE55-1001 and up. [New Yorker Deluxe] Detroit numbers were N55-1001 to N55-49395 and Los Angeles-built cars had numbers NSSL-1001 to NSSL-3560. Engine numbers began with NE55-1001 and up. [Chrysler 300] Detroit-built cars numbered 3N55-1001 to 3N55-2724. Engine numbers ranged from 3NE55-1001 and up.

Windsor Deluxe Series

Model Number	Body/Style Number	Body Type & Seating	Factory Price	Shipping Weight	Production Total
C67	Note 1	4-dr Sedan-6P	$2,660	3,915 lbs.	63,896
C67	Note 1	2-dr Nassau-6P	$2,703	3,920 lbs.	18,474
C67	Note 1	2-dr Newport-6P	$2,818	3,915 lbs.	13,126
C67	Note 1	2-dr Convertible-6P	$3,090	4,075 lbs.	1,395
C67	Note 1	Town & Country Wagon-6P	$3,331	4,295 lbs.	1,983

NOTE 1: *Code numbers to provide positive identification of body type were not provided.*

NOTE 2: *Production totals for special hardtops and sedans are included in totals for standard offerings.*

NEW YORKER DELUXE SERIES — (8-CYLINDER): This top-drawer Chrysler continued to use the 331.1-cid Hemi engine, although horsepower increased. The two-door hardtop came as a standard Newport and an upgraded St. Regis, the latter noted for its unique two-tone styling. Later, a summer sales special used the St. Regis curved upper bodyside trim on the standard New Yorker Deluxe Newport, providing a rather unusual two-toning effect. The "Forward Look" made a successful debut with new styling and engineering changes. Insignia was placed at the rear of the bodyside color sweep on standard cars and to the rear, below the horizontal molding, on the St. Regis.

The ordinary New Yorker sedan had a long, narrow color sweep all the way down the side of the car. It was common for this sweep to be white in contrast to the rest of the car.

The lower grille opening, which was empty on the Windsor, held a long grille guard bar, and the parking lights were on each end of that bar on the New Yorker. This treatment was imitated on the rear of the car, where a long bumper guard on top of the rear bumper held the backup lights.

New Yorker Deluxe Series

Model Number	Body/Style Number	Body Type & Seating	Factory Price	Shipping Weight	Production Total
C68	Note 1	4-dr Sedan-6P	$3,494	4,160 lbs.	33,342
C68	Note 1	2-dr Newport-6P	$3,652	4,140 lbs.	5,777
C68	Note 1	2-dr St. Regis-6P	$3,690	4,125 lbs.	11,076
C68	Note 1	2-dr Convertible-6P	$3,924	4,255 lbs.	946
C68	Note 1	T & C Wagon-6P	$4,208	4,430 lbs.	1,036
C68	Note 1	Chassis	—	—	1

NOTE 1: *Code numbers to provide positive identification of body type were not provided.*

NOTE 2: *Production totals for midyear additions to the line are included in the totals for standard offerings.*

CHRYSLER 300 SERIES — (8-CYLINDER): The most powerful automobile of the year sported a much-modified 331.1 cid Hemi engine developing 300 brake horsepower. Two four-barrel carburetors, a full race camshaft and heavy-duty suspension, coupled with an Imperial grille and full leather interior, marked this car as something special. Performance and styling, combined in one package of such magnitude, created an aura that was to last for more than a decade.

The 300 used the same two grille halves as the Imperial, but it was less fancy, and the parking lights mounted to the body under the headlights as they did on the Windsor. The 300 was only available in three colors – white, red, or black – and the interior was only a solid tan. The 300 was a stripped-down, yet expensive car with enough weight to control the power and speed, and the plainness of the car added to its image as a semi-racing machine that didn't pretend to pamper the occupants.

300 Series

Model Number	Body/Style Number	Body Type & Seating	Factory Price	Shipping Weight	Production Total
C68-300	Note 1	2-dr Hardtop Coupe	$4,109	4,005 lbs.	1,725

NOTE 1: *Code numbers to provide positive identification of body type were not provided.*

"...the '55 [Chrysler] emerges as a car that has improved in every important aspect, something that few can say..."

Pete Molson, Motor Trend, May 1955

To stimulate sales in 1955, Chrysler Corporation brought out special models like this Blue Heron version.

Beauty and beast in one machine— the 1955 Chrysler C-300. It was a car that would shatter records wherever it raced.

WINDSOR DELUXE ENGINE: V-8. Overhead valve. Cast iron block. Displacement: 301 cid. Bore and stroke: 3.625 x 3.625 inches. Compression ratio: 8.0:1. Brake hp: 188 at 4400 rpm. Hydraulic valve lifters. Carburetors: (standard shift) Carter BBD 2180S, 2180SA, 2180SB. (PowerFlite) BBD 2162S, 2162SA, 2162SB.

NEW YORKER DELUXE ENGINE: V-8. Overhead valve with hemispherical combustion chambers. Displacement: 331.1 cid. Bore and stroke: 3.81 x 3.63 inches. Brake hp: 250 at 4600 rpm. Five main bearings. Hydraulic valve lifters. Dual exhaust system. Compression ratio: 8.5:1. Carburetor: Carter WCFB 2126S.

CHRYSLER 300 ENGINE: V-8. Overhead valve with hemispherical combustion chambers. Cast iron block. Displacement: 331.1 cid. Bore and stroke: 3.81 x 3.63 inches. Brake hp: 300 at 5200 rpm. Compression ratio: 8.5:1. Solid lifters with full-race camshaft. Two four-barrel carburetors.

CHASSIS FEATURES: Wheelbase: (all) 126 inches. Overall length: (Windsor Deluxe) 218.6 inches; (all other models) 218.8 inches. Tires: (Windsor) 7.60 x 15-inch; (New Yorker) 8.00 x 15-inch; (New Yorker and Town & Country with wire wheels) 8.20 x 15-inch. Six-volt positive ground electrical system.

OPTIONS: PowerFlite transmission on Windsor Deluxe. Power steering. White sidewall tires. Chrome wire wheels. Air Temp air conditioning. Power brakes. Radio. Heater. Solex glass. Fog lights. Spotlamps. Rear seat radio speaker. Windshield washers. Outside rearview mirror. Two-tone paint. Power windows. Power front seat.

HISTORICAL FOOTNOTES: The Chrysler and Imperial lines for 1955 (including Nassau and St. Regis hardtops) were introduced Nov. 17, 1954. Chrysler Town & Country station wagons were added to the line Jan. 5, 1955. The Chrysler 300 was added to the line Feb. 10, 1955. Chrysler took second place in the high-priced sales field this season.

The Million Dollar Look" came forward with a tasteful face-lift. The busy, multi-piece 1955 grille disappeared from the Windsors and New Yorkers, and the grilles took on a much cleaner, more modern neatness that ridded the cars of any remaining vestiges of 1940s ornamentation. The 300s and Imperials kept the two-piece grilles from 1955. All Chrysler lines also ridded themselves of attached taillights, and the taillights were integrated into the ends of the higher, more fin-like rear fenders. From the rear, the Forward Look was showing through the "100 Million Dollar Look." The term "Flight Sweep" was added to the advertising for Chrysler Corporation cars as fins, or what Exner called "stabilizers" grew out back.

The Chryslers all kept the 1955 dashes with the fun addition of push-button controls for the PowerFlite automatic transmission tucked under the dash on the left-hand side, replacing the dash-mounted finger-tip shift levers of 1955. A new pillarless four-door hardtop body-style also announced that the 1960s were coming. Chrysler Corporation replaced its six-volt, positive-ground electrical system with a 12-volt-negative-ground system. The company began phasing out the anchored brake shoes and replacing them with floating shoes arranged with the same geometry under the trade name Center-Plane Brakes.

The 1956 Chrysler New Yorker was most popular in the sedan form.

WINDSOR SERIES — (8-CYLINDER): Three horizontal grille bars floated within a chrome surround. The Windsor was cleaner—some would say plainer—than the 1955 version, but the cleanness of the design allowed for more of the car's style to come from its shape, rather than from added-on ornamentation. Two-toned Windsors highlighted the growing fins with contrasting color.

CHRYSLER I.D. NUMBERS: Serial numbers were found on the left front hinge post. Engine numbers were located on the block behind the water pump. [Windsor] Detroit-built cars were numbered W56-1001 to W56-75206. Los Angeles-built cars were numbered W56L-1001 to W56L-7091. Engine numbers ranged from WE56-1001 to WE56-81623. [New Yorker] Detroit-built cars were numbered N56-1001 to N56-36162. Los Angeles-built cars were numbered N56L-1001 to N56L-5197. Engine numbers ranged from NE56-1001 to NE56-40609. [300-B] Production of Chrysler 300 Letter Cars took place exclusively in Detroit, with numbers ranging from 3N56-1001 to 3N56-2150. Engine numbers were 3NE56-1001 to 3NE56-2174.

Windsor Series

Model Number	Body/Style Number	Body Type & Seating	Factory Price	Shipping Weight	Production Total
C71	Note 1	4-dr Sedan-6P	$2,770	3,900 lbs.	53,119
C71	Note 1	2-dr Convertible-6P	$3,235	4,100 lbs.	1,011
C71	Note 1	Town & Country Wagon-6P	$3,498	4,290 lbs.	2,700
C71-1	Note 1	2-dr Nassau-6P	$2,804	3,910 lbs.	11,400
C71-2	Note 1	2-dr Newport-6P	$2,941	3,920 lbs.	10,800
C71-2	Note 1	4-dr Newport-6P	$3,028	3,990 lbs.	7,050

NOTE 1: *Code numbers to provide positive identification of body type were not used.*

NEW YORKER SERIES — (8-CYLINDER): The New Yorker used a more finely detailed, more screen-like grille and different bumpers to set it apart from the Windsor. Eight chrome teeth appeared on the side of the car above the side spear, and this became a New Yorker styling touch for years to come. Additional moldings created unique two-tone paint combinations and a tri-tone combination in the St. Regis series. Big news this year was the first size increase for the Hemi engine, to 354 cid. This increased brake horsepower, in standard form, by more than 10 percent.

New Yorker Series

Model Number	Body/Style Number	Body Type & Seating	Factory Price	Shipping Weight	Production Total
C72	Note 1	4-dr Sedan-6P	$3,673	4,110 lbs.	24,749
C72	Note 1	2-dr Convertible-6P	$4,136	4,360 lbs.	921
C72	Note 1	Town & Country Wagon-6P	$4,417	4,460 lbs.	1,070
C72-1	Note 1	2-dr Newport-6P	$3,845	4,175 lbs.	4,115
C72-1	Note 1	4-dr Newport-6P	$3,995	4,220 lbs.	3,599
C72-2	Note 1	2-dr St. Regis-6P	$3,889	4,175 lbs.	6,686

300-B SERIES — (8-CYLINDER): The 300-B's styling reflected the same unique flavor of the first Chrysler Letter Car introduced in 1955. Changes were essentially limited to tail lamp alterations, in line with those appearing on other Chryslers, and the 300 wore the cleaner styling as well. The cleaner styling made the 1956 Chrysler 300 look faster. The 300 was still a stripped-down hot rod with no hint that it would ever become more luxurious with time, and it was still only available in three colors with tan leather upholstery.

300-B Series

Model Number	Body/Style Number	Body Type & Seating	Factory Price	Shipping Weight	Production Total
C72-300	Note 1	2-dr Hardtop Coupe-6P	$4,242	4,360 lbs.	1,102

NOTE 1: *Code numbers to provide positive identification of body type were not used.*

WINDSOR ENGINE: V-8. Overhead valve. Cast iron block. Displacement: 331.1 cid. Bore and stroke: 3.81 x 3.63 inches. Compression ratio: 8.5:1. Brake hp: 225 at 4400 rpm. (Optional engine with dual exhaust and single four-barrel carburetor produced 250 brake horsepower.) Hydraulic

The 1956 Chrysler dashboards were as fancy as ever but the upholstery styles were moving toward being a little cleaner and simpler.

valve lifters. Carburetors: (standard shift) Carter BBD 2312S; (PowerFlite) Carter 2313S; (Power package, with all transmissions) Carter WCFB 2367S or 2367SA.

NEW YORKER ENGINE: V-8. Overhead valve. Cast iron block. Displacement: 354 cid. Bore and stroke: 3.94 x 3.63 inches. Brake hp: 280 at 4600 rpm. Compression ratio: 9.0:1. Five main bearings. Hydraulic valve lifters. Carburetor: Carter WCFB 2314S or 2314SA.

300-B ENGINE: V-8. Overhead valve. High-lift camshaft. Extra stiff valve springs. Cast iron block. Displacement: 354 cid. Bore and stroke: 3.94 x 3.63 inches. Brake hp: 340 at 5200 rpm (with optional 10.0:1 compression ratio, brake horsepower became 355 at 5200 rpm).

CHASSIS FEATURES: Three-speed column-mounted transmission standard on the Windsor (available by special order on 300-B). PowerFlite transmission standard on New Yorker and 300B. Late 300-Bs used three-speed TorqueFlite transmissions. Wheelbase: (all models) 126 inches. Overall length: (Windsor) 220.5 inches; (New Yorker) 221 inches; (New Yorker Town & Country) 221.2 inches; (Windsor Town & Country) 220.4 inches. It was the last year for front coil springs combined with rear leaf springs.

OPTIONS: Power steering. Power brakes. Power front seat. Hi-Way Hi-Fi record player. Air Temp air conditioning. Electric window lifts. Power radio antenna. Hot water heater. Instant gas heater. Solex safety glass. Whitewall tires. Steering wheel mounted clock. Power package on Windsor (included dual exhaust and four-barrel carburetor).

HISTORICAL FOOTNOTES: The 300-B, America's fastest and highest powered car in 1956, set the World Passenger Car Speed Record at Daytona Beach, Fla., averaging 133.9 mph. In trials there, NASCAR driver Tim Flock had a one-way best of 142.91 mph while Vickie Wood set the pace for women drivers at 136.081 mph, reportedly in the same car. The mighty 300-Bs finished 1-2-3 in NASCAR Grand National competition in 1956.

Technically, this was the third year of Chrysler's catchy "Forward Look" trade name, but this was the year the name took on real meaning. Chrysler enthusiasts usually think of the 1957 to '59 Chrysler Corporation lineup as *the* Forward Look cars. The cars were longer, lower, wider, and had a flatter, flying-under-the-radar look.

The grille smiled broadly without any interfering badges or ornaments. The rear of the car swept upward into the American auto industry's most functional set of tail fins. Every styling aspect of the new Chrysler was integrated without any sense of ill-fit or added-on styling elements. The bulbous, rounded, balloon-like styling of the late 1940s and early 1950s were over, and the flat, creased and sculpted 1960s were on the way.

The Forward Look took a big step with models like the 1957 Chrysler. The New Yorker retained clean, sweeping trim and a simple taillight.

The 1957 Chrysler was new from the ground-up, and the car was packed with mechanical innovations. The front of the car no longer sat atop coil springs. Torsion-Aire suspension replaced it. The long torsion bars were attached to the lower control arms and twisted with variations in the road. Chryslers and all the 1957 Chrysler Corporation cars remained flat and sure through sharp turns and panic swerves. The four-year-old PowerFlite automatic transmission still served lower-priced Dodges and Plymouths, but the Chrysler received the new three-speed TorqueFlite automatic. While early examples proved troublesome, the TorqueFlite became one of the toughest, simplest automatics on the road.

In spite of all the innovations and changes, the new Chrysler was still a Chrysler. The tail fins ended in integrated, bar-like taillights as they had in 1956, and the driver operated TorqueFlite from the dash-mounted push-button cluster on the driver's left side.

As the year began, safety laws restricted cars to having only two headlights, but Chrysler was ready for the legal change everyone knew was coming, and part-way into the model-year run, Chrysler adopted the four-headlight system and got the jump on the rest of the industry.

Chrysler mounted the rearview mirror on the dash on a flexible stem, and while it was an attractive Space Age feature, a person sitting in the middle of the front or rear seat blocked the driver's view. The dash-top-mounted mirrors were known to vibrate so badly that they were nearly useless. Chrysler seemed to have corrected the vibration problem over time as the mirrors in 1960 models seemed to sit still more.

WINDSOR — (8-CYLINDER): The Windsor got even plainer for 1957, but the styling of the car came almost exclusively from its shape, and the Windsor was a sweeping, stylish car for its class. The Windsor had very little side trim, and its identifying feature was its sweep of contrasting color toward the rear, under the fin.

CHRYSLER I.D. NUMBERS: Serial numbers were found on the left front door hinge post. Engine numbers were located on the block behind the water pump. [Windsor] Detroit-built cars were numbered W57-1001 and up. Los Angeles-built cars were numbered W57L-1001 and up. Engine numbers ranged from WE57-1001 to WE57-48864. [Saratoga] Detroit-built cars were numbered L57-1001 and up. Los Angeles-built cars were numbered L57L-1001 and up. Engine numbers ranged from LE57-1001 and up. [New Yorker] Detroit-built cars were numbered N57-1001 and up. Los Angeles-built cars were numbered N57L-1001 and up. Engine numbers ranged from NE57-1001 to NE57-35552. [300] Serial numbers were 3N57-1001 and up. Engine numbers ranged from 3NE57-1001 to 3NE57-3338. All production of Chrysler 300s was quartered in Detroit.

Windsor Series

Model Number	Body/Style Number	Body Type & Seating	Factory Price	Shipping Weight	Production Total
C75-1	145	4-dr Sedan-6P	$3,088	3,995 lbs.	17,639
C75-1	146	2-dr Hardtop-6P	$3,153	3,925 lbs.	14,027
C75-1	149	4-dr Hardtop-6P	$3,217	4,030 lbs.	14,354
C75-1	148	Town & Country Wagon-6P	$3,574	4,210 lbs.	2,035

SARATOGA SERIES — (8-CYLINDER): The Saratoga name returned after an absence of five years. This mid-line Chrysler, based on Windsor components, featured upgraded upholstery, a higher horsepower engine with dual exhaust, back-up lamps and brake warning signals. The TorqueFlite automatic transmission, stainless steel wheel covers, and power steering were standard equipment. A single horizontal trim molding ran from front to rear, giving the car a long sweeping look that reflected Virgil Exner's design inspiration. Two-tone finish was optional and popular. The Saratoga insignia was located below the horizontal trim line, just left of the front wheelhouse opening.

Saratoga Series

Model Number	Body/Style Number	Body Type & Seating	Factory Price	Shipping Weight	Production Total
C75-2	255	4-dr Sedan-6P	$3,718	4,165 lbs.	14,977
C75-2	256	2-dr Hardtop-6P	$3,754	4,075 lbs.	10,633
C75-2	259	4-dr Hardtop-6P	$3,832	4,195 lbs.	11,586

NEW YORKER SERIES — (8-CYLINDER): This top-of-the-line model featured the largest production car engine available in 1957. The Hemi engine's bore and stroke were increased. Displacement was raised nearly 10 percent. A narrow, dart-like color sweep distinguished the sides of the New Yorker. Cars with two-tone finish had the roof color added to the side trim area. Advertised as, "The most glamorous cars in a generation," all body styles were included in this series. Dual rear antennas were a popular option that emphasized the sweep of the tailfins.

In addition to its attention getting fin treatment, Chrysler used canted radio aerials, often with stylish dual rear mountings.

Coming or going, the 1957 Chrysler's second wave of the Forward Look left GM's styling looking fat, bloated and old fashioned.

New Yorker Series

Model Number	Body/Style Number	Body Type & Seating	Factory Price	Shipping Weight	Production Total
C76	165	4-dr Sedan-6P	$4,173	4,315 lbs.	12,369
C76	166	2-dr Hardtop-6P	$4,202	4,220 lbs.	8,863
C76	169	4-dr Hardtop-6P	$4,259	4,330 lbs.	10,948
C76	163	2-dr Convertible-6P	$4,638	4,365 lbs.	1,049
C76	168	Town & Country Wagon-6P	$4,746	4,490 lbs.	1,391

300-C SERIES — (8-CYLINDER): The third version of the 300 continued as the fastest and most powerful production car in the country. The 300 featured full leather interior trims and a new trapezoidal grille that was unlike any other Chrysler that year. Exterior ornamentation was kept to a minimum with single spear-like moldings on the lower rear quarter panels. The round 300 medallion, with a red-white-blue background and model numbers and lettering made its debut and the checkered flag badges were discontinued. Medallions were placed on the side spears, one on each hubcap, one each on the hood, deck lid, glovebox and another within the steering wheel center hub. Only the two on the spears carried both numbers and letters. The others had only the 300 designation. The colors of the emblem were claimed to be representative of the high-performance nature of the American car-buying public. With smaller, 14-inch wheels being used, it was found necessary to provide for additional brake cooling on the Chrysler 300. This was accomplished by adding a rectangular opening below the headlamps that admitted air and guided it, via a duct, to the front brakes. Monotone colors were used exclusively on the 300 and the front did not have the short, narrow vertical bumper guards found on other 1957 Chryslers. The 300s were considered a part of the New Yorker series, but were actually a world apart from most other U.S. production automobiles of the day. While 200 lbs. heavier than the C-300 or 300-B versions, the 1957 300-C was a better-handling car.

300-C Series

Model Number	Body/Style Number	Body Type & Seating	Factory Price	Shipping Weight	Production Total
C76-300	566	2-dr Hardtop-6P	$4,929	4,235 lbs.	1,918
C76-300	563	2-dr Convertible-6P	$5,359	4,390 lbs.	484

WINDSOR ENGINE: V-8. Overhead valve. Cast iron block. Displacement: 354 cid. Bore and stroke: 3.94 x 3.63 inches. Compression ratio: 9.25:1. Brake hp: 285 at 4800 rpm. Five main bearings. Hydraulic valve lifters. Carburetor: Carter two-barrel, Type BBD Model 2527S.

SARATOGA ENGINE: V-8. Overhead valve. Cast iron block. Displacement: 354 cid. Bore and stroke: 3.94 x 3.63 inches. Compression ratio: 9.25:1. Brake hp: 295 at 4600 rpm. Five main bearings. Hydraulic valve lifters. Carburetor: Carter WCFB2589S four-barrel (dual exhaust).

NEW YORKER ENGINE: V-8. Cast iron block. Overhead valve with hemispherical combustion chambers. Displacement: 392 cid. Bore and stroke: 4.00 x 3.90 inches. Compression ratio: 9.25:1. Brake hp: 325 at 4600 rpm. Five main bearings. Solid valve lifters. Carburetor: Carter WCFB Model 2590S four-barrel (dual exhaust).

300-C ENGINE: V-8. Cast iron block. Overhead valve with hemispherical combustion chambers. Displacement: 392 cid. Bore and stroke: 4.00 x 3.90 inches. Compression ratio: 9.25:1. Brake hp: 375 at 5200 rpm. Five main bearings. Carburetor: Two Carter Model WCFB 2334S four-barrel.

OPTIONAL 300-C ENGINE: V-8. Cast iron block. Overhead valve with hemispherical combustion chambers. Displacement: 392 cid. Bore and stroke: 4.00 x 3.90 inches. Compression ratio: 9.25:1. Brake hp: 390 at 5400 rpm. Five main bearings. Carburetor: Two Carter Model WCFB 2334S four-barrel. This extra-cost solid lifter competition engine was intended mainly for acceleration trials and stock racing cars. It was available only with stickshift (adapted from a Dodge column-mounted three-speed) and no power options. It had a 10.0:1 compression ratio, four-bolt cast iron exhaust headers and a 2 ½-inch low back-pressure exhaust system. Solid valve lifters and twin four-barrel carburetors were used.

CHASSIS FEATURES: Manual shift was standard on the Windsor. TorqueFlite optional on Windsor; standard on Saratoga, New Yorker and 300-C. Wheelbase: 126 inches. Separate body and frame construction. Hotchkiss drive. Hypoid rear axle. Total-Contact brakes. Overall length: (Windsor, Saratoga, New Yorker and 300-C) 219.2 inches; (Town & Country wagon) 218.9 inches. Safety wheel rims. Tires: (Windsor and Saratoga) 8.50 x 14 inches; (New Yorker and 300C) 9.00 x 14-inches. Front tread: (Windsor and Saratoga) 61 inches; (New Yorker) 61.2 inches. Rear tread: (Windsor and Saratoga) 59.7 inches; (New Yorker) 60 inches. Width: (all models) 78.8 inches. Torsion-Aire torsion bar front suspension.

OPTIONS: Power steering on Windsor (standard on other series). Handbrake warning signal option on Windsor. Back-up lights optional on Windsor. Dual headlamps (became standard on all lines shortly after production commenced). Air-Temp air conditioning. Power brakes. Power window lifts. Six-way power seat. Whitewall tires. Nylon tires. Chrome stainless steel wheel covers on Windsor. Radio with Music Master or Electro-Touch tuner. Dual rear antennas. Power front antenna. Rear seat speaker. Fresh air heater. Instant Air heater. Two-tone finish. Tinted glass. Rear window defroster. Windshield washer. Undercoating. Non-slip differential. Outside mirrors. Full-flow oil filter on Windsor. Captive-Aire tires on Town & Country station wagon. Highway Hi-Fi phonograph.

HISTORICAL FOOTNOTES: The 1957 Chrysler models were introduced on Oct. 29, 1956. Output in 1957 was 156,679 cars of which 118,733 were Chryslers and 37,946 Imperials. Since 1926, when the first Chrysler Imperial 80 was produced, Imperials had been built in the corporation's East Jefferson plant at Detroit, along with Chryslers. Beginning in 1955, the Imperial was given a distinctively different styling treatment and, by 1957, there were no longer any body parts interchangeable with Chrysler. "Chrysler in 1957 aggressively established Imperial as a volume automobile line," said Chrysler Corporation president L.L. "Tex" Colbert.

The 1958 Chrysler 300-D was the final year for the original hemi V-8.

The 1958 Chrysler was a tasteful update of the 1957 styling. The car's shape was the same, and the clean, smiling 1957 grille gave way to a flatter bumper with a car-width slot in it. Chrysler still distinguished itself from De Soto by having the rear fin end in a bar-like taillight, but the taillight shrunk for 1958 and floated in a sea of bright metal. The rear treatment was still attractive, but begged the question of why the taillights shrunk. Perhaps the idea was to add glitz by surrounding the lenses in bright metal. While the 1957 TorqueFlite three-speed automatic had a reputation for being troublesome in its first year, collectors report the 1958 TorqueFlites to have been more refined and trouble-free.

WINDSOR SERIES — (8-CYLINDER): The Windsor used a smaller Dodge chassis under the skin, and while the car had solidly Chrysler styling motifs, the front end sheet metal was capped off with a chrome eyebrow running from side-to-side above the headlamps. The 1958 grille was tastefully adapted to the Dodge-like front end. Side trim on the standard offering was a single molding, at mid-level, running horizontally from the rear to just aft of the front wheelhouse opening. In the spring, a Dartline package was introduced, which added some flair to the Windsor's styling. The Dartline package was an addition to the hardtop line. Besides additional trim on the front fender and a metal insert, this option included bright sill moldings, special roof trim and three slim moldings on each side of the rear deck license plate housing. The standard two-door hardtop used a sweep of color similar to the 1957 version with the major difference being the sharper pointed front part of the sweep on the 1958 model. A nine-passenger wagon with a rear-facing third seat appeared in the Windsor line. Auto-Pilot speed control debuted.

"…it's a rare demand you can make of a 300-D that will not be fulfilled."

William Carroll, Motor Trend, February 1958

CHRYSLER I.D. NUMBERS: Serial numbers were found on the left front hinge post. Engine numbers were located on the block behind the water pump. [Windsor] Detroit-built cars were numbered LC1-1001 and up. Los Angeles-built cars were numbered LC1L-1001 and up. Engine numbers ranged from 58W-1001 and up. [Saratoga] Detroit-built cars used numbers LC2-1001 and up. Los Angeles-built cars used numbers LC2L-1001 and up. Engine numbers ranged from SAS-1001 and up. [New Yorker] Detroit-built cars were numbered LC3-1001 and up. Los Angeles-built cars were numbered LC3L-1001 and up. Engine numbers ranged from 58N-1001 and up. [300D] All 300s were built in Detroit and serial numbers began with LC4-1001 and up. Engine numbers started at 58N3-1001 and up.

The 1958 Chrysler 300-D also received the memorable shrinking taillight.

Windsor Series

Model Number	Body/Style Number	Body Type & Seating	Factory Price	Shipping Weight	Production Total
LC1-L	513	4-dr Sedan-6P	$3,129	3,895 lbs.	12,861
LC1-L	512	2-dr Hardtop-6P	$3,214	3,860 lbs.	6,205
LC1-L	514	4-dr Hardtop-6P	$3,279	3,915 lbs.	6,254
LC1-L	571	Town & Country Wagon-6P	$3,616	4,155 lbs.	862
LC1-L	572	Town & Country Wagon-9P	$3,803	4,245 lbs.	791
LC1-L	515	2-dr Convertible-6P	—	—	2

SARATOGA SERIES — (8-CYLINDER): This series continued almost unchanged from 1957. Instrument panel background color changed, as did the metal background of the radio and heater control panels. The side trim began at the forward edge of the front door and continued rearward to the taillamp bezel. The Saratoga nameplate was placed to the rear of the front fender, directly in line with the side trim molding. A color spear was available at extra cost. On cars with this option, the extra trim began at the middle of the front door and rose slightly, in a gentle line, as it ran rearward.

Saratoga Series

Model Number	Body/Style Number	Body Type & Seating	Factory Price	Shipping Weight	Production Total
LC2-M	533	4-dr Sedan-6P	$3,818	4,120 lbs.	8,698
LC2-M	532	2-dr Hardtop-6P	$3,878	4,045 lbs.	4,456
LC2-M	534	4-dr Hardtop-6P	$3,955	4,145 lbs.	5,322

NEW YORKER SERIES — (8-CYLINDER): The New Yorker got the same face-lift as the less expensive models. The New Yorker had the Saratoga-style mid-line body trim molding, but a unique emblem, placed just rearward of the front door, set New Yorkers apart. A color spear of anodized aluminum graced the area between the two trim pieces and covered the rear portion of the car. While not as substantial or as long as the color sweep of 1957, it helped distinguish this model from its brethren. Auto-Pilot and remote-control outside rearview mirrors were new options. Interior fabric was "Fountainebleu" Jacquard and metallic vinyl and was slightly richer than the "Chainmail" fabric and metallic vinyl used on the Saratoga (Windsors used "Bahama" Jacquard and metallic vinyl trim combinations). The Town & Country station wagon now had a third seat option, with the seat facing the rear of the car. All hardtops sported the new domed windshield introduced on 1957 convertibles. The New Yorker's trademark hashmarks sat above the side spear on the rear fenders.

New Yorker Series

Model Number	Body/Style Number	Body Type & Seating	Factory Price	Shipping Weight	Production Total
LC3-H	553	4-dr Sedan-6P	$4,295	4,195 lbs.	7,110
LC3-H	552	2-dr Hardtop-6P	$4,347	4,205 lbs.	3,205
LC3-H	554	4-dr Hardtop-6P	$4,404	4,240 lbs.	5,227
LC3-H	555	2-dr Convertible Coupe-6P	$4,761	4,350 lbs.	666
LC3-H	575	Town & Country Wagon-6P	$4,868	4,435 lbs.	775
LC3-H	576	Town & Country Wagon-9P	$5,083	4,445 lbs.	428

300-D SERIES — (8-CYLINDER): This super high-performance car was again a subseries of the New Yorker. It carried forward the design motifs of 1957 with only minor alterations. The windshield on the hardtop now conformed to the windshield style (domed) of the convertible. Hubcaps now had red finish, painted in the depressed outer areas of the wheel covers. Instrument face backgrounds were identical to those of other 1958 Chryslers. Large red-white-blue rear quarter panel medallions returned for the second year, but the letter "D" replaced the "C" used in 1957. In all, there were 10 locations for the various sized 300 medallions on the car: glovebox, grille, deck lid, steering hub, hubcaps and the aforementioned rear quarters. A limited number of 300-Ds were built with an electronic fuel injection system called the Bendix Electrojector. This marked the first use of a computer in a Chrysler product. Because of problems with the system, a recall program was instituted in late summer 1958, and most of the EFI units were replaced by conventional dual four-barrel carburetors like those standard on all 300s. It was also the last year for the Firepower Hemi engine.

As it was previously, the Chrysler 300-D was cleaner looking than other Chryslers.

300-D Series

Model Number	Body/Style Number	Body Type & Seating	Factory Price	Shipping Weight	Production Total
LC3-S	592	2-dr Hardtop-6P	$5,173	4,305 lbs.	618
LC3-S	595	2-dr Convertible Coupe-6P	$5,603	4,475 lbs.	191

The shrunken taillight was a curious feature on the 1958 Chrysler. While the style was the same as the 1957, the smaller lens floated in a field of textured pot metal.

WINDSOR ENGINE: V-8. Overhead valve. Cast iron block. Displacement: 354 cid. Bore and stroke: 3.94 x 3.63 inches. Compression ratio: 10.0:1. Brake hp: 290 at 4600 rpm. Five main bearings. Hydraulic valve lifters. Carburetor: Carter Type BBD Model 2733S two-barrel.

SARATOGA ENGINE: V-8. Overhead valve. Cast iron block. Displacement: 354 cid. Bore and stroke: 3.94 x 3.63 inches. Compression ratio: 10.0:1. Brake hp: 310 at 4600 rpm. Five main bearings. Hydraulic valve lifters. Carburetor: Carter four-barrel.

NEW YORKER ENGINE: V-8. Cast iron block. Overhead valve with hemispherical combustion chambers. Displacement: 392 cid. Bore and stroke: 4.00 x 3.90 inches. Compression ratio: 10.0:1. Brake hp: 345 at 4600 rpm. Five main bearings. Hydraulic valve lifters. Carburetor: Carter Type AFB four-barrel Model 2651S. Dual exhaust.

300-D ENGINE: V-8. Cast iron block. Overhead valve with hemispherical combustion chambers. Adjustable valve lifters. Displacement: 392 cid. Bore and stroke: 4.00 x 3.90 inches. Compression ratio: 10.0:1. Brake hp: 380 at 5200 rpm. Dual Carter WCFB four-barrel carburetors.

EFI ENGINE: Optional Bendix fuel-injected engine produced 390 brake horsepower at 5200 rpm. Low back pressure exhaust system available.

CHASSIS FEATURES: Manual shift was standard on Windsor. TorqueFlite optional on Windsor and standard on Saratoga, New Yorker and 300-D. Wheelbase: 122 inches on Windsor; 126 inches on all other series. Constant control power steering optional on Windsor and standard on other series. Torsion-Aire front suspension sway bar and Oriflow shock absorbers standard on all models. 300-D used larger diameter torsion bars. Windsor length was 218 inches (217.7 inches on Town & Country). The Saratoga was 220 inches in length. New Yorkers were 220.2 inches (Town & Country was 219.9 inches). Tire size: 8.00 x 14-inch for Windsor; 8.50 x 14-inch for Saratoga and 9.00 x 14-inch for the New Yorker and 300-D. Safety rim wheels were standard on all models.

OPTIONS: Power steering and TorqueFlite on Windsor. Power brakes. Power windows. Power seat. Air-Temp air conditioning. White sidewall rayon tires (nylon tubeless super soft cushion tires in black and white optional). Stainless wheel covers on Windsor. Remote control mirror. Radios. Antennas including power antenna. Two-tone finish. Tinted glass. Heaters. Rear window defroster. Windshield washer. Undercoating. Non-slip differential. Highway Hi-Fi. Auto-Pilot.

HISTORICAL FOOTNOTES: Dealer introductions of 1958 Chryslers were held on Nov. 1, 1957. Production included 26,500 Windsors; 18,300 New Yorkers and 15,700 Saratogas. Emphasizing the Imperial as a separate line was a major step in the division's 1958 activities.

Passenger car production for calendar year 1958 was 63,186 units, including Imperial's share of 13,673 or 21.6 percent of the total. Installation rates of the leading equipment items continued at a high rate on 1958 models. Such accessories as automatic transmission, power steering, heater and windshield washer, neared 100 percent for Chrysler. Auto-Pilot was Chrysler's unique driver assist option. First introduced in 1958, the device permitted drivers to dial a speed and remove their foot from the accelerator.

Stunning in white is the 1959 Chrysler 300-D two-door hardtop.

1959 Chrysler was a more square-like car all around, but especially in the front. The grille carried forward its horizontal flair, but the lower section now wrapped around the fender and ran back nearly to the wheelhouse opening. Bumpers, front and rear, were noticeably different and the rear license plate was no longer embedded in the deck lid. It was now positioned at the center inset of the rear bumper. Taillamps were placed in a higher, notched housing, totally unlike previous designs. A unique feature was the "outlined roof" treatment. It was an option that could be ordered in colors that matched the bodyside sweep inserts. A new, wedge-like combustion chamber "Golden Lion" V-8 engine was used on all 1959 Chryslers. This engine was a derivative of the B-block introduced in 1958 for De Soto, Dodge and Plymouth. All hardtops and convertibles used the dome-like windshield pioneered on 1957 convertibles.

WINDSOR — (8-CYLINDER): The low-line Windsor used the same Dodge-sized body structure of the earlier versions. The Town & Country name continued to identify the station wagons. Interior upholstery came in 14 color and fabric choices using "Times Square" metallic threaded cloth with pleated vinyl inserts. Swivel seats were available on all body styles, except the station wagon, and were standard on Chrysler 300Es. The Windsor continued to be built on the Dodge chassis.

CHRYSLER I.D. NUMBERS: Serial numbers were found on the left front hinge post. Engine numbers were located on the boss behind the water pump. Chrysler instituted a new serial number coding system that consisted of 10 symbols. [Windsor] First symbol "M" indicated 1959. The second digit "5" indicated Chrysler. The third digit "1" indicated Windsor and the fourth digit indicated the assembly plant, as follows: 1=Detroit; 4=Los Angeles. The last six symbols represented the production sequence number, beginning with 100001. Detroit-built cars were numbered M511-100001 and up. Los Angeles-built cars were numbered M514-100001 and up. Detroit-built station wagons were numbered M571-100001 and up. Los Angeles-built station wagons were numbered M574-100001 and up. [Saratoga] Detroit-built cars used numbers M531-100001 and up. Los Angeles-built cars used numbers M534-100001 and up. The coding system was the same used on all Chryslers. The third symbol "2" indicated Saratoga. [New Yorker] Detroit-built cars used numbers M551-100001 and up. Los Angeles-built cars used numbers M554-100001 and up. Detroit-built station wagons used serial numbers M571-100001. Los Angeles-built station wagons used numbers M574-100001 and up. The third symbol "3" indicated New Yorker/300-E. [300-E] All cars were built in Detroit and were numbered M591-100001 and up.

Windsor Series

Model Number	Body/Style Number	Body Type & Seating	Factory Price	Shipping Weight	Production Total
MC1-L	513	4-dr Sedan-6P	$3,204	3,800 lbs.	19,910
MC1-L	512	2-dr Hardtop Coupe-6P	$3,289	3,735 lbs.	6,775
MC1-L	514	4-dr Hardtop Sedan-6P	$3,353	3,830 lbs.	6,084
MC1-L	515	2-dr Convertible-6P	$3,620	3,950 lbs.	961
MC1-L	576	Town & Country Wagon-6P	$3,691	4,045 lbs.	992
MC1-L	577	Town & Country Wagon-9P	$3,878	4,070 lbs.	751

SARATOGA SERIES — (8-CYLINDER): The Saratoga used the long wheelbase chassis (126 inches). From the cowl area back, the sheet metal was identical to that of the Windsor. However, the front end sheet metal was four inches longer. A new color sweep began at the lower rear quarter panel and arched upward, in a graceful manner, to a mid-body location. It then ran forward to the tip of the front fender. Standard two-tone color combinations had the body and roof panel insert in the same color and contrasting finish on the color sweep, roof outline and C-pillar. A Saratoga nameplate was located just forward of the taillamp housing. A Golden Lion medallion was used in Chrysler's new promotional theme, "Chrysler 1959 — presenting the Lion-hearted Car that's every inch a New Adventure." An array of options included the unique swivel seat. Interiors were all vinyl. Optional were seat inserts made of Jacquard material called Mayfair.

Saratoga Series

Model Number	Body/Style Number	Body Type & Seating	Factory Price	Shipping Weight	Production Total
MC2-M	533	4-dr Sedan-6P	$3,966	4,010 lbs.	8,783
MC2-M	532	2-dr Hardtop Coupe-6P	$4,026	3,970 lbs.	3,753
MC2-M	534	4-dr Hardtop Sedan-6P	$4,104	4,035 lbs.	4,943

The 1959 Chrysler 300-D convertible

NEW YORKER SERIES — (8-CYLINDER): The B-series engine was used for the first time in a New Yorker. The Hemi engine was no longer available. Horsepower was up slightly, as was displacement. Engine weight, simplicity of design and lower manufacturing costs were the principal reasons for the change in power plant. The New Yorker used a spear-like color sweep with horizontal top trim. The lower trim molding dipped and broadened, at the rear, running to bumper level height. An anodized insert ran from front to rear, within the color spear, and seven slash-type strips were added at the rear. They continued the same pattern used on previous New Yorkers. The Golden Lion insignia rode below the New Yorker script at the rear portion of the front fender. Upholstery options consisted of 22 combinations of vinyl and Jacquard fabric. The instrument panel and dashboard were relatively unchanged from the two previous years.

The squaring and apparent raising of the Chrysler rear fenders and taillights fit the 300-D well. It kept with the performance car theme.

New Yorker Series

Model Number	Body/Style Number	Body Type & Seating	Factory Price	Shipping Weight	Production Total
MC3-H	553	4-dr Sedan-6P	$4,424	4,120 lbs.	7,792
MC3-H	552	2-dr Hardtop Coupe-6P	$4,476	4,080 lbs.	2,435
MC3-H	554	4-dr Hardtop Sedan-6P	$4,533	4,165 lbs.	4,805
MC3-H	555	2-dr Convertible-6P	$4,890	4,270 lbs.	286
MC3-H	578	Town & Country Wagon-6P	$4,997	4,295 lbs.	444
MC3-H	579	Town & Country Wagon-9P	$5,212	4,360 lbs.	564
MC3-H	—	Chassis	—	—	2

1959 Chrysler Saratoga two-door hardtop

Phil Hall Collection

300-E SERIES — (8-CYLINDER): Considered a part of the New Yorker series, the "Beautiful Brute" continued the tradition of luxurious, high-performance driving pleasure. Minor styling revisions and the use of a wedge-shaped combustion chamber engine were changes. The new engine was said to have performance equal to or slightly better than the Hemi engine, which left no doubt as to the car's heritage. A revised grille, on the familiar theme, eliminated the vertical bar look. A 300 insignia was placed on the driver's side of the hood, in line with the headlamps. Swivel bucket seats were available and the red-white-blue medallion was positioned in its usual place. The letter "E" was added to the medallion to signify the new model as the 300-E. This was the last year for separate body and frame design.

300-E Series

Model Number	Body/Style Number	Body Type & Seating	Factory Price	Shipping Weight	Production Total
MC3-H	592	2-dr Hardtop-6P	$5,319	4,290 lbs.	550
MC3-H	595	2-dr Convertible-6P	$5,749	4,350 lbs.	140

WINDSOR ENGINE: V-8. Cast iron block. Displacement: 383 cid. Bore and stroke: 4.03 x 3.75 inches. Compression ratio: 10.1:1. Brake hp: 305 at 4800 rpm. Five main bearings. Hydraulic valve lifters. Carburetor: Carter Type BBD two-barrel Model 2872S.

SARATOGA ENGINE: V-8. Cast iron block. Displacement: 383 cid. Bore and stroke: 4.03 x 3.75 inches. Compression ratio: 10.1:1. Brake hp: 325 at 4600 rpm. Five main bearings. Hydraulic valve lifters. Carburetor: Carter Type AFB four-barrel Model 2797S.

NEW YORKER ENGINE: V-8. Cast iron block. Displacement: 413 cid. Bore and stroke: 4.18 x 3.75 inches. Compression ratio: 10.0:1. Brake hp: 350 at 4600 rpm. Five main bearings. Hydraulic valve lifters. Carburetor: Carter Type AFB four-barrel.

300-E ENGINE: V-8. Cast iron block. Displacement: 413 cid. Bore and stroke: 4.18 x 3.75 inches. Compression ratio: 10.1:1. Brake hp: 380 at 5000 rpm. Five main bearings. Hydraulic valve lifters. Carburetors: Two Carter four-barrel Type AFB Model 2798S.

CHASSIS FEATURES: Wheelbase: (Windsor) 122 inches; (Saratoga) 126 inches; (New Yorker) 126 inches; (300-E) 126 inches. Overall length: (Windsor) 216.6 inches; (Saratoga) 220.6 inches; (New Yorker) 220.9 inches; (300-E) 220.9 inches. Front tread: (Windsor) 60.9 inches; (Saratoga) 60.9 inches; (New Yorker) 61.2 inches; (300-E) 61.2 inches. Rear tread: (Windsor) 59.8 inches; (Saratoga) 59.8 inches; (New Yorker) 60.0 inches; (300-E) 60.0 inches. Tires: (Windsor) 8.00 x 14-inch; (Saratoga) 8.50 x 14-inch; (New Yorker) 9.00 x 14-inch and (300-E) 9.00 x 14-inch.

OPTIONS: Power steering (Windsor). TorqueFlite (Windsor). Power brakes (Windsor). Power windows. Power seat. Swivel seats. Air-Temp air conditioning. Custom super-soft cushion rayon tires. White sidewall tires. Nylon and Captive-Air tires. Stainless steel wheel covers on Windsor (standard on Windsor Town & Country). Remote control mirror. Radios. Antennas (including power antenna). Two-tone finish. Solex glass. Heater. Rear window defroster. Auto-Pilot. Windshield washer. Undercoating. Non-slip differential. Handbrake warning lights. Back-up light (Windsor). Sill moldings (Windsor).

HISTORICAL FOOTNOTES: It was the first year for "B" block engines and the last year for the separate body and frame construction. The "Golden Lion" was the new advertising theme. The 1959 models were introduced on Oct. 24, 1958.

Chrysler promoted the lion image in 1959 advertising. The lion was in gold trim. The outside mirrors reflected the flight-inspired Forward Look styling.

The famed push-button gear selectors had become very familiar on Chrysler Corporation cars with automatic transmissions by 1959.

De Soto

Clockwise: The Sportsman expressed a new openness that fit the 1950s.

Walter P. Chrysler named the car after Spanish explorer Hernando De Soto. His glowing likeness guided drivers as they explored highways.

The De Soto Sportsman logo told everyone this was a new era for the car.

The 1950 De Soto Custom Sportsman hardtop used the convertible's windshield and doors and its color-coordinated instrument panel.

De Soto began the 1950s with a handsome face-lift of its 1949 styling. The grille continued its vertical theme from the previous year, but the grille now had 28 strong chrome bars with a painted panel down the middle, holding an elaborate crest. The grille had less chrome than the 1949 grille, but it seemed more massive, and the dividing panel made it seem less added-on than the previous grille. The optional light-up hood ornament that made Hernando De Soto's face glow a bright amber when the headlights were switch on gave the De Soto added glitz over all the other corporation divisions.

Also reducing the added-on elements of the car was the elimination of the elaborate multi-purpose housing (trunk handle/license plate frame/brake light/back-up light/license plate light) on the trunk lid. This one-device-does-all was a handsome, chrome-laden Art Deco artifact belonging more to the 1930s than the 1950s. Its elimination brought the 1950 De Soto further into the new decade. In keeping with the bigger-on-the-inside/smaller-on-the-outside theme, the 1949 rear fenders had narrowed toward the rear of the car, and the rear bumpers did not extend beyond the width of the car. For 1950, the rear fender flared outward more toward the rear, and the bumpers extended beyond the fenders, adding to the 1950 model's more modern appearance compared with the 1949. The 1950 De Soto used the same dash as the 1949, but the dash no longer was woodgrained and was only available in a medium solid gray or a sort of "brown sugar" color. The removal of woodgraining also brought the car further from the Art Deco 1930s and seemed more modern.

Chryslers and De Sotos continued the Feather-Light steering from 1949. The steering gear sat on its side on the frame with the pitman arm swinging front-to-back instead of side-to-side. The pitman arm's series of connections to the tie rods added leverage and eased the steering effort.

DELUXE SERIES — (6-CYLINDER): The Deluxe series was the lower trim level, and its lack of rear fender gravel guards and painted rubber steering wheel are its identifying features. Deluxes also had plainer upholstery choices. Other than these minor traits, the Deluxe had all the trim of the higher-lever Custom series. The Deluxe nameplate was on the front doors below the vent pane.

DE SOTO I.D. NUMBERS: Serial numbers were located on the left front door hinge pillar post. Letters shown in midsection of lines, before the serial numbers, identified the assembly plant as follows: D=Detroit, Mich.; LA=Los Angeles, Calif.; W=Windsor, Ontario, Canada. These letters were not part of the serial number. Deluxes built in Detroit had serial numbers 6233501 to 6262653; those built in Los Angeles had serial numbers 60005001 to 60009175. Taxis were numbered 5116001 to 5118350. Customs built in Detroit had serial numbers 50062001 to 50148412. Cars built in Los Angeles had serial numbers 62011501 to 62023225. Engine numbers were located on the left side of the block below the cylinder head between first and second cylinders. Engine numbers began with S13-1001 and ran through S13-93581.

Deluxe Series

Model Number	Body/Style Number	Body Type & Seating	Factory Price	Shipping Weight	Production Total
Standard Wheelbase					
S14-1	Note 1	2-dr Club Coupe-6P	$1,976	3,450 lbs.	10,703
S14-1	Note 1	4-dr Sedan-6P	$1,986	3,525 lbs.	18,489
S14-1	Note 1	4-dr Carry-All-6P	$2,191	3,600 lbs.	3,900
Long Wheelbase					
S14-1	Note 1	4-dr Sedan-8P	$2,676	3,995 lbs.	235

NOTE 1: *Code numbers identifying body style were not used.*

NOTE 2: *The production totals above include 2,350 taxicabs in the Deluxe series.*

ENGINE: L-head. Six-cylinder. Cast iron block. Displacement: 236.7 inches. Bore and stroke: 3.438 x 4.25 inches. Compression ratio: 7.0:1. Brake hp: 112 at 3600 rpm. Carburetors: (Fluid Drive or M-6) B-B E7L3 or B-B E7L4; (standard transmission) EX2R or EX3R.

CUSTOM SERIES — (6-CYLINDER): The Custom series had chrome gravel shields that melded gracefully with the rocker trim and a mottled, plastic steering wheel. The Sportsman was the new

You could always tell a De Soto by what many called its "toothy grin," the vertical bars that made up its front grille.

The Sportsman (left) had a more open-air feeling that reflected the 1950s while the club coupe (right) still had the closed, protected look of the 1930s and 1940s.

The De Soto club coupe's rear window was nearly a foot from the edge of the trunk lid, as opposed to the hardtop and sedan roofs that stretched to the trunk.

A look at the interior of the 1950 De Soto.

Phil Hall Collection

The dashboard of the 1950 De Soto.

Phil Hall Collection

1950 De Soto station wagon

Phil Hall Collection

two-door hardtop, and while early factory photos show the "Sportsman" name under the vent pane as the Deluxe and Custom names are, the mass-produced Sportsmans had the name above the chrome spears on the doors. De Soto debuted its first all-steel station wagon in the Custom series. Factory two-tone paint schemes were available in several combinations on Custom sedans and club coupe with even more two-tone choices available on the Sportsman hardtops.

1950 De Soto
Custom sedan

Custom Series

Model Number	Body/Style Number	Body Type & Seating	Factory Price	Shipping Weight	Production Total
Standard Wheelbase					
S14-2	Note 1	4-dr Sedan-6P	$2,174	3,640 lbs.	72,664
S14-2	Note 1	2-dr Club Coupe-6P	$2,156	3,575 lbs.	6,100
S14-2	Note 1	2-dr Sportsman HT-6P	$2,489	3,735 lbs.	4,600
S14-2	Note 1	2-dr Convertible Coupe-6P	$2,578	3,815 lbs.	2,900
S14-2	Note 1	4-dr Station Wagon-6P	$3,093	4,035 lbs.	600
S14-2	Note 1	4-dr Steel Station Wagon-6P	$2,717	3,900 lbs.	100
Long Wheelbase					
S14-2	Note 1	4-dr Sedan-8P	$2,863	4,115 lbs.	734
S14-2	Note 1	4-dr Suburban-8P	$3,179	4,400 lbs.	623

NOTE 1: *Code numbers identifying body style were not used.*

ENGINE: L-head. Six-cylinder. Cast iron block. Displacement: 236.7 inches. Bore and stroke: 3.438 x 4.25 inches. Compression ratio: 7.0:1. Brake hp: 112 at 3600 rpm. Carburetor: (Fluid Drive or M-6) B-B E7L3 or B-B E7L4; (Standard transmission) EX2R or EX3R.

CHASSIS FEATURES: Wheelbase (long wheelbase models) 139.5 inches; (all others) 125.5 inches. Tires: 7.60 x 15 for all standard wheelbase models; 8.20 x 15 for others. Three-speed manual transmission was standard on Deluxes. Tip-Toe Hydraulic shift with Gyrol Fluid Drive was standard equipment on Customs and $121 extra on Deluxes.

OPTIONS: Tip-Toe Hydraulic Shift with Gyrol Fluid Drive on Deluxe models ($121); standard on Custom models. Radio. Heater. Chrome full wheel covers. Directional signals (Deluxe). Backup lights (Deluxe). Whitewalls. Electric clock. Lighted hood ornament. Two-tone paint.

HISTORICAL FOOTNOTES: De Soto came in 14th in the production race with 127,430 assemblies for the 1950 calendar year.

The 1951 De Soto Custom sedan seemed "de-trimmed" up front after the chrome-dripping 1950 models.

Jerry Marshall

The 1951 De Soto looks noticeably plainer than the 1950 models, but in some ways the design was a little more modern. The hood was flatter, and the front of it sloped back more, giving the car a slightly sleeker profile. The massive chrome teeth floated in an otherwise empty grille opening. There was no trim around the grille, making it appear more mouth-like. The parking lights looked a little less added-on as part of the grille instead of being attached to the grille or stuck to the body. Unlike all the other Chrysler Corporation divisions, the De Soto had no chrome trim spears on the front fenders and doors. The rear treatment remained exactly as it had been in 1950, and the same optional light-up Hernando De Soto hood ornament glowed at night. The pod that faced the driver in 1950 was gone and was replaced by three dials. Woodgraining made a reappearance.

DELUXE SERIES — (6-CYLINDER): The 1951 De Soto S15 lineup continued with the same models as the previous year. Deluxe models lacked front door nomenclature and came standard with small hubcaps.

DE SOTO I.D. NUMBERS: Serial numbers were located on the left front door hinge pillar post. Letters shown in midsection of lines, before the serial numbers, identified the assembly plant as follows: D=Detroit, Mich.; LA=Los Angeles, Calif.; W=Windsor, Ontario, Canada. These letters were not part of the serial number. Only serial numbers were to be used for identification purposes. Deluxe models built in Detroit had serial numbers 6269001 to 6283459. Deluxe models built in Los Angeles had serial numbers 60011001 to 60012889. Custom models built in Detroit had serial numbers 50155001 to 50230003. Custom models built in Los Angeles had serial numbers 62024001 to 62032486. Engine numbers were located on the left side of the block below the cylinder head between first and second cylinders. Engine numbers were S15-1001 and up for models and series and were continued into 1952 without interruption.

The 1951 De Soto Custom sedan seems suspended in space in this brochure artwork.

Phil Hall Collection

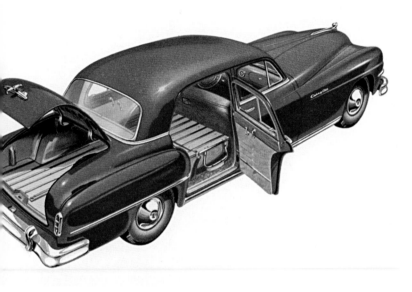

The famed chair-height seat from the 1951 De Soto.

Phil Hall Collection

The versatile 1951 De Soto Carry-All sedan. *Phil Hall Collection*

The bed of the 1951 De Soto's All-Steel wagon.

Phil Hall Collection

This 1951 De Soto Custom club coupe is prized by its owners.

Jennifer Bruzina

Deluxe Series

Model Number	Body/Style Number	Body Type & Seating	Factory Price	Shipping Weight	Production Total
Standard Wheelbase					
S15-1	Note 1	4-dr Sedan-6P	$2,227	3,570 lbs.	Note 2
S15-1	Note 1	2-dr Club Coupe-6P	$2,215	3,475 lbs.	Note 2
S15-1	Note 1	4-dr Carry-All-6P	$2,457	3,685 lbs.	Note 2
Long Wheelbase					
S15-1	Note 1	4-dr Sedan-8P	$3,001	4,005 lbs.	Note 2

NOTE 1: *Body style code numbers were not provided.*

NOTE 2: *Production for 1951 and 1952 was lumped together, with no breakouts available for individual model year production. See Historical Footnotes for additional production data.*

ENGINE: L-head. Six-cylinder. Cast iron block. Displacement: 250.6 cid. Bore and stroke: 3.438 x 4.50 inches. Compression ratio: 7.0:1. Brake hp: 116 at 3600 rpm. Five main bearings. Carburetors: Stromberg 380359; (with M-6 transmission) Stromberg 380349; (also with M-6 transmission) Carter E9AI.

CUSTOM SERIES — (6-CYLINDER): Various models in the Custom series were distinguished by the words Custom, Sportsman or Suburban on the front fenders. The Custom series also had more exterior color choices and interior fabric and color choices. These 1951 models were carried into the 1952 model year due to manufacturing sanctions imposed by involvement in the Korean War.

Custom Series

Model Number	Body/Style Number	Body Type & Seating	Factory Price	Shipping Weight	Production Total
Standard Wheelbase					
S15-2	Note 1	4-dr Sedan-6P	$2,438	3,685 lbs.	Note 2
S15-2	Note 1	2-dr Club Coupe-6P	$2,418	3,585 lbs.	Note 2
S15-2	Note 1	2-dr Sportsman HT-6P	$2,761	3,760 lbs.	Note 2
S15-2	Note 1	2-dr Convertible Coupe-6P	$2,862	3,840 lbs.	Note 2
S15-2	Note 1	4-dr Station Wagon-6P	$3,047	3,960 lbs.	Note 2
Long Wheelbase					
S15-2	Note 1	4-dr Sedan-8P	$3,211	4,155 lbs.	Note 2
S15-2	Note 1	4-dr Suburban-9P	$3,566	4,395 lbs.	Note 2

NOTE 1: *Body style code numbers were not provided.*

NOTE 2: *Production for 1951 and 1952 was lumped together, with no breakouts available for individual year production. See the historical footnotes for additional production data.*

The stern-looking Hernando de Soto image glowed amber in the optional light-up ornament.

Jennifer Bruzina

ENGINE: L-head. Six-cylinder. Cast iron block. Displacement: 250.6 cid. Bore and stroke: 3.438 x 4.50 inches. Compression ratio: 7.0:1. Brake hp: 116 at 3600 rpm. Five main bearings. Carburetors: Stromberg 380359; (with M-6 transmission) Stromberg 380349; (also with M-6 transmission) Carter E9AI.

CHASSIS FEATURES: Wheelbase: (long wheelbase models) 139.5 inches; (all others) 125.5 inches. Three-speed manual transmission was standard in Deluxe models. Tip-Toe Shift Fluid Drive (Prest-O-Matic) was optional on Deluxes and standard on Customs. As an option it was priced at $132. The number of cars built with automatic transmission (semi-automatic in De Sotos) was governed by rules established by the National Price Administration (NPA). The permissible NPA attachment rates varied in relation to a car's sales price bracket. In the De Soto price class, the limit was established at 65 percent. Tire sizes: (short wheelbase models) 7.60 x 15-inch; (long wheelbase models) 8.20 x 15-inch.

OPTIONS: Radio. Heater. Whitewall tires. Full wheel covers. Lighted hood ornament. Directional signals. Back-up lights. Two-tone paint.

HISTORICAL FOOTNOTES: The 1951 De Sotos were introduced in showrooms on Jan. 27, 1951. Due to the Korean War, production for the 1951 and 1952 model years was counted as a single total. However, industry sources record that 121,794 De Sotos (2.28 percent of total industry output) were built in the 1951 model year. Of these, 3,910 were Custom convertibles; 6,775 were Custom hardtops and 1,637 were Custom station wagons. Calendar year production stood at 120,757 units, which put De Soto 12th in the industry. On Dec. 16, 1950, the Economic Stabilization Agency (ESA) froze prices of automobiles at the Dec. 1 level. This freeze lasted until March 1, 1951.

"[the 1951 De Soto Suburban] pulled our trailer coach through desert heat and over mountains, from Burbank to St. Paul and home again... How's that for engineering integrity and durability?"

Charles Gayman, WPC News, April 1976

DE SOTO-PLYMOUTH Dealers present **GROUCHO MARX** in "You Bet Your Life" every week on both RADIO and TELEVISION...NBC networks.

*1952 De Soto
FireDome 8 sedan*

The big news for the 1952 was De Soto's first-ever V-8. The corporation installed a smaller, 276-cubic-inch version of its hemi-head V-8 into the De Soto with Fluid Torque and the Tip-Toe Shift semi-automatic transmission behind it. The new V-8 De Soto was now more competitive marketing-wise with the V-8 Oldsmobile, and vastly superior to the Mercury V-8 which dated back to the 1930s.

The 1952 De Soto was nearly identical to the 1951 models. The light-up hood ornament disappeared, and a small hood scoop appeared. The stylized, cursive "De Soto" script on the front of the hood was replaced by a series of large block letters. The taillights and back-up lights were more integral with the car's back end design.

DELUXE SERIES — (6-CYLINDER): The Deluxes followed the same de-trimmed, lower-priced theme as they had since 1950. The Deluxe had fewer interior and exterior colors than the Custom, but the Deluxe series still had the Carry-All sedan. Even though its sales totals equaled the station wagon, the Carry-All sedan seemed redundant due to the popularity of the all-steel station wagons.

DE SOTO I.D. NUMBERS: Serial numbers were located on the left front door hinge pillar post. Letters shown in midsection of lines, before the serial numbers, identified the assembly plant as follows: D=Detroit, Mich.; LA=Los Angeles, Calif.; W=Windsor, Ontario, Canada. These letters were not part of the serial number. Only serial numbers were to be used for identification purposes. Deluxe models built in Detroit had serial numbers 6283601 to 6288250. Deluxe models built in Los Angeles had serial numbers 60013001 to 60013651. An important phase of De Soto operations was the manufacture of taxicabs built on the long wheelbase platform with body shell furnished to taxicab manufacturer's specifications. Taxis had serial numbers 5121401 to 5122684. Custom models built in Detroit had serial numbers 50203101 to 50261940. Custom models built in Los Angeles had serial numbers 62032601 to 62036371. Firedome models built in Detroit had serial numbers 5500001 to 55040155. Firedome models built in Los Angeles had serial numbers 64001001 to 64005899. Six-cylinder engine numbers were located on the left side of the block below the cylinder head between the first and second cylinders. These numbers were S15-145987 and up for Deluxes and Customs and continued into 1952 without interruption. On the V-8, the engine number was positioned atop the engine block under the water outlet elbow. Engine numbers S17-1001 to S17-46488 were used at both assembly plants.

De Luxe Series

Model Number	Body/Style Number	Body Type & Seating	Factory Price	Shipping Weight	Production Total
Standard Wheelbase					
S15-1	Note 1	4-dr Sedan-6P	$2,333	3,540 lbs.	13,506
S15-1	Note 1	2-dr Club Coupe-6P	$2,319	3,435 lbs.	6,100
S15-1	Note 1	4-dr Carry-All-6P	$2,572	3,650 lbs.	1,700
Long Wheelbase					
S15-1	Note 1	4-dr Taxi-6P	N/A	N/A	3,550
S15-1	Note 1	4-dr Sedan-8P	$3,142	4,035 lbs.	343

NOTE 1: *Code numbers identifying body style were not used.*

NOTE 2: *Production totals are a combination of 1951 and 1952 output, with no breakouts per model year available. See Historical Footnotes in 1951 section for additional production data. Totals for Deluxe models include 3,550 California taxicabs. For the 1952 calendar year, De Soto produced 97,585 cars, including 5,325 hardtops, 1,319 station wagons and 1,150 convertibles. These body styles were available with Custom trim only.*

1952 De Soto FireDome 8 convertible

Phil Hall Collection

1952 De Soto FireDome 8 Sportsman   Phil Hall Collection

ENGINES: L-head. Six-cylinder. Cast iron block. Displacement: 250.6 cid. Bore and stroke: 3.438 x 4.50 inches. Compression ratio: 7.0:1. Brake hp: 116 at 3600 rpm. Five main bearings. Carburetors: Stromberg 380359; (with M-6 transmission) Stromberg 380349; (also with M-6 transmission) Carter E9AI.

CUSTOM SERIES — (6-CYL): The Custom six was also a carryover from 1951 with the same changes outlined in Deluxe models plus upgraded upholstery choices. The word Custom appeared on the front fenders. Late models used the Air-Vent-type hood similar to the Firedome V-8.

Custom Series

Model Number	Body/Style Number	Body Type & Seating	Factory Price	Shipping Weight	Production Total
Standard Wheelbase					
S15-2	Note 1	4-dr Sedan-6P	$2,552	3,660 lbs.	88,491
S15-2	Note 1	2-dr Club Coupe-6P	$2,531	3,565 lbs.	19,000
S15-2	Note 1	2-dr Sportsman HT-6P	$2,890	3,720 lbs.	8,750
S15-2	Note 1	2-dr Convertible Coupe-6P	$2,996	3,865 lbs.	3,950
S15-2	Note 1	4-dr Station Wagon-6P	$3,189	4,020 lbs.	1,440
Long Wheelbase					
S15-2	Note 1	4-dr Sedan-8P	$3,362	4,155 lbs.	769
S15-2	Note 1	4-dr Suburban-9P	$3,734	4,370 lbs.	600

NOTE 1: Code numbers identifying the body style were not used.

NOTE 2: Production totals are a combination of 1951 and 1952 output, with no breakouts per model year available. See 1952 De Soto Deluxe specifications chart notes for additional production data.

1952 De Soto FireDome 8 sedan

Phil Hall Collection

ENGINE: L-head. Six-cylinder. Cast iron block. Displacement: 250.6 cid. Bore and stroke: 3.438 x 4.50 inches. Compression ratio: 7.0:1. Brake hp: 116 at 3600 rpm. Five main bearings. Carburetor: Stromberg 380359; (with M-6 transmission) Stromberg 380349; (also with M-6 transmission) Carter E9AI.

FIREDOME SERIES — (V-8): Essentially, the Firedome models were Customs with suitable modifications to accommodate the new V-8. Nomenclature consisted of the name "Firedome 8" placed on front fender sides and an "8" positioned on the deck lid. Shortly after introduction, the "8" emblems were replaced by a V-8 insignia for the deck.

Firedome Series

Model Number	Body/Style Number	Body Type & Seating	Factory Price	Shipping Weight	Production Total
Standard Wheelbase					
S17	Note 1	4-dr Sedan-6P	$2,740	3,760 lbs.	35,651
S17	Note 1	2-dr Club Coupe-6P	$2,718	3,675 lbs.	5,699
S17	Note 1	2-dr Sportsman HT-6P	$3,078	3,850 lbs.	3,000
S17	Note 1	2-dr Convertible Coupe-6P	$3,183	3,950 lbs.	850
S17	Note 1	4-dr Station Wagon-6P	$3,377	4,080 lbs.	550
Long Wheelbase					
S17	Note 1	4-dr Sedan-8P	$3,547	4,325 lbs.	80

NOTE 1: *Code numbers identifying the body style were not used. This series was offered exclusively in 1952 and production totals for Firedome models are for this model year only.*

ENGINE: V-8. Overhead valve. Hemispherical combustion chambers. Displacement: 276.1 cid. Bore and stroke: 3.626 x 3.344 inches. Compression ratio: 7.0:1. Brake hp: 160 at 4400 rpm. Five main bearings. Hydraulic valve lifters. Carburetors: Carter WCD two-barrel Models 884S, 884SA and 884SC. Also used were Models 901S with Fluid Drive or Torque Convertor and M-6 transmission; 905S with standard transmission; 906S with standard transmission in combination with overdrive. Later Firedome V-8s used Models 908S, 909S and 910S, which carried over into 1953 production.

CHASSIS FEATURES: Wheelbase: (long wheelbase models) 139-½ inches; (short wheelbase models) 125-½ inches. Overall length: (long wheelbase models) 224-⅜ inches; (short wheelbase models) 208-⅜ inches. Front tread: (all) 56-5/16 inches. Rear tread: (all) 59-9/16 inches. Tires: (eight-passenger) 8.20 x 15-inch; (all others) 7.60 x 15-inch.

OPTIONS: Power steering ($199). Overdrive ($102). Tip-Toe Shift with Fluid Torque Drive ($257). Tip-Toe Shift with Fluid Drive ($132). Solex tinted glass. Electric window lids. Radio. Heater. White sidewall tires. Power brakes. Two-tone paint.

HISTORICAL FOOTNOTES: Actual building of Firedome V-8s commenced Oct. 18, 1951. About 85 percent of De Sotos were built at the Wyoming Avenue assembly plant in Detroit. Engines were built at the Warren Avenue plant, a so-called "push-button" facility. The "transfermatic" machinery in this factory had a capacity of 60 V-8 power plants per hour. Calendar year output of 97,585 cars put De Soto 12th in the industry.

The 1953 De Soto was in tune with its era with very little that reminded drivers of the previous decades. The only indication was a bulging rear fender.

Dave Kopesky

The De Soto was nearly all-new for 1953. It was the same car under the skin, but the new body moved away from the closed, upright feel that kept sedan styling rooted in the 1930s and 1940s through 1952. The profile of the 1953 Chrysler products more closely approximated the silhouette of the offerings from Oldsmobile and Buick. The front fender line extended front to rear and the back fenders were now integral with the body structure. The taillights sat high on the ends of the rear fenders and were more in keeping with the times. The roofline now faded into the rear deck in a more pleasing fashion. The windshield was one piece and curved, and the sedans now used the three-piece rear window the Sportsman hardtops had featured since 1950. The De Soto added two more teeth to the grille for a wider-smiling total of 11, and the large, oval parking lights sat way out on the ends of the grille, adding to the feeling of greater width. The cars had no trim on the front fenders, which made them look plainer than they should have for their price range, and plain compared to their competition. Changes from 1952 included a new combination tail, stop and back-up lights and a gas cap positioned below the deck lid on the left side. The Custom and Deluxe names were gone. The station wagons and eight-passenger sedans used the 1952 styling from the windshield back.

This would be the last year for the semi-automatic transmissions. The corporation was testing the fully-automatic PowerFlite transmission on Chryslers late in the 1953 model run. Also, air conditioning was offered for the first time on De Sotos.

POWERMASTER SIX SERIES — (6-CYLINDER): The Powermaster was the equivalent of the low-priced Deluxe series of 1949 to 1952. The Powermaster had fewer interior and exterior color choices and had no side trim—only the Powermaster name on the front fenders.

DE SOTO I.D. NUMBERS: Serial numbers were located on the left front door hinge pillar post. Letters shown in midsection of lines, before the serial numbers, identified the assembly plant as follows: D=Detroit, Mich.; LA=Los Angeles, Calif.; W=Windsor, Ontario, Canada. These letters were not part of the serial number. Only serial numbers were to be used for identification purposes. Powermasters built in Detroit had serial numbers 50266001 to 50304981. Powermasters built in Los Angeles had serial numbers 6209001 to 62042345. Taxis were numbered 5124001 to 5125701. Firedome models built in Detroit had serial numbers 55050001 to 55127622. Firedome models built in Los Angeles had serial numbers 64008001 to 64015691. Six-cylinder engine numbers were located on the left side of the block below the cylinder head between the first and second cylinders. These numbers were S18-1001 and up for Powermasters. On the V-8, the engine number was positioned atop the engine block under the water outlet elbow. Engine numbers S16-1001 and up were used.

Powermaster Six Series

Model Number	Body/Style Number	Body Type & Seating	Factory Price	Shipping Weight	Production Total
S18	Note 1	2-dr Club Coupe-6P	$2,434	3,495 lbs.	8,063
S18	Note 1	4-dr Sedan-6P	$2,456	3,555 lbs.	33,644
S18	Note 1	4-dr Sedan-8P	$3,266	4,070 lbs.	225
S18	Note 1	2-dr Sportsman HT-6P	$2,781	3,596 lbs.	1,470
S18	Note 1	4-dr Station Wagon-6P	$3,093	3,855 lbs.	500

NOTE 1: *Code numbers identifying body style were not used. Production totals include 1,700 California taxicabs. Eight-passenger models were on the long wheelbase chassis.*

ENGINE: L-head. Six-cylinder. Cast iron block. Displacement: 250.6 cid. Bore and stroke: 3.438 x 4.50 inches. Compression ratio: 7.0:1. Brake hp: 116 at 3600 rpm. Five main bearings. Carburetor: Stromberg 380359; (with M-6 transmission) Stromberg 380349; (also with M-6 transmission) Carter E9AI.

FIREDOME SERIES — (V-8): This was the second year for the V-8 models. They shared most features of the six-cylinder series and offered the same six body styles as seen in 1952. The words "Firedome V-8" appeared on both front fenders and the word "Eight" was affixed on the right side, below the deck lid. A chrome trim slash was seen on the front fenders of all models except the eight-passenger sedan and the station wagon.

Under its skin, and behind its front grille, the Powermaster model still used the old six-cylinder engine, but the Firedome V-8 was in step with the 1950s.

Dave Kopesky

Another look at the front grille area of the 1953 De Soto Firedome.

John Lee

Firedome Series

Model Number	Body/Style Number	Body Type & Seating	Factory Price	Shipping Weight	Production Total
S16	Note 1	2-dr Club Coupe-6P	$2,718	3,640 lbs.	14,591
S16	Note 1	4-dr Sedan-6P	$2,740	3,705 lbs.	64,211
S16	Note 1	4-dr Sedan-8P	$3,544	4,290 lbs.	200
S16	Note 1	2-dr Convertible Coupe-6P	$3,172	3,965 lbs.	1,700
S16	Note 1	2-dr Sportsman HT-6P	$3,069	3,675 lbs.	4,700
S16	Note 1	4-dr Station Wagon-6P	$3,366	3,990 lbs.	1,100

NOTE 1: *Code numbers identifying body style were not used. Eight-passenger models were on the long wheelbase chassis.*

ENGINE: V-8. Overhead valve. Hemispherical combustion chambers. Displacement: 276.1 cid. Bore and stroke: 3.626 x 3.344 inches. Compression ratio: 7.0:1. Brake hp: 160 at 4400 rpm. Five main bearings. Hydraulic valve lifters. Carburetors: Same as 1952 late-year models.

CHASSIS FEATURES: Wheelbase: (long wheelbase models) 139-½ inches; (short wheelbase models) 125-½ inches. Overall length: (long wheelbase models) 224 inches; (short wheelbase models) 213-⅜ inches; (station wagon) 212-¾ inches. Front tread: (all) 56-5/16 inches. Rear tread: (all) 59-9/16 inches. Tires: (eight-passenger) 8.20 x 15-inch; (all others) 7.60 x 15-inch.

OPTIONS: Overdrive ($98). Tip-Toe Shift with Fluid Torque Drive ($237). Tip-Toe Shift with Fluid Drive ($130). Power steering ($177). Power brakes. Solex safety glass. Electric window lifts. White sidewall tires. Air conditioning. Continental tire kit. Wire spoke wheel covers. Full wheel covers. Radio. Heater.

HISTORICAL FOOTNOTES: Calendar year production of 129,959 units put De Soto 12th in the industry this year. Chrysler purchased the Briggs Manufacturing Co. this year for $35,000,000. This was the 25th Anniversary for De Soto, but no special models were offered. The De Soto Adventurer experimental show car was seen during 1953. The model year started in November 1952. Air conditioning was introduced in January, which seems a bit odd!

The De Soto's rear deck area was in tune with many other 1953 cars. John Lee

The modern 1954 De Soto, with its fully automatic Powerflite transmission and V-8, was a big breakaway from the car's previous image.

The De Soto grille smiled even wider for 1954, and the grille opening widened to encompass the entire toothy theme. The parking lights got smaller and were round, and they were part of the grille rather than being outside it as they had been in 1953. The silhouette of the car was the same as 1953 with greater amounts of trim that seemed to fit the styling of the car better and more deliberately. New step-down chrome moldings stretched down the front fenders and doors. The rear fender side moldings now stretched completely to the rear of the cars from the redesigned gravel shields. Headlight and taillight clusters were updated with decorative bezels on top. The dash and interior trim were completely redesigned.

De Soto brought out the Coronado—its first special trim package since the Fifth Avenue of 1942. The Coronado came out as a "spring special" and had a Cadiz Blue body and Sahara Beige roof, or the more rare reverse, and the interior was color-coordinated with this exterior. The Coronados were all four-door sedans and went for the luxury sedan market rather than the sporty hardtop market.

A factory sales brochure said, "As for beauty, the 1954 De Soto Automatic has a brilliant new 'forward' look!'" The statement foreshadowed great things to come for the entire corporation in the following several years.

POWERMASTER SERIES — (6-CYLINDER): The Powermaster name was incorporated into the front fender moldings, and a Powermaster crest adorned the hood. Even the Powermaster seemed more dressed-up than the previous year, and as such, it was a little more in keeping with being an expensive type car as the Deluxes had been in 1950. The Powermaster seems also to have had more choices in colors and interior patterns as well.

DE SOTO I.D. NUMBERS: Serial numbers were located on the left front door hinge pillar post. Letters shown in midsection of lines, before the serial numbers, identified the assembly plant as follows: D=Detroit, Mich.; LA=Los Angeles, Calif.; W=Windsor, Ontario, Canada. These letters were not part of the serial number. Only serial numbers were to be used for identification purposes. Powermasters built in Detroit were numbered 50306001 to 50322514; in Los Angeles 62043001 to 62043897; taxicabs 5126001 to 5128005. Firedomes built in Detroit were numbered 55130001 to 55182504; in Los Angeles 64017001 to 64020704. Six-cylinder engine numbers were located on the left side of the block below the cylinder head between the first and second cylinders. These numbers were S20-1001 through S20-21082. On the V-8, the engine number was positioned atop the engine block under the water outlet elbow. Engine numbers S19-1001 to S19-57604 were used.

Powermaster Six Series

Model Number	Body/Style Number	Body Type & Seating	Factory Price	Shipping Weight	Production Total
S20	Note 1	2-dr Club Coupe-6P	$2,364	3,525 lbs.	3,499
S20	Note 1	4-dr Sedan-6P	$2,386	3,590 lbs.	14,967
S20	Note 1	4-dr Sedan-8P	$3,281	4,120 lbs.	263
S20	Note 1	2-dr Special Club Coupe-6P	$2,893	3,815 lbs.	250
S20	Note 1	4-dr Station Wagon-6P	$3,108	3,855 lbs.	225

NOTE 1: *Code numbers identifying body style were not used. Powermaster production totals include 2,005 taxicabs.*

NOTE 2: *Records show no Powermaster hardtops were sold in the U.S. They were sold in Canada only and were called Powermaster 6 Special Club Coupes (not Sportsman) although they were true pillarless hardtops.*

NOTE 3: *Eight-passenger sedan was on the long wheelbase chassis.*

The De Soto identified itself clearly as having a V-8 under the hood in 1954.

ENGINE: L-head. Six-cylinder. Displacement: 250.6 cid. Bore and stroke: 3.438 x 4.50 inches. Compression ratio: 7.0:1. Brake hp: 116 at 3600 rpm. Carburetors: Carter BBD two-barrel: (with standard transmission) Model 2067S; (with overdrive) Model 2068S; (with PowerFlite) Model 2070S.

FIREDOME SERIES — (V-8): The word Firedome, incorporated between the step down front fender moldings, identified the V-8 models for 1954. There were also prominent V-8 emblems on the front of the hood and rear fender sides, plus a V-shaped insignia on the rear deck lid. Seven models appeared at introduction time and a luxury four-door Coronado sedan was added in the spring. Exterior embellishments on this car included special rear fender signature logos and small medallions on the rear roof C-pillar. A one-piece rear window was seen on the Sportsman V-8.

Firedome Series

Model Number	Body/Style Number	Body Type & Seating	Factory Price	Shipping Weight	Production Total
S19	Note 1	2-dr Club Coupe-6P	$2,652	3,685 lbs.	5,762
S19	Note 1	4-dr Sedan-6P	$2,673	3,750 lbs.	45,095
S19	Note 1	4-dr Sedan-8P	$3,559	4,275 lbs.	165
S19	Note 1	2-dr Convertible Coupe-6P	$3,144	3,995 lbs.	1,025
S19	Note 1	2-dr Sportsman HT-6P	$2,923	3,775 lbs.	4,382
S19	Note 1	4-dr Station Wagon-6P	$3,361	4,025 lbs.	946

The 1954 De Soto was still behind Oldsmobile and Buick stylistically and that was deadly for sales in the early 1950s.

DE SOTO AUTOMATIC with POWERFLITE TRANSMISSION

ENGINE: V-8. Overhead valve. Cast iron block. Displacement: 276.1 cid. Bore and stroke: 3.625 x 3.344 inches. Compression ratio: 7.5:1. Brake hp: 170 at 4400 rpm. Five main bearings. Hydraulic valve lifters. Carburetor: Carter BBD two-barrel Model 2070S; (with standard transmission) Models 2067S or 2129S; (with overdrive) Models 2068S or 2130S. Carter Models 2250S and 2131S also saw applications on PowerFlite-equipped cars. Larger diameter valves were used in some Firedome V-8 models late in the year.

CHASSIS FEATURES: Three-speed manual column-mounted transmission was standard. Overdrive manual transmission was optional at $98 extra. PowerFlite automatic transmission was optional at $189 extra. Wheelbase: (standard) 125-½ inches; (eight-passenger) 139-½ inches. Overall length: (standard) 214-½ inches; (eight-passenger) 223-⅞ inches. Front tread: (all) 56-5/16 inches. Rear tread: (all) 59-⅝ inches. Tires: (eight-passenger) 8.20 x 15-inch; (all others) 7.60 x 15-inch.

OPTIONS: Power steering ($140). Power brakes ($37). Power windows ($101). Radio ($101). Heater ($78). Air Temp air conditioning ($643). Electric clock ($33). Solex tinted glass ($33). Fog lights ($33). White sidewall tires ($33 plus exchange). Wire spoke wheel rims. Wheel covers. Rear seat radio speaker. Windshield washers. Outside rearview mirror.

HISTORICAL FOOTNOTES: De Soto ranked as the 12th largest volume manufacturer in the industry this year, based on calendar year production of 69,844 cars. Only 1.27 percent of American cars were De Sotos. The 1954 models were promoted as "De Soto Automatics" to spotlight the new, fully-automatic PowerFlite transmission. The Coronado was a midyear spring model. Chrysler Corp. held elaborate dedication ceremonies for its new proving grounds, at Chelsea, Michigan, during 1954. The Ghia-built Adventurer II show car appeared this year.

A dramatic cutaway used a 1954 De Soto in a Chrysler Corporation ad.

The top-of-the line 1955 De Soto Fireflite was all new but carried a definite De Soto identity.

"...longer, lower, and wider, with a stylish contemporary new 'forward look' which expresses fleetness, power, and outstanding performance." So said De Soto for the 1955 model introduction.

De Soto styling was all-new for 1955. The refinements that had helped De Soto in 1953 and had failed somewhat in 1954 evolved into what seemed to be a completely new car for 1955, even though, under the skin, these were nearly the very same cars they had been in 1940. The 1955 De Soto shared its new body with Chrysler as had been its habit for 20 years. While the Chrysler was stylish but dignified, the De Soto was a glittery, flashy, wildly two-toned car. Collectors often say the 1955 and '56 De Sotos have some of the greatest two-toning of the 1950s.

The cars were much longer and wider and had no hint of the "bigger-on-the-inside/smaller-on-the-outside" feel from 1949 through 1954. The 1955 Chrysler products were firmly up-to-date. While the Chrysler had chrome taillight housings that lengthened and heightened the ends of the rear fenders, the De Soto did not hide the downward slope of the rear fenders and allowed the rear of the car to have a low, ground-hugging appearance. The taillights were part of the rear fender rather than fancy add-ons like Chrysler's. Comforting to the traditional De Soto buyer, the grille retained De Soto's trademark toothy look.

The dash had two panels—one in front of the driver and one in front of the passenger—divided by a painted piece that matched the interior of the car. Some say this dash mimicked an aircraft dash. The PowerFlite gear selector, called the "Flite-Control" lever, was stuck out of the dash between the steering column and the radio. Higher-trim models had a bullet-shaped, pod-like clock mounted on the top of the dash above the radio that clearly imitated an aircraft compass.

De Soto was all V-8 in 1955. The Firedome moved down to the lower-priced slot, and the new Fireflite took over the expensive position.

FIREDOME — (V-8): Cars in this line were identifiable by the Firedome name, in script, on their front fenders. Bodyside decorations took the form of constant width chrome moldings running front to rear, with a slight kickup above the rear wheel housing. There were nameplates and round medallions, mounted to the rear roof pillar, to help in picking out Sportsman models. Shortly after production began, Fireflite color sweep treatments became a Firedome option. The two-toned Firedome distinguishes itself from the Fireflite by having lighter chrome spears defining its two-toning and by the lack of front fender-top spears. Firedome hardtops do not have the heavy chrome trim piece where the rear quarter of the roof meets the body.

FIREDOME I.D. NUMBERS: Serial numbers and engine numbers were in the previous locations. Serials numbers are usable for identification. Cars built in Detroit were numbered 55185001 to 55256392; in Los Angeles 64022001 to 64026847; taxicab numbers began at 5130001. Engine numbers were S22-1001 to S22-76620.

Firedome Series

Model Number	Body/Style Number	Body Type & Seating	Factory Price	Shipping Weight	Production Total
S22	Note 1	4-dr Sedan-6P	$2,498	3,870 lbs.	46,388
S22	Note 1	2-dr Convertible Coupe-6P	$2,824	4,010 lbs.	625
S22	Note 1	2-dr Sportsman HT	$2,654	3,805 lbs.	28,944
S22	Note 1	2-dr Special Coupe-6P	$2,541	3,810 lbs.	(Notes 1, 2)
S22	Note 1	4-dr Station Wagon-6P	$3,125	4,175 lbs.	1,803

NOTE 1: *Code numbers to provide positive identification of body type were not provided.*

NOTE 2: *Production totals include taxicabs. The production of Fireflite Special two-door hardtop coupes was counted in the figures for Sportsman hardtops. All De Sotos were on a common wheelbase this season.*

FIREFLITE SERIES — (V-8): Identification features included Fireflite front fender script, plus chrome fender top ornaments running back from the headlamps and the rocker panel beauty trim. Special side color sweep beauty panels were standard on Fireflite convertibles and hardtops, optional on other De Soto models. Once again, the Coronado was an added springtime model. It was a sedan featuring a leather interior and three-tone exterior finish treatment with a turquoise, black, and white used in three possible combinations on the body, sweep, and roof. The fuel filler was now located behind a door on the right rear quarter panel. There were V-8 emblems on the rear quarter panel, set lower and forward inside the color sweep. Cars without color sweep styling treatments had the V-8 emblem slightly offset, forward of the gas filler and even with the taillamp centerline. A sun cap visor treatment clung to the top of the windshield. Genuine leather-trimmed upholstery was provided in the Fireflite Sportsman. Others had silky nylon upholstery and nylon carpeting, too. A 200-hp four-barrel V-8 with hemispherical segment combustion chambers was another Fireflite standard.

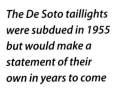

The De Soto taillights were subdued in 1955 but would make a statement of their own in years to come

The 1955 De Soto dash had a definite aeronautical feel. The instrument panel had clearly evolved from the 1954 model.

FIREFLITE I.D. NUMBERS: Code number locations were the same as previous. Detroit numbers were 50330001 to 50364093; Los Angeles numbers were 62045001 to 62047586. Engine numbers were S21-1001 to S21-35660.

Fireflite Series

Model Number	Body/Style Number	Body Type & Seating	Factory Price	Shipping Weight	Production Total
S21	Note 1	4-dr Sedan-6P	$2,727	3,395 lbs.	26,637
S21	Note 1	4-dr Coronado Sedan-6P	N/A	N/A	Note 2
S21	Note 1	2-dr Convertible Coupe-6P	$3,151	4,090 lbs.	775
S21	Note 1	2-dr Sportsman-6P	$2,939	3,490 lbs.	10,313

NOTE 1: Code numbers to provide positive identification of body type were not provided.

NOTE 2: Coronado sedan production included in total for Fireflite four-door sedan.

Engines:

FIREDOME V-8. OVERHEAD VALVE. CAST IRON BLOCK. DISPLACEMENT: 291 cid. Bore and stroke: 3.72 x 3.344 inches. Compression ratio: 7.5:1. Brake hp: 185 at 4400 rpm. Five main bearings. Hydraulic valve lifters. Carburetors: (standard transmission) Carter BBD two-barrel Model 2067S; (overdrive transmission) Carter BBD Model 2177S-SA; (PowerFlite transmission) Carter BBD Model 2178S-SA.

FIREFLITE V-8. OVERHEAD VALVE. CAST IRON BLOCK. DISPLACEMENT: 291 cid. Bore and stroke: 3.72 x 3.344 inches. Compression ratio: 7.5:1. Brake hp: 200 at 4400 rpm. Five main bearings. Hydraulic valve lifters. Carburetor: Carter WCFB four-barrel Model 2210S.

The 1955 De Soto Coronado three color combinations appeared on the car's body, side sweep and roof. All Coronados are rare, with the aqua roof the rarest.

CHASSIS FEATURES: Three-speed manual column-mounted transmission was standard. Overdrive manual transmission was optional at $108 extra. PowerFlite automatic transmission with "Flite-Control" selector lever protruding from dashboard was $189 extra. Wheelbase: (all) 126 inches. Overall length: (station wagon) 218.6 inches; (all others) 217.9 inches. Front tread: (all) 60.2 inches. Rear tread: (all) 59.6 inches. Tires: tubeless blackwalls of 7.60 x 15-inch size.

OPTIONS: Power steering ($113). Power brakes ($40). Power front seat ($70). Four-barrel power package for Firedome series ($40). Radios ($110 and $128). Heater ($92). Power windows ($102). Air conditioning ($567). Directional signals. White sidewall tires. Other standard accessories.

The early production 1955 De Soto station wagons used the "twin tower" Chrysler Windsor taillights.

The 1955 De Soto station wagon put style in the simple tasks of hauling people and cargo. De Soto wagons got their own taillights later in the 1955 model run.

HISTORICAL FOOTNOTES: Dual exhaust was available on all models, except station wagons, at extra cost. Three famous Ghia-built experimental show cars with De Soto running gear appeared this year at auto shows. They were the Falcon roadster, Flight Sweep I convertible and Flight Sweep II coupe.

1956 De Soto Firedome convertible

Even the front of the 1956 De Soto was designed with speed and motion in mind.

The 1956 De Soto is a favorite among 21st century Chrysler enthusiasts because of its seemingly perfect two-toning and its three big taillights—a De Soto feature over four consecutive model years. The refinement of the '55 styling was beautiful. The side sweep kicked up slightly right at the end of the now-higher and more fin-like rear fenders. Each rear fender housed two large red taillights with the back-up lights between, adding to the Jet-Age/Space Age character of the car. The grille was a fine mesh, which is loved by some for being more modern and disliked by others for seeming cheap compared to the heavy chrome teeth of previous years. A big set of bumper guards stylistically jumped off the front of the car, and they contained the parking/signal lights. Station wagons with two-toning kept the shape of the 1955 sweep that dropped down toward the rear. Rear fender fins were obviously bolted-on.

The interiors were basically the same as the 1955 models, and the cars used the same dash, but the unique dash-mounted "Flite-Control" PowerFlite gear selector lever from 1955 was replaced by a pod of push-buttons at the driver's left hand.

FIREDOME — (V-8): The Firedome was once again the entry-level De Soto, and the chrome bordering the top of its side color sweep was thinner and lighter-looking than on the higher-priced Fireflite. The interiors seems less fancy and are not as color-coordinated with the exterior. The Firedome used chrome headlight bezels that only slightly hung over the headlights, and there were not fender-top spears on top of the front fenders above the headlights. Low-priced hardtops were designated as Sevilles and a four-door pillarless model was introduced.

FIREDOME I.D. NUMBERS: Serial and engine numbers were in the usual locations. Use serial number only for identification purposes. Cars built in Detroit were numbered 55258001 to 55329506; in Los Angeles 64028001 to 64034406. Engine numbers S23-1001 to S23-79267 were used.

Firedome Series

Model Number	Body/Style Number	Body Type & Seating	Factory Price	Shipping Weight	Production Total
S23	Note 1	2-dr Seville HT-6P	$2,684	3,865 lbs.	19,136
S23	Note 1	4-dr Seville HT-6P	$2,833	3,940 lbs.	4,030
S23	Note 1	2-dr Sportsman-6P	$2,783	3,910 lbs.	4,589
S23	Note 1	4-dr Sportsman-6P	$2,954	3,920 lbs.	1,645
S23	Note 1	4-dr Sedan-6P	$2,805	3,855 lbs.	44,909
S23	Note 1	2-dr Convertible Coupe-6P	$3,032	4,230 lbs.	646
S23	Note 1	4-dr Station Wagon-6P	$3,321	4,230 lbs.	2,950

NOTE 1: *Code numbers to provide positive identification of body type were not used.*

Around back, De Soto conceived a new trademark, a set of three vertically arranged taillights.

The push-button gear selector came to De Soto and the rest of Chrysler Corporation in 1956.

De Soto featured a clock in 1956 that was nicknamed the "egg cup."

Positioned trackside, the 1956 De Soto Adventurer seems ready for racing.

FIREFLITE — (V-8): Fireflite models had suitable front fender nameplates and painted headlight hoods with chrome strips on top extending back along the peak of the front fenders. The upper arm of color sweep panels on Fireflites extended in a solid line from in back of headlights to the extreme tip of the tailfin. A double molding was used and grew wider at the front edge of the front door, spreading to an even wider flare at the rear fender, giving the side color sweep treatment a heavier look than the Firedome's. On four-door sedans, the side trim was available in the color sweep format or an optional format that utilized the upper double molding only. Fireflite four-doors with the latter choice are considered rare today. All Fireflite De Sotos had PowerFlite automatic transmissions as standard equipment. This transmission now incorporated push-button gear selection controls. On Jan. 11, 1956, De Soto announced that a Fireflite convertible with heavy-duty underpinnings, but standard engine, would pace the Indianapolis 500 and that a limited-edition Pacesetter convertible would be available to the public. These cars had the same special features and a heavy complement of power accessories, but were not lettered like the authentic pace car.

The Fireflite interiors were more colorful and coordinated with the exterior color. The Fireflite hardtop had a heavy chrome trim piece where the rear quarter of the roof met the belt-line.

FIREFLITE I.D. NUMBERS: Serial and engine numbers were in the usual locations with serial numbers meant for identification purposes. Cars built in Detroit were numbered 50366001 to 50392114; in Los Angeles 62048001 to 62051424. Engine numbers S24-1001 to S24-29811 were used.

Fireflite Series

Model Number	Body/Style Number	Body Type & Seating	Factory Price	Shipping Weight	Production Total
S24	Note 1	2-dr Sportsman-6P	$3,256	4,030 lbs.	7,479
S24	Note 1	4-dr Sedan-6P	$3,029	4,005 lbs.	18,207
S24	Note 1	4-dr Sportsman-6P	$3,341	4,015 lbs.	3,350
S24	Note 1	2-dr Convertible Coupe-6P	$3,454	4,125 lbs.	1,485
S24	Note 1	2-dr Convertible Pacesetter-6P	$3,565	4,070 lbs.	(Note 2)

NOTE 1: *Code numbers to provide positive identification of body type were not used.*

NOTE 2: *Production of Pacesetter convertibles is included in base convertible totals.*

In 1956, De Soto led the Indianapolis 500 racing field. Indianapolis Motor Speedway

An interesting timepiece is this image of the ABC De Soto dealership in Minneapolis, Minnesota, in 1956.

"The De Soto is quite a satisfactory car if you like 'em big and roomy with excellent driver and passenger comfort and riding qualities."

"When you squeeze on the floorboard, you know things are happening under the hood."

Racer Brown, Hot Rod, June 1956

ADVENTURER — (V-8): The Adventurer two-door hardtop coupe was introduced as a limited production specialty car on Feb. 18, 1956. It was technically a Fireflite sub-series and was sometimes called the Golden Adventurer. It had a special high-performance engine, dual exhaust and custom appointments and finish. Standard equipment included power brakes, whitewall tires, dual tailpipe extensions, dual outside rearview mirrors, rear-mounted manual radio antennas, padded instrument panel, power front seat, electric windows, windshield washers, electric clock and heavy-duty suspension. Adventurers were only available in two color combinations—white with a gold sweep and roof, or black with a gold sweep and roof. The wheel covers and grille were gold anodized, as was the V on the trunk lid.

ADVENTURER I.D. NUMBERS: Coding on Adventurers was the same as on Detroit-built Fireflites in terms of serial numbers. Engine numbers S24A-1001 to S24A-29811 were used in Adventurers.

Adventurer Sub-series

Model Number	Body/Style Number	Body Type & Seating	Factory Price	Shipping Weight	Production Total
S24A	Note 1	2-dr Hardtop Coupe-6P	$3,678	3,870 lbs.	996

NOTE 1: Code numbers to provide positive identification of body type were not used.

Engines:

FIREDOME: V-8. Overhead valve. Cast iron block. Displacement: 330.4 cid. Bore and stroke: 3.72 x 3.80 inches. Compression ratio: 8.5:1. Brake hp: 230 at 4400 rpm. Five main bearings. Hydraulic valve lifters. Carburetors: Carter BBD two-barrel (with standard transmission) Model 2308S; (overdrive transmission) Model 2309S; (PowerFlite transmission) 2310S.

FIREFLITE: V-8. Overhead valve. Cast iron block. Displacement: 330.4 cid. Bore and stroke: 3.72 x 3.80 inches. Compression ratio: 8.5:1. Brake hp: 255 at 4400 rpm. Five main bearings. Hydraulic valve lifters. Carburetors: Carter WCFB four-barrel Model 2311S (primary and secondary).

ADVENTURER: V-8. Overhead valve with enlarged valve ports, high-lift camshaft, large diameter valves and stiffer valve springs. Cast iron block with modified slipper pistons, heavy-duty connecting rods and shot-peened crankshaft. Displacement: 341.4 cid. Bore and stroke: 3.78 x 3.80 inches. Compression ratio: 9.25:1. Brake hp: 320 at 5200 rpm. Five main bearings. Hydraulic valve lifters. Carburetors: Carter dual four-barrel WCFB type: (front) Model 2476S; (rear) Model 2445S.

CHASSIS FEATURES: Three-speed column-mounted transmission was standard on Firedome and not normally available on Fireflite. Overdrive transmission was $108 on the Firedome and not normally available on the Fireflite series. PowerFlite automatic transmission was optional on the Firedome for $189 extra and was standard on the Fireflite. Push-button PowerFlite controls were adopted. Wheelbase: (all) 126 inches. Overall length: (four-door sedan and Sportsman) 217.9 inches; (all two-doors) 220.9 inches; (station wagon) 218.6 inches. Front tread: (all) 60.4 inches. Rear tread: (all) 59.6 inches. Tires: 7.60 x 15-inch.

OPTIONS: Power steering ($97). Feather Touch power brakes ($40). Power front seat ($70). Highway Hi-Fi record player. Air Temp air conditioning. Electric window lifts. Power radio antenna. Hot water heater. Instant heat. "Conditionair" (operated on a gasoline burner). Solex safety glass. Whitewall tires. Steering wheel mounted clock. Seat belts. Other standard accessories.

HISTORICAL FOOTNOTES: An Adventurer hardtop paced the 1956 Pike's Peak Hill Climb. Another Adventurer competed in the Daytona Speed Weeks and recorded a top speed of 137.29 mph. Another Adventurer recorded a top speed of 114 mph at the Chrysler Proving Grounds. A reported 0 to 60 time for the Adventurer was 10.5 seconds.

The 1957 De Soto was all new from the ground up. Gone completely was any remnant of the chassis design that had served Chrysler Corporation since 1940. The new bodies were lower and longer with high, upswept fins. The 1956 two-toning was ingeniously adapted to the totally new car, making it one of the most natural all-new-model evolutions of the time. The grille was part of a massive bumper arrangement. As usual, De Soto used the same body as the Chrysler, and the space that carried the bar-like taillights on the Chrysler housed the three large, round taillights that had defined a De Soto the previous year. The rear view mirror was mounted on the dash.

Like Chrysler, the De Soto started off in 1957 with only two headlights, but as the state laws changed, they allowed for the four-headlight system. De Soto was ready, and part-way through the 1957 season, De Soto was suddenly the only American car in its class with four headlights.

Like the rest of the entire corporation, De Soto glided down the road and held it lightly with its torsion bar front suspension.

FIRESWEEP SERIES — (V-8): The Firesweep was really a Dodge in disguise, and Dodge plants built the Firesweep. It rode on the shorter (122-inch wheelbase) Dodge chassis, and while the Firesweep looked all De Soto from the side and back, its Dodge roots showed up front where the two headlight housings are connected by a chrome band across the front edge of the hood like a Dodge. The Firesweep made for a light, nimble De Soto price leader.

FIRESWEEP I.D. NUMBERS: Serial numbers and engine numbers were in their familiar locations. Cars built in Detroit were numbered 58001001 to 58038408; in Los Angeles 60014001 to 60017360. Engine numbers KDS-1001 to KDS-287531 were used. Firesweep models were actually manufactured by Chrysler Corporation's Dodge Division.

The second wave of the Forward Look hit De Soto in 1957 with new styling from the ground up.

Ed Petrus

Firesweep Series

Model Number	Body/Style Number	Body Type & Seating	Factory Price	Shipping Weight	Production Total
S27	Note 1	2-dr Sportsman-6P	$2,836	3,645 lbs.	13,333
S27	Note 1	4-dr Sedan-6P	$2,777	3,675 lbs.	17,300
S27	Note 1	4-dr Sportsman-6P	$2,912	3,720 lbs.	7,168
S27	Note 1	4-dr Station Wagon-6P	$3,169	3,965 lbs.	2,270
S27	Note 1	4-dr Station Wagon-9P	$3,310	3,970 lbs.	1,198

The De Soto and other Chrysler models made a statement with the 1957 iteration of the Forward Look. The challenge was to keep the task of innovation coming.

Ed Petrus

NOTE 1: *Code numbers designating body style were not provided. The six-passenger station wagon was called the "Shopper" and the nine-passenger station wagon was called the "Explorer."*

Firedome Series

Model Number	Body/Style Number	Body Type & Seating	Factory Price	Shipping Weight	Production Total
S25	Note 1	2-dr Sportsman-6P	$3,085	3,910 lbs.	12,179
S25	Note 1	4-dr Sedan-6P	$2,958	3,955 lbs.	23,339
S25	Note 1	4-dr Sportsman-6P	$3,142	3,960 lbs.	9,050
S25	Note 1	2-dr Convertible Coupe-6P	$3,361	4,065 lbs.	1,297

Though the 1957 De Soto bore no resemblance to the 1956 edition, Chrysler designers ingeniously brought the 1956 two-tone paint pattern to the new car.

NOTE 1: *Code numbers designating body style were not provided.*

Something as simple as the Jiffy Jet windshield washer fluid bag evokes a memory of the 1950s for De Soto enthusiasts. Ed Petrus

Though the seats were low and hard by traditional Chrysler standards, the 1957 De Soto Adventurer's interior presented a sparkling, modern package.

The 1957 De Soto Adventurer dash was both ornate and clean. Ed Petrus

1957 De Soto Adventurer convertible

The fins and taillights seemed like they would continue growing taller on all 1957 De Sotos, including the Adventurer convertible.

A shot of the power top opening on the 1957 De Soto Adventurer convertible.

FIREFLITE SERIES — (V-8): For identification, models in the top line series had Fireflite rear fender nameplates. In addition, medallions were seen at the front fender side moldings. Headlights were positioned separate of the grille as on Firedomes with cutback notches in the sides of the hood. Dual color sweep moldings were standard on all models. The six-passenger station wagon was again referred to as the "Shopper," while the nine-passenger model was called the "Explorer." The convertible coupe used a distinctive, dome-like windshield, which became standard on all 1958 Sportsman models. Front fender-top chrome ornaments appeared in mixed applications on some Fireflite models. TorqueFlite automatic transmission; foam seat cushions; back-up lights and full wheel covers were standard.

FIREFLITE I.D. NUMBERS: Serial numbers and engine numbers were in their familiar locations. Cars built in Detroit were numbered 50396001 to 50426380; in Los Angeles 62053001 and up. Engine numbers S26-1001 to S26-29541 were used.

Fireflite Series

Model Number	Body/Style Number	Body Type & Seating	Factory Price	Shipping Weight	Production Total
S26	Note 1	2-dr Sportsman-6P	$3,614	4,000 lbs.	7,217
S26	Note 1	4-dr Sedan-6P	$3,487	4,025 lbs.	11,565
S26	Note 1	4-dr Sportsman-6P	$3,671	4,125 lbs.	6,726
S26	Note 1	2-dr Convertible Coupe-6P	$3,890	4,085 lbs.	1,151
S26	Note 1	4-dr Station Wagon-6P	$3,982	4,250 lbs.	837
S26	Note 1	4-dr Station Wagon-9P	$4,124	4,290 lbs.	934

NOTE 1: *Code numbers designating body style were not used.*

1957 De Soto Fireflite Shopper station wagon Phil Hall Collection

The famous rear-facing third seat was used in the 1957 De Soto Fireflite Shopper station wagon.

Phil Hall Collection

Pick a mount with the DE SOTO brand, pardner!

ADVENTURER SERIES — (V-8): This was a high-powered, performance car line. The Adventurer hardtop coupe was unveiled two months after regular De Soto introductions on Oct. 30, 1956. An Adventurer convertible was marketed even later. Both models had special gold-colored trim accents to carry forward the tradition begun in 1956. They also featured TorqueFlite automatic transmission, power brakes, dual exhaust, dual rear radio antenna, dual outside rearview mirrors, white sidewall tires, padded dashboards and special paint and trim as standard equipment. Distinctive nameplates appeared on the rear fender and bright metal strips graced the rear deck lid. A special V-8 with dual four-barrel carburetors provided one horsepower per cubic inch of displacement.

ADVENTURER I.D. NUMBERS: Serial numbers and engine numbers were in their familiar locations. All Adventurers were built at the Detroit factory, according to reference sources, with serial numbers 50396001 to 50426380 utilized. This range of numbers is the same as listed for Detroit-built Fireflites, which indicates the Adventurer was a sub-series of this line. Engine numbers also fell into the previously listed Fireflite sequence.

Adventurer Series

Model Number	Body/Style Number	Body Type & Seating	Factory Price	Shipping Weight	Production Total
S26A	Note 1	2-dr Hardtop Coupe-6P	$3,997	4,040 lbs.	1,650
S26A	Note 1	2-dr Convertible Coupe-6P	$4,272	4,235 lbs.	300

NOTE 1: Code numbers designating body style were not used.

FIRESWEEP: V-8. Overhead valve. Cast iron block. Displacement: 325 cid. Bore and stroke: 3.69 x 3.80 inches. Compression ratio: 8.5:1. Brake hp: 245 at 4400 rpm. Five main bearings. Hydraulic valve lifters. Carburetor: Carter two-barrel Model 2532S.

FIREDOME: V-8. Overhead valve. Cast iron block. Displacement: 341.4 cid. Bore and stroke: 3.78 x 3.80 inches. Compression ratio: 9.25:1. Brake hp: 270 at 4600 rpm. Five main bearings. Hydraulic valve lifters. Carburetor: Carter two-barrel Model 2522S.

FIREFLITE: V-8. Overhead valve. Cast iron block. Displacement: 341.4 cid. Bore and stroke: 3.78 x 3.80 inches. Compression ratio: 9.25:1. Brake hp: 295 at 4600 rpm. Five main bearings. Hydraulic valve lifters. Carburetor: Carter four-barrel Model 2588S.

ADVENTURER: V-8. Overhead valve. Cast iron block. Displacement: 345 cid. Bore and stroke: 3.80 x 3.80 inches. Compression ratio: 9.25:1. Brake hp: 345 at 5200 rpm. Five main bearings. Hydraulic valve lifters. Carburetor: Carter dual-quad induction.

CHASSIS FEATURES: Automatic transmissions were now considered standard De Soto equipment at a slight additional cost for lower cost models and at no extra cost for Fireflites and Adventurers. PowerFlite automatic transmission was offered only in Firesweep models at approximately $180 extra. TorqueFlite automatic transmission was offered in all lines at approximately $220 extra. Push-button gear shifting was featured with both transmissions. Three-speed manual transmission with column-mounted gear shifting was an infrequently ordered "deduct option." Wheelbase: (S27/Firesweep) 122 inches; (all others) 126 inches. Overall length: (S27/Firesweep station wagon) 217.4 inches; (S27/Firesweep passenger cars) 215.8 inches; (Adventurer) 221 inches; (all other station wagons) 219.5 inches; (all other passenger cars) 218 inches. Front tread: (S27) 60.9 inches; (all others) 61 inches. Rear tread: (all) 59.7 inches. Tires: (S26A) 9.00 x 14-inch; (S26 and S25) 8.50 x 14-inch and (S27) 8.00 x 14-inch.

OPTIONS: Power brakes ($39). Power steering ($106). Power window lifts ($106). Six-way power seat ($101). Dual exhaust, except standard on Adventurer ($34). Whitewalls, except standard on Adventurer ($42-$45). Radio with antenna ($120). Electro Tune radio with antenna ($120). Dual rear antenna ($16). Rear seat speaker ($15). Single rear power antenna ($24). Fresh Air heater ($89). Instant Air heater ($157). Standard two-tone finish ($19). Special finish, solid or two-tone ($71). Tinted glass ($32). Electric clock ($18). Self-winding steering wheel clock ($30). Windshield washer ($12). Variable speed windshield wiper, except standard on Firedome and Fireflite ($7). Air Foam seat cushions, except standard on Fireflite and Firedome ($11). Armrest on four-door and sport models ($27). Air conditioning with Fresh Air heater ($493). Air conditioning group order ($404). Padded safety panel (dash) except standard on Adventurer ($21). Firesweep back-up lights ($12). Engine four-barrel power-pack, Firesweep only ($45). Undercoating ($14). Wheel covers ($16). Front and rear carpets in Firesweep ($14). Rear window defogger ($21). Non-Slip differential ($50). Outside mirror ($6).

HISTORICAL FOOTNOTES: The 1957 De Soto Adventurer was the first base model U.S. car to provide one horsepower per cubic inch of displacement, as the 345-hp engine was not considered optional equipment. The 1956 Chrysler 300-B and 1957 Chevrolet were also available with one-horsepower-per-cubic-inch V-8s as optional equipment. De Soto earned 1.63 percent of total U.S. auto sales for 1957. It was the third best year in the division's history. The Firesweep line made De Soto the only maker in the medium-low price field to achieve a gain in new car sales over the previous season. The availability of overdrive transmission was discontinued this year. When equipped with the optional Power-Pack four-barrel V-8, the 1957 De Soto Firesweep models were rated 260 hp at 4400 rpm, a gain of 15 hp over the base two-barrel engine. The 1957 De Soto received "Car of the Year" honors from both Motor Trend and Car Life magazines.

In 1957, Chrysler Corporation introduced a new version of its De Soto Diplomat, an export only vehicle built in Detroit since 1946. Previously, these De Sotos were basically Plymouth bodies with some De Soto trim and the "toothy" grille. In 1957, the Diplomat featured the Firesweep front clip with the Plymouth body. De Soto Diplomats came in Deluxe and Custom editions and a two-door station wagon called the Commercial Utility. They used the American 230-cid six and the 301-cid V-8.

The rear view of the 1958 De Soto changed little from the 1957 version.

The small dip in the middle of the 1958 De Soto bumper with small teeth on each side made the grille seem a lot more elaborate than the 1957 grille had been.

Styling was characterized by a minor face-lift of the 1957 model. Changes included a honeycomb grille insert, a dip in the center of the middle grille bar and round parking lights at the outboard ends of the lower grille opening. Quad headlights were standard on all models. Hemi engines disappeared on all De Sotos in 1958, leaving them with an array of wedge-head engines that breathed nearly as easily as the Hemi with fewer moving parts, less weight, and a simpler design.

Two-toning no longer swept downward to encompass the rear wheel well but, rather, swept upward to accentuate the tail fin, and the various model names resided in this triangular color panel where it widened just in front of the fin.

FIRESWEEP SERIES — (V-8): This series continued to use the Dodge chassis. There were Firesweep rear fender nameplates, and a continuous Dodge-like band of metal again decorated the front lip of the hood and climbed over the headlamp hoods. Sportsman models had the dome-like windshield seen on 1957 convertibles, while sedans continued with a visored windshield header. An upgraded interior, similar to that fitted inside Firedome models, was an available option.

FIRESWEEP I.D. NUMBERS: Serial numbers and engine numbers were in the familiar locations. Cars built in Detroit had serial numbers LS1-1001 to 18900; in Los Angeles LS1L-1001 and up. Engine numbers L350-1001 and up were used.

The 1958 version of the De Soto Fireflite logo.

Firesweep Series

Model Number	Body/Style Number	Body Type & Seating	Factory Price	Shipping Weight	Production Total
LS1-L	Note 1	2-dr Sportsman-6P	$2,890	3,660 lbs.	5,635
LS1-L	Note 1	4-dr Sedan-6P	$2,819	3,660 lbs.	7,646
LS1-L	Note 1	4-dr Sportsman-6P	$2,953	3,720 lbs.	3,003
LS1-L	Note 1	2-dr Convertible Coupe-6P	$3,219	3,850 lbs.	700
LS1-L	Note 1	4-dr Station Wagon-6P	$3,266	3,955 lbs.	1,305
LS1-L	Note 1	4-dr Station Wagon-9P	$3,408	3,980 lbs.	1,125

NOTE 1: *Code numbers designating body style were not used. The six-passenger station wagon was the Shopper. The nine-passenger station wagon was the Explorer.*

FIREDOME SERIES — (V-8): Firedome nameplates on the rear fenders identified De Soto's one-step-up line. Firedome models had the same side trim as Firesweeps, but not the same frontal molding treatment. Wind-split ornaments for tops of front fenders were optional. A richer interior was featured. Upholstery materials were defined as Frontier Homespun fabric in combination with grained vinyl, colored to harmonize with exterior finish. These same interiors could be had in selected Firesweep models at a slight extra cost.

FIREDOME I.D. NUMBERS: Serial numbers and engine numbers were in the familiar locations. Cars built in Detroit had serial numbers LS2-1001 to 17409. Some reference sources indicate no Los Angeles production. Others indicate that Los Angeles numbers ran from LS2L-1001 and up. Engine numbers L360-1001 and up were used.

Firedome Series

Model Number	Body/Style Number	Body Type & Seating	Factory Price	Shipping Weight	Production Total
LS2-M	Note 1	4-dr Sedan-6P	$3,085	3,855 lbs.	9,505
LS2-M	Note 1	2-dr Sportsman-6P	$3,178	3,825 lbs.	4,325
LS2-M	Note 1	4-dr Sportsman-6P	$3,235	3,920 lbs.	3,130
LS2-M	Note 1	2-dr Convertible Coupe-6P	$3,489	4,065 lbs.	519

NOTE 1: *Code numbers designating body style were not used.*

FIREFLITE SERIES — (V-8): Identifiers for the top rung series included specific rear fender nameplates and a distinctive upper body side molding that extended the full length of the car and incorporated special medallions on the sides of the front fenders. Wind split fender-top ornaments were standard equipment. Color sweep trim was standard on hardtops and convertibles. Eighty-six two-tone and 14 solid color schemes were offered for De Sotos. The Fireflites used the same new V-8 that featured a rigid, deep skirt block; inline overhead valves employing a single shaft in each cylinder head; a reduced weight of 640 pounds; and wedge-shaped combustion chambers. A springtime trim package was released as an option for all models except Adventurers. It featured two groups of four vertical, bright metal deck lid slashes, with one group affixed to each side of the recessed license plate housing. New exterior colors were announced about the same time. Fireflite interiors were done in metallic Damask and vinyl and incorporated integrated armrests with aluminum finish recesses above them.

FIREFLITE I.D. NUMBERS: Serial numbers and engine numbers were in their familiar locations. Reference sources give Detroit numbers only. They run from LS3-1001 to 13552. Engine numbers were L360-1001 and up.

Fireflite Series

Model Number	Body/Style Number	Body Type & Seating	Factory Price	Shipping Weight	Production Total
LS3-H	Note 1	4-dr Sedan-6P	$3,583	3,990 lbs.	4,192
LS3-H	Note 1	2-dr Sportsman-6P	$3,675	3,920 lbs.	3,284
LS3-H	Note 1	4-dr Sportsman-6P	$3,731	3,980 lbs.	3,243
LS3-H	Note 1	2-dr Convertible Coupe-6P	$3,972	4,105 lbs.	474
LS3-H	Note 1	4-dr Station Wagon-6P	$4,030	4,225 lbs.	318
LS3-H	Note 1	4-dr Station Wagon-9P	$4,172	4,295 lbs.	609

NOTE 1: *Code numbers designating body style were not used. The six-passenger station wagon was the Shopper; the nine-passenger station wagon was the Explorer.*

ADVENTURER SERIES — (V-8): The Adventurer models again represented a sub-series. Like the Fireflites that they were based on, these high-performance cars came standard with TorqueFlite transmission, back-up lamps and full wheel covers. But there were some other extras, too, such as power brakes, dual exhaust, dual rear radio antennas, dual outside rearview mirrors, white sidewall tires, dashboard safety panel and special paint and trim. The latter included gold highlights, twin groupings of four deck lid bars, triangular rear side sweep inserts and special upholstery. This specialty series was announced at the 1958 Chicago Auto Show on January 4 of that year. Other De Soto models had been introduced Nov. 1, 1957. A new option was an electronic fuel injection system manufactured by Bendix. Cars so equipped wore special nameplates above the front fender medallions and were later recalled to the factory for reconversion into "standard," dual-quad carburetor form.

1958 De Soto Firesweep sedan

1958 De Soto Fireflite Sportsman two-door hardtop

1958 De Soto Golden Adventurer Two-Door Hardtop

"No bad habits, a good ride, plenty of performance, handling and braking with the best… and a price structure that leaves little to quibble about. It's an impressive fuselage."

William Carroll, Motor Trend, June 1958

ADVENTURER I.D. NUMBERS: As a Fireflite sub-series, the Adventurers used corresponding serial and engine numbers.

Adventurer Series

Model Number	Body/Style Number	Body Type & Seating	Factory Price	Shipping Weight	Production Total
LS3-S	Note 1	2-dr Hardtop Coupe-6P	$4,071	4,000 lbs.	350
LS3-S	Note 1	2-dr Convertible Coupe-6P	$4,369	4,180 lbs.	82

NOTE 1: Code numbers designating body style were not used.

Engines:

FIRESWEEP: V-8. Overhead valve. Cast iron block. Displacement: 350 cid. Bore and stroke: 4.06 x 3.38 inches. Compression ratio: 10.0:1. Brake hp: 280 at 4600 rpm. Five main bearings. Hydraulic valve lifters. Carburetor: Carter two-barrel (part number 1855633).

FIREDOME: V-8. Overhead valve. Cast iron block. Displacement: 361 cid. Bore and stroke: 4.12 x 3.38 inches. Compression ratio: 10.0:1. Brake hp: 295 at 4600 rpm. Five main bearings. Hydraulic valve lifters. Carburetor: Carter two-barrel (part number 1855633).

FIREFLITE: V-8. Overhead valve. Cast iron block. Displacement: 361 cid. Bore and stroke: 4.12 x 3.38 inches. Compression ratio: 10.0:1. Brake hp: 305 at 4600 rpm. Five main bearings. Hydraulic valve lifters. Carburetor: Carter (part number 1822053).

ADVENTURER: V-8. Overhead valve. Cast iron block. Displacement: 361 cid. Bore and stroke: 4.12 x 3.38 inches. Compression ratio: 10.25:1. Brake hp: 345 at 5000 rpm. Five main bearings. Hydraulic valve lifters. Carburetor: two four-barrel Carter carburetors (front carburetor part number 1826081; rear carburetor part number 1826082).

CHASSIS FEATURES: Automatic transmission was still considered "standard" De Soto equipment, but again cost extra on Firesweep and Firedome models. There was no charge for automatic transmission in Fireflite and Adventurer models. PowerFlite two-speed automatic transmission was available only in Firesweeps at $180 extra. TorqueFlite three-speed automatic transmission was offered in all lines and cost $220 extra in Firesweeps and Firedomes. Push-button gear shifting was used again, too. Three-speed manual transmission with column-mounted controls was an infrequently ordered "deduct option." The Bendix-built EFI (fuel-injection) system was a $637.20 option in Adventurers only. It was installed in a limited number of 1958 Adventurers, Chrysler 300-Ds, Dodge D-500s and Plymouth Furys. These cars were originally built with dual-quad carburetors and were then converted to fuel injection at the De Soto factory. Adventurers so equipped were rated 355 hp at 5000 rpm. As previously noted, these cars were factory recalled for reconversion to "standard" carburetion systems, although some may have escaped the call-back. Wheelbase: (LS1-L) 122 inches; (all others) 126 inches. Overall length: (LS1-L station wagon) 218.1 inches; (LS1-L passenger cars) 216.5 inches; (Adventurer) 221 inches; (all other station wagons) 220.2 inches; (all passenger cars) 218.6 inches. Front tread: (LS1-L) 60.9 inches; (all others) 61 inches. Rear tread: (all) 59.7 inches. Tires: (Adventurer) 9.00 x 14; (LS1-L and LS2-M) 8.50 x 14 and (LS3-H) 8.00 x 14. Several sources indicate that 9.00 x 14 tires were used on 1957 and 1958 Adventurers and that six-ply 8.50 x 14 tires were used on Explorer station wagons. Other references do not confirm this information, however.

OPTIONS: Power brakes ($39). Power steering ($106). Power window lifts ($106). Six-way power seat ($101). Dual exhaust, except standard on Adventurer ($34). Whitewalls, except standard on Adventurer ($42-$45). Radio with antenna ($120). Electro Tune radio with antenna ($120). Dual rear antenna ($16). Rear seat speaker ($15). Single rear power antenna ($24). Fresh Air heater

($89). Instant Air heater ($157). Standard two-tone finish ($19). Special finish, solid or two-tone ($71). Tinted glass ($32). Electric clock ($18). Self-winding steering wheel clock ($30). Windshield washer ($12). Variable speed windshield wiper, except standard on the Firedome and Fireflite ($7). Air Foam seat cushions, except standard on the Fireflite and Firedome ($11). Armrest on four-door and sport models ($27). Air Conditioning with Fresh Air heater ($493). Air conditioning group order ($404). Padded safety panel (dash), except standard on Adventurer ($21). Firesweep back-up lights ($12). Engine four-barrel power-pack, Firesweep only ($45). Undercoating ($14). Wheel covers ($16). Front and rear carpets in Firesweep ($14). Rear window defogger ($21). Non-Slip differential ($50). Outside mirror ($6). EFI fuel injection ($637.20)*.

 * According to Allpar.com and Hemmings Classic Car writer George Mattar, this rare and expensive option was the Bendix fuel injection system called the "Electrojector." It included a transistor modulator that received a timed electrical signal from the car's ignition distributor. Sensors located at various points in the engine offered temperature, throttle position, manifold pressure and air density. The modulator translated the sensor data and actuated fuel injectors. Most of the cars equipped with the visionary but troubled Bendix "Electrojector" space-age fuel injection system were recalled and were replaced with carburetors. Today, one De Soto Adventurer is recognized as the only car retaining its fuel injection system by Chrysler Historical Records. The Bendix manual lists two Plymouth Furys, 16 Chrysler 300-D models, 12 Dodge D-500s and five De Sotos that were originally equipped with the Bendix "Electrojector" system.

An advertisement for the 1958 De Soto Adventurer.

**1959 De Soto
Firedome sedan**

The 1959 De Soto shared Chrysler's body as usual and had the same slightly more square look that Chrysler brought out in 1959. The De Soto only had a narrow grille at the top of the front of the car. Most of the air got to the radiator through two slot-like scoops in the massive front bumper, and through one car-width slot below the bumper. The front of the De Soto doesn't have a grille so much as it has a series of scoops. The more squared-off theme appeared on the rear of the car as well. The fins were more upright and started further forward on the car, so they didn't seem to sweep more and more upward as they progressed to the back of the car, and they formed more of a straight line from their point of origin to their ends. The ends of the fins still carried De Soto's now characteristic three vertical taillights. The rear end carried a large double bumper with beauty panels between the top and bottom members.

The side spear was a massive, obtrusive design that streaked toward the rear of the car but took a dip behind the rear wheel openings and then curved upward towards the tips of tall tailfins, forming a design that looked like a giant "check mark."

FIRESWEEP — (V-8): There were no series nameplates on Firesweeps, and silver colored inserts along the sides were optional. The Firesweep did not have the same outward clues to its Dodge roots as the previous two years had. The four-door sedan had painted side window trim. At the start of the season, four body styles appeared in this line, but two Seville hardtops were introduced as mid-run additions. Standard equipment included front foam cushions, dual exhaust on the convertible, four black nylon Captive Air tires on three-seat station wagons and front and rear carpets except on the six-passenger station wagon and four-door sedan.

FIRESWEEP L.D. NUMBERS: Serial numbers and engine numbers were in their familiar locations. Cars built in Detroit were numbered M412-100001 and up; in Los Angeles M414-100001 and up. Station wagons were numbered M471-100001 and up and were all assembled in Detroit.

Collectible today, the 1959 De Soto and other Chrysler Corporation cars were quickly losing the light, innovative styling that had challenged the auto industry in 1957.

Firesweep Series MS1-L

Model Number	Body/Style Number	Body Type & Seating	Factory Price	Shipping Weight	Production Total
413	41	4-dr Sedan-6P	$2,904	3,670 lbs.	9,649
414	43	4-dr Sportsman-6P	$3,038	3,700 lbs.	2,875
412	23	2-dr Sportsman-6P	$2,967	3,625 lbs.	5,481
415	27	2-dr Convertible Coupe-6P	$3,315	3,840 lbs.	596
476	45A	4-dr Station Wagon-6P	$3,366	3,950 lbs.	1,054
477	45B	4-dr Station Wagon-9P	$3,508	3,980 lbs.	1,179

NOTES: *Two-digit body model (style) numbers were now provided. Two- and four-door Seville hardtops were midyear models included in production figures for two- and four-door Sportsman. The six-passenger four-door station wagon was the Shopper; the nine-passenger four-door station wagon was the Explorer.*

FIREDOME — (V-8): For identification a series nameplate was affixed to the front fenders. Silver color sweeps were optional. Side window trim on four-door sedans was of bright metal. Standard equipment was the same as in Firesweeps plus back-up lights, padded dash panel, rear foam cushions, front and rear carpets, wheel covers, special steering wheel and vari-speed windshield wipers. The Firedome shared the Chrysler body and wheel base and was a little longer than the Firesweep.

FIREDOME L.D. NUMBERS: Serial numbers and engine numbers were in their familiar locations. Cars built in Detroit were numbered M43-10001 and up. No California production is noted in standard reference sources.

The radically-finned 1959 De Soto looked heavier while competition from Oldsmobile and Pontiac predicted 1960s styling with finless, angular lines.

A side chrome sweep and decorative badge indicated the De Soto lineage.

Practical touches like the rub strip on the tailgate and the passenger step on the rear bumper were carefully styled on De Soto and other Chrysler cars of the era.

Firedome Series MS2-M

Model Number	Body/Style Number	Body Type & Seating	Factory Price	Shipping Weight	Production Total
433	41	4-dr Sedan-6P	$3,234	3,840 lbs.	9,171
434	43	4-dr Sportsman-6P	$3,398	3,895 lbs.	2,862
432	23	2-dr Sportsman-6P	$3,341	3,795 lbs.	2,744
435	27	2-dr Convertible Coupe-6P	$3,653	4,015 lbs.	299

NOTE 1: Seville two- and four-door hardtops added at midyear are included in Sportsman production figures.

FIREFLITE SERIES — (V-8): Fireflites looked similar to Firedomes, but could be distinguished by a different series nameplate on the front fenders and by large medallions above the dip in the side trim on the rear fenders. Standard equipment matched all found on Firedomes plus TorqueFlite transmission, front and rear bumper guards, electric clock, handbrake warning light, color sweep molding, roof molding package, molding package number 2, windshield washer and 8.50 x 14 tires. Three-seat station wagons came with a power tailgate and four-ply black nylon Captive Air tires as regular features.

FIREFLITE I.D. NUMBERS: Serial numbers and engine numbers were in their familiar locations. All cars were built in Detroit and were numbered M451-100001 and up.

The 1959 De Soto station wagon was both stylish and practical.

Fireflite Series MS4-M

Model Number	Body/Style Number	Body Type & Seating	Factory Price	Shipping Weight	Production Total
453	41	4-dr Sedan-6P	$3,763	3,920 lbs.	4,480
454	43	4-dr Sportsman-6P	$3,888	3,950 lbs.	2,364
452	23	2-dr Sportsman-6P	$3,831	3,910 lbs.	1,393
455	27	2-dr Convertible Coupe-6P	$4,152	4,105 lbs.	186
478	45A	4-dr Station Wagon-6P	$4,216	4,170 lbs.	271
479	45B	4-dr Station Wagon-9P	$4,358	4,205 lbs.	433

NOTES: *The six-passenger station wagon was the Shopper; the nine-passenger station wagon was the Explorer.*

ADVENTURER SERIES — (V-8): Cars in this line had Adventurer nameplates on their front fenders. Gold color sweep inserts were affixed and the grille was also finished in gold. A narrow vertical medallion was placed at the dip in the side trim on the rear fenders. Wheel cutout moldings were used. The two-door hardtop had simulated Scotch-grain leather finish for the roof. Standard equipment was the same as for Fireflites plus power steering, power brakes, dual exhaust, dual rear radio antennas, dual outside rearview mirrors, white sidewall tires constructed of Rayon (size 8.50 x 14), brushed aluminum sweep insert, deck lid moldings, swivel front driver's seat, and high-performance Adventurer dual four-barrel carbureted V-8 with high-lift camshaft.

ADVENTURER I.D. NUMBERS: Serial numbers and engine numbers were in their familiar locations. Adventurers were assembled in Detroit and had serial numbers M491-100001 and up.

Adventurer Series MS3-H

Model Number	Body/Style Number	Body Type & Seating	Factory Price	Shipping Weight	Production Total
492	23	2-dr Sportsman-6P	$4,427	3,980 lbs.	590
495	27	2-dr Convertible Coupe-6P	$4,749	4,120 lbs.	97

Engines:

FIRESWEEP: V-8. Overhead valve. Cast iron block. Displacement: 361 cid. Bore and stroke: 4.12 x 3.38 inches. Compression ratio: 10.0:1. Brake hp: 295 at 4600 rpm. Five main bearings. Hydraulic valve lifters. Carburetor: Carter BBD two-barrel Model 2870S.

FIREDOME: V-8. Overhead valve. Cast iron block. Displacement: 383 cid. Bore and stroke: 4.25 x 3.38 inches. Compression ratio: 10.1:1. Brake hp: 305 at 4600 rpm. Five main bearings. Hydraulic valve lifters. Carburetor: Carter BBD two-barrel Model 2871S.

FIREFLITE: V-8. Overhead valve. Cast iron block. Displacement: 383 cid. Bore and stroke: 4.25 x 3.38 inches. Compression ratio: 10.1:1. Brake hp: 325 at 4600 rpm. Five main bearings. Hydraulic valve lifters. Carburetor: Carter BBD four-barrel Model 2794.

ADVENTURER: V-8. Overhead valve. Cast iron block. Displacement: 383 cid. Bore and stroke: 4.25 x 3.38 inches. Compression ratio: 10.1:1. Brake hp: 350 at 5000 rpm. Five main bearings. Hydraulic valve lifters. Carburetor: Two Carter AFB four-barrel Model 2794.

A 1959 De Soto Adventurer convertible on display in 2002 at Manitowoc, Wisconsin.

Tom Collins

Another angle shows the interior of this well-preserved 1959 De Soto Adventurer convertible.

Tom Collins

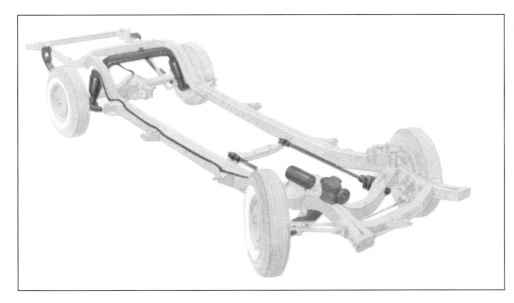

CHASSIS FEATURES: Three-speed manual transmission was the base price attachment on Firesweep and Firedome models, although automatic transmission was often referred to as standard equipment. TorqueFlite automatic transmission was included in the price of Fireflite and Adventurer models. Wheelbase: (Firesweep) 122 inches; (all others) 126 inches. Overall length: (MS1-L passenger cars) 217.1 inches; (MS1-L station wagons) 216.1 inches; (MS3-H station wagons) 220.1 inches; (all other passenger cars) 221.1 inches. Tires: (Firesweep) 8.00 x 14-inch; (all others) 8.50 x 14-inch.

OPTIONS: TorqueFlite transmission ($227). PowerFlite transmission ($189). Power steering ($106). Power brakes ($43). Power window lifts ($106). Six-way seat ($101). Firedome/Fireflite power front swivel seat ($187). Adventurer power swivel passenger seat ($101). Manual swivel seat ($86). (Note: Swivel seats were not available on the Firedome four-door sedan and the Fireflite station wagon. They were available with the Firesweep Sportsman.) Dual exhaust as option ($34). Whitewall 8.00 x 14 four-ply Rayon tires on all, but Explorer ($42). Whitewall 8.50 x 14 four-ply Rayon tires on all, but Explorer ($46). Whitewall 9.80 x 14 four-ply Rayon tires ($147). Radio with antenna ($94). Electric Tuner radio with antenna ($94). Rear seat speaker ($17). Manual dual rear antenna ($16). Hot water heater ($98). Instantaneous heater ($135). Standard two-tone paint ($21). Special solid or two-tone paint ($71). Color sweep trim ($21). Solex tinted glass ($43). Electric clock ($18). Windshield washer ($12). Variable speed windshield wiper ($7). Air foam cushion as option ($11). Air conditioning with hot water heater ($501). Air conditioning with accessory groups ($404). Dual air conditioning with hot water heater for station wagons ($710). Padded dash as option ($21). Firesweep back-up lights ($12). Undercoating ($14). Full wheel covers ($18). Firesweep front and rear carpets ($14). Rear window defogger ($21). Sure-Grip differential ($50). Outside rearview mirror ($6). Remote control outside rearview mirror on Adventurer ($11); on others ($18). Photo electric tilt rearview mirror ($23). Power tailgate on six-passenger station wagon ($40). Rear air suspension ($140). Aluminum sweep insert ($21). Automatic headlamp beam changer ($50). Front bumper guards ($12). Front and rear bumper guards ($24). Adventurer dual four-barrel V-8 for Firesweep ($142); for Firedome ($122); for Fireflite ($108). Station wagon luggage locker ($31). Adventurer deck lid molding ($11). Sill and lower deck molding package ($27). Number 1 roof molding package for four-door sedans and station wagons ($14). Number 2 roof molding package for Firesweep and Firedome Sportsman ($38). Special plastic steering wheel ($10). Panoramic rear window ($24).

HISTORICAL FOOTNOTES: Special appointments, including plaid upholstery, padded dash, and custom steering wheel were added to the Firedome standard equipment list in the spring. This was the last season for De Soto convertibles and station wagons as well as the final year for separate frame and body construction.

DODGE

Top to bottom: Dodge introduced its first hardtop in 1950, the Coronet Diplomat. A handsome package for its price range, the Diplomat was available in a variety of two-tone combinations.

The 1950 Dodge Diplomat hardtop's dash was painted the same color as the lower exterior of the car's body.

The elaborate radio harkened back to the Art Deco era of the 1930s. Dark woodgrain made the chrome even more striking.

1950-1959

Dodge received a handsome facelift of the "Daring New Dodge" body of 1949. Dodge simplified the complicated egg-crate 1949 grille into cleaner design. The grille had three heavy horizontal bars, with the upper bar curving down at the ends. The second and third bars formed a long oval with round parking lights incorporated at the ends. A large chrome center plaque contained the Dodge crest.

The front chrome and logo was meant to portray quality of workmanship over flash and fad.

Also reducing the added-on elements of the car was the elimination of the elaborate multi-purpose housing on the trunk lid that served as a handle/license plate frame/brake light/back-up light and license plate light housing. This one-device-does-all was a handsome, chrome-laden Art-Deco artifact belonging more to the 1930s than the 1950s. Its elimination brought the 1950 Dodge into the new decade. In keeping with the Chrysler Corporation bigger-on-the-inside/smaller-on-the-outside theme, the 1949 Dodge's rear fenders had narrowed toward the rear and the rear bumpers did not extend beyond the width of the car. Instead, the 1950 Dodge rear fenders flared outward more toward the rear, and the bumpers extended beyond the fenders, adding to the 1950 model's more modern appearance. The 1950 Dodge used the same dash as the 1949 – a dark woodgrain with three chrome-trimmed square dials in front of the driver and a huge chrome, radio grille in the middle. A single horizontal chrome strip was located on each front and rear fender. The model name was located along the chrome strip on the front fenders, behind the front wheel well, and this name plate also told whether the car was equipped with Fluid Drive or Gyro-Matic.

WAYFARER SERIES — (6-CYLINDER): As in 1949, the Wayfarer was the base trim level. The model name Wayfarer was located on the front fenders. The Wayfarer was a small car with only three body styles – a three-passenger coupe, a true roadster without roll-up side windows, and a turtle-backed two-door sedan. The side chrome spear ran the length of the front fender but stopped at the edge of the door.

WAYFARER I.D. NUMBERS: Wayfarer numbers were: (Detroit) 37060001 to 37129622; (San Leandro, Calif.) 48004001 to 48007069; (Los Angeles) 48502001 to 48504748.

The 1950 Dodge Wayfarer rode on a shorter wheelbase and was available as a three-window coupe, convertible roadster and two-door sedan.

Bill Meyer

Wayfarer Series

Model Number	Body/Style Number	Body Type & Seating	Factory Price	Shipping Weight	Production Total
D33	Note 1	2-dr Sedan-6P	$1,738	3,200 lbs.	65,000
D33	Note 1	2-dr Coupe-3P	$1,611	3,095 lbs.	7,500
D33	Note 1	2-dr Roadster-3P	$1,727	3,190 lbs.	2,903

NOTE 1: *Owners seeking parts were advised: "There is no way to positively identify the type of body. When in doubt, specify the vehicle serial number and vehicle body number when ordering parts."*

MEADOWBROOK SERIES — (6-CYLINDER): The Meadowbrook was the base trim level four-door sedan and came in only one body. The Meadowbrook did not have rear fender gravel shields and had plainer interiors than the Coronet.

MEADOWBROOK I.D. NUMBERS: Meadowbrook numbers were: (Detroit) 31420001 to 31660411; (San Leandro, Calif.) 45064001 to 45077531; (Los Angeles) 45505001 to 45515652. Engine numbers began at D34-1001 and went to D34-341043.

Meadowbrook Series

Model Number	Body/Style Number	Body Type & Seating	Factory Price	Shipping Weight	Production Total
D34	Note 1	4-dr Sedan-6P	$1,848	3,395 lbs.	Note 2

NOTE 1: *Owners seeking parts were advised: "There is no way to positively identify the type of body. When in doubt, specify the vehicle serial number and vehicle body number when ordering parts."*

NOTE 2: *Total Meadowbrook and Coronet four-door sedan production was 221,791.*

A view of the 1950 Dodge Wayfarer dash. It offered both a sense of style and no-nonsense practicality. Bill Meyer

A 1950 Dodge Coronet sedan, with matching sun visor and fender skirts, seems at home in this rural Nebraska setting.

John Lee

The 1950 Dodge Coronet was available in sedan and club coupe versions with a longer wheelbase than the Mercury or Pontiac. Harry Wisser

A shiny 1950 Dodge Coronet club coupe glistened in the sun as it was presented for viewing at a regional car show held at Antigo, Wisconsin.

Tom Collins

CORONET SERIES — (6-CYLINDER): The Coronet series continued as the top trim level for 1950 and included all the features of the Meadowbrook plus chrome trim rings on the wheels or full wheel covers, rear fender gravel guards, somewhat plusher interior colors and fabrics, more options, and a full array of body styles. The Diplomat two-door hardtop appeared in June, 1950. Dodge dropped the Town Sedan upgraded interior in February 1950. Many Coronets were equipped with the Gyro-Matic automatic transmission, and the Coronet logo on the front fender included the Gyro-Matic name.

CORONET I.D. NUMBERS: Coronet numbers were: (Detroit) 31420001 to 31660411; (San Leandro, Calif.) 45064001 to 45077531; (Los Angeles) 45505001 to 45515652. Engine numbers began at D34-1001 and went to D34-341043.

Coronet Series

Model Number	Body/Style Number	Body Type & Seating	Factory Price	Shipping Weight	Production Total
D34	Note 1	4-dr Sedan-6P	$1,927	3,405 lbs.	Note 2
D34	Note 1	4-dr Town Sedan-6P	$2,030	3,410 lbs.	Note 2
D34	Note 1	2-dr Club Coupe-6P	$2,012	3,410 lbs.	38,502
D34	Note 1	2-dr Hardtop Coupe-6P	$2,223	3,515 lbs.	3,600
D34	Note 1	2-dr Convertible-6P	$2,329	3,590 lbs.	1,800
D34	Note 1	4-dr Station Wagon-6P	$2,865	3,850 lbs.	600
D34	Note 1	4-dr Metal Station Wagon-6P	$2,865	3,726 lbs.	100
D34	Note 1	4-dr Sedan-8P	$2,617	4,045 lbs.	1,300

NOTE 1: Owners seeking parts were advised: "There is no way to positively identify the type of body. When in doubt, specify the vehicle serial number and vehicle body number when ordering parts."

NOTE 2: There was no breakout of four-door sedan production between the Meadowbrook and the Coronet series. Total production in both series was 221,791.

NOTE 3: The four-door metal station wagon was called the Sierra.

ENGINE: Inline. L-head. Six-cylinder. Cast iron block. Displacement: 230 cid. Bore and stroke: 3.25 x 4.33 inches. Compression ratio: 7.1:1. Brake hp: 103 at 3600 rpm. Four main bearings. Solid valve lifters. Carburetor: Stromberg BXVD 3-93.

CHASSIS FEATURES: Wheelbase: (Wayfarer) 115 inches; (Meadowbrook and Coronet) 123.5 inches; (eight-passenger) 137.5 inches. Overall length: (Wayfarer roadster) 194.38 inches; (Wayfarer sedan) 196.3 inches; (Meadowbrook and Coronet) 202.9 inches. Tires: (Wayfarer) 6.70 x 15 tube-type black sidewall; (Meadowbrook and Coronet) 7.10 x 15 tube-type black sidewall. Three-speed manual with Fluid-Drive was once again the standard transmission in 1950.

CONVENIENCE OPTIONS: Electric clock. Turn signals. Radio. Heater. Gyro-Matic semi-automatic transmission. White sidewall tires.

HISTORICAL FOOTNOTES: The standard Dodge line was introduced Jan. 4, 1950, and the Diplomat appeared in dealer showrooms June 11, 1950. Model year production peaked at 350,000 units. Calendar year sales of 332,782 cars were recorded. L.L. "Tex" Colbert was again president of the Dodge Division. W.C. Newberg became the divisional vice-president, a role he would fill through 1951. Dodge held a 4.99 percent total market share. This was the final year that K. T. Keller was the president of Chrysler Corporation.

A new grille design gave the 1951 Dodge Coronet a wider, less boxy appearance.

Dodge was nowhere as sleek as its competition from Pontiac and Oldsmobile, but Dodge took steps in the right direction with a flatter hood that leaned back more, giving the car a little sleeker appearance from the side. A bold horizontal bar dominated the grille and extended around the parking lights at both ends. Bumpers had a rounded cross-section. The Dodge crest sat in the center of the redesigned hood, directly above the Dodge name, in block letters. The rear of the car remained just about the same. Dodge redesigned its dash with a gray woodgraining, less chrome, and a shape that rounded under at the bottom.

WAYFARER SERIES — (6-CYLINDER): As in 1950, the Wayfarer was the base trim level. The model name Wayfarer was located on the front fenders. The Wayfarer was a small car with only three body styles – a three-passenger coupe, a true roadster without roll-up side windows, and a turtle-backed two-door sedan. The side chrome spear ran the length of the front fender but stopped at the edge of the door.

WAYFARER I.D. NUMBERS: Wayfarer numbers were: (Detroit) 37135001 to 37174914; (San Leandro, Calif.) 48008001 to 48009814, (Los Angeles) 48506001 to 48507517. Engine numbers began at D42-1001 and went up.

The windshield area of the 1951 Dodge Coronet convertible.

As with all Chrysler Corporation cars of the early 1950s, the 1951 Dodge Coronet convertible had the dash painted in the body color.

Wayfarer Series

Model Number	Body/Style Number	Body Type & Seating	Factory Price	Shipping Weight	Production Total
D41	Note 1	2-dr Sedan-6P	$1,895	3,210 lbs.	70,700
D41	Note 1	2-dr Coupe-3P	$1,757	3,125 lbs.	6,702
D41	Note 1	2-dr Roadster-3P	$1,884	3,175 lbs.	1,002

NOTE 1: Owners seeking parts were advised: "There is no way to positively identify the type of body. When in doubt, specify the vehicle serial number and vehicle body number when ordering parts."

NOTE 2: Production figures are totals for 1951 and 1952 model years.

The 1951 Dodge ram's head reached its record size in 1951.

A period press photo offers an attractive presentation of the 1951 Dodge Coronet sedan.

MEADOWBROOK SERIES — (6-CYLINDER): The Meadowbrook was the base trim level four-door sedan and had no chrome rear fender gravel guards. The Meadowbrook came with small hubcaps and plain interiors.

MEADOWBROOK I.D. NUMBERS: Meadowbrook numbers were: (Detroit) 31663001 to 31867688; (San Leandro, Calif.) 45079001 to 45090488; (Los Angeles) 45518001 to 45527385. Engine numbers began at D42-1001 and went up.

Meadowbrook Series

Model Number	Body/Style Number	Body Type & Seating	Factory Price	Shipping Weight	Production Total
D42	Note 1	4-dr Sedan-6P	$2,016	3,415 lbs.	Note 2

NOTE 1: Owners seeking parts were advised: "There is no way to positively identify the type of body. When in doubt, specify the vehicle serial number and vehicle body number when ordering parts."

NOTE 2: Total Meadowbrook and Coronet four-door sedan production was 329,202. This figure is the total for 1951 and 1952 model years.

CORONET SERIES — (6-CYLINDER): The Coronet series continued as the top trim level for 1951 and included all the features of the Meadowbrook, plus chrome trim rings on the wheels or full wheel covers and a few more interior color and fabric choices. Many Coronets were equipped with the Gyro-Matic automatic transmission, and the Coronet logo on the front fender included the Gyro-Matic name.

CORONET I.D. NUMBERS: Coronet numbers were: (Detroit) 31663001 to 31867688; (San Leandro, Calif.) 45079001 to 45090488; (Los Angeles) 45518001 to 45527385. Engine numbers began at D42-1001 and went up. See Meadowbrook series.

Coronet Series

Model Number	Body/Style Number	Body Type & Seating	Factory Price	Shipping Weight	Production Total
D42	Note 1	4-dr Sedan-6P	$2,103	3,415 lbs.	Note 2
D42	Note 1	2-dr Club Coupe-6P	$2,088	3,320 lbs.	56,103
D42	Note 1	2-dr Diplomat Hardtop-6P	$2,426	3,515 lbs.	21,600
D42	Note 1	2-dr Convertible-6P	$2,514	3,575 lbs.	5,550
D42	Note 1	4-dr Metal Station Wagon-6P	$2,710	3,750 lbs.	4,000
D42	Note 1	4-dr Sedan-6P	$2,855	3,935 lbs.	1,150

NOTE 1: *Owners seeking parts were advised: "There is no way to positively identify the type of body. When in doubt, specify the vehicle serial number and vehicle body number when ordering parts."*

NOTE 2: *There was no breakout of four-door sedan production between the Meadowbrook and Coronet series. Total production in both series was 329,202.*

NOTE 3: *Production figures are totals for 1951 and 1952 model years.*

NOTE 4: *The metal station wagon is the Sierra.*

The business end of the 1951 Dodge Coronet station wagon offered plenty of cargo room.

John Lee

ENGINE: Inline. L-head. Six-cylinder. Cast iron block. Displacement: 230 cid. Bore and stroke: 3.25 x 4.38 inches. Compression ratio: 7.1:1. Brake hp: 103 at 3600 rpm. Four main bearings. Solid valve lifters. Carburetor: Stromberg Type BXVD one-barrel Model 3-93.

CHASSIS FEATURES: Wheelbase: (Wayfarer) 115 inches; (Meadowbrook and Coronet) 123.5 inches; (eight-passenger) 137.5 inches. Overall length: (Wayfarer roadster) 194.38 inches; (Wayfarer sedan) 196.3 inches; (Meadowbrook and Coronet) 202.9 inches; (eight-passenger) 222.9 inches. Front tread: (all models) 56 inches. Rear tread: (all models) 59 inches. Tires: (Wayfarer) 6.70 x 15; (Meadowbrook and Coronet) 7.10 x 15; (Sierra) 7.60 x 15; (eight-passenger) 8.20 x 15.

POWERTRAIN OPTIONS: Fluid-Drive was standard. Gyro-Matic transmission ($95). Heavy-duty air cleaner. Available rear axle gear ratios: 3.73:1; 3.90:1; 4.00:1.

CONVENIENCE OPTIONS: Electric clock. Turn signals. Mopar radio. Heater (called the "All Weather Comfort System"). Chrome wheel trim rings (standard on Coronet). Back-up lights. Gyro-Matic semi-automatic transmission (with Sprint-Away passing gear). Whitewall tires.

HISTORICAL FOOTNOTES: The 1951 Dodges were introduced Jan. 20, 1951. Model year production peaked at 292,000 units. Calendar year sales of 325,694 cars were recorded. W.C. Newberg became president of Dodge Division this year. Dodge earned a 6.1 percent share of total market. The Sierra all-steel station wagon and eight-passenger sedans were discontinued late in the calendar year, when production of models built to 1952 specifications commenced (November 1951). Nearly 90 percent of Dodge Division output was quartered at its Hamtramck, Michigan, plant, which was called "Dodge Main." Some nicknamed it "Chrysler Rouge" because of its productivity. This large factory offered 5,480,312 square feet of floor space. Preparations began, late in the season, for production of an all-new Dodge V-8.

Potential car buyers could "delight their eyes" by looking at a 1951 Dodge.

"Roominess and comfort front and rear are tops and luggage space is more than ample."

"The Dodge is no powerhouse, just solid transportation with plenty of style and safety."

Griffith Borggeson, Motor Trend, August 1951

One magazine ad portrayed the 1951 Dodge as "beauty to behold."

A 1951 magazine ad put it quite simply saying "Dodge is a honey."

A harbor scene with relaxed water skiers and a bright new 1952 Dodge Coronet convertible suggested the hope and optimism of the 1950s lifestyle.

While 1951 and 1952 Dodges are nearly identical, there are some minor revisions in the later year models. Dodge was involved heavily in the massive war effort during the Korean conflict and was so busy with the construction of military vehicles, that the passenger car line was continued nearly the same. Some of the subtle changes included a painted lower grille louver, red reflector dot below the taillight lenses, minor hubcap restyling, a new trunk handle, plus new interior trim and a revised dashboard finish. The rear fender moldings and taillight bezels were no longer connected.

WAYFARER SERIES — (6-CYLINDER): It was the last year for the low trim level, short wheelbase Wayfarer series, which was identified by the Wayfarer name on the front fenders. The Wayfarer roadster was dropped, leaving only the three-passenger coupe and the turtle-backed two-door sedan.

WAYFARER I.D. NUMBERS: Wayfarer models, if assembled in Detroit, began at 37175001 and went to 37207644. If assembled in San Leandro, Calif., began at 48009901 and went to 48011259 and if assembled in Los Angeles, began at 48507601 and went to 48508754. Engine numbers continued where 1951 models left off and went up to D42-419735.

Wayfarer Series

Model Number	Body/Style Number	Body Type & Seating	Factory Price	Shipping Weight	Production Total
D41	Note 1	2-dr Sedan-6P	$2,034	3,140 lbs.	Note 2
D41	Note 1	2-dr Coupe-3P	$1,886	3,050 lbs.	Note 2
D41	Note 1	2-dr Roadster-3P	$1,924	3,100 lbs.	Note 2

NOTE 1: *Owners seeking parts were advised: "There is no way to positively identify the type of body. When in doubt, specify the vehicle serial number and vehicle body number when ordering parts."*

NOTE 2: *Production figures were not separated between 1951 and 1952 models. Therefore, production figures shown for 1951 models represented totals for both 1951 and 1952 model years.*

MEADOWBROOK SERIES — (6-CYLINDER): As in the last three years, the Meadowbrook was the base trim level four-door sedan and the series was offered only in that particular configuration. The Meadowbrook did not have chrome rear fender gravel guards, and only had small hubcaps.

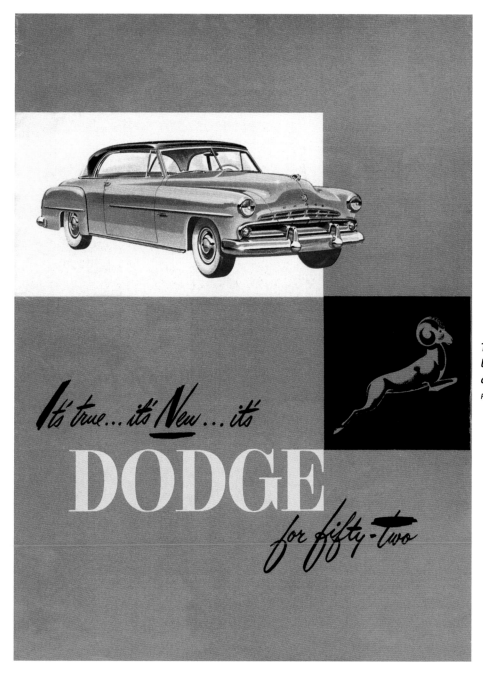

The 1952 Dodge brochure promised a "New Look."

Phil Hall Collection

MEADOWBROOK I.D. NUMBERS: Meadowbrook series sedans, if assembled in Detroit, began at 31887801 and went to 32038822. If assembled in San Leandro, Calif., began at 45090601 and went to 45100113. If assembled in Los Angeles, began at 45527501 and went to 45534770. Engine numbers continued where 1951 models left off and went up to D42-419735.

Meadowbrook Series

Model Number	Body/Style Number	Body Type & Seating	Factory Price	Shipping Weight	Production Total
D41	Note 1	4-dr Sedan-6P	$2,164	3,355 lbs.	Note 2

NOTE 1: *Owners seeking parts were advised: "There is no way to positively identify the type of body. When in doubt, specify the vehicle serial number and vehicle body number when ordering parts."*

NOTE 2: *See Note 2, 1952 Wayfarer series.*

CORONET SERIES — (6-CYLINDER): The Coronet series continued as the top trim level for 1952 and included all the features of the Meadowbrook plus chrome trim rings or full wheel covers. The Coronet had chrome rear fender gravel guards and more interior color choices. Many Coronets were equipped with the Gyro-Matic semi-automatic transmission, and the Coronet logo on the front fender included the Gyro-Matic name.

CORONET I.D. NUMBERS: Coronets, if assembled in Detroit, began at 31867801 and went to 32038822. If assembled in San Leandro, Calif., began at 45090601 and went to 45100113. If assembled in Los Angeles, began at 45527501 and went to 45534770. Engine numbers continued where 1951 models left off and went up to D42-419735.

Coronet Series

Model Number	Body/Style Number	Body Type & Seating	Factory Price	Shipping Weight	Production Total
D42	Note 1	4-dr Sedan-6P	$2,256	3,385 lbs.	Note 2
D42	Note 1	2-dr Club Coupe-6P	$2,240	3,290 lbs.	Note 2
D42	Note 1	2-dr Diplomat HT-6P	$2,602	3,475 lbs.	Note 2
D42	Note 1	2-dr Convertible-6P	$2,698	3,520 lbs.	Note 2
D42	Note 1	4-dr Sierra Wagon-6P	$2,908	3,735 lbs.	Note 2
D42	Note 1	4-dr Sedan-8P	$3,064	3,935 lbs.	Note 2

NOTE 1: Owners seeking parts were advised: "There is no way to positively identify the type of body. When in doubt, specify the vehicle serial number and vehicle body number when ordering parts."
NOTE 2: See Note 2, 1952 Wayfarer series.

ENGINE: Inline. L-head. Six-cylinder. Cast iron block. Displacement: 230 cid. Bore and stroke: 3.25 x 4.265 inches. Compression ratio: 7.0:1. Brake hp: 103 at 3600 rpm. Four main bearings. Solid valve lifters. Carburetor: Stromberg Type BXVD one-barrel Model 3-93.

CHASSIS FEATURES: Wheelbase: (Wayfarer) 115 inches; (Meadowbrook and Coronet) 123.5 inches; (eight-passenger) 137.5 inches. Overall length: (Wayfarer roadster) 194.3 inches; (Wayfarer sedan) 196.3 inches; (Meadowbrook and Coronet) 202.9 inches; (eight-passenger) 222.5 inches. Tires: (Wayfarer) 6.70 x 15 tube-type black sidewall; (Meadowbrook and Coronet) 7.10 x 15 tube-type black sidewall; (Sierra station wagon) 7.60 x 15 tube-type black sidewall; (eight-passenger) 8.20 x 15 tube-type black sidewall. A three-speed manual with Fluid-Drive continued to be the standard transmission, with Gyro-Matic semi-automatic as an option on all models except the Wayfarer roadster.

1952 Dodge Coronet Sierra station wagon

Phil Hall Collection

The "Dependable Dodge" was advertised in 1952.

CONVENIENCE OPTIONS: Electric clock. Turn signals. Mopar radio. Heater (called the "All Weather Comfort System"). Chrome wheel trim rings (standard on Coronet). Back-up lights. Gyro-Matic semi-automatic transmission (with Sprint-Away passing gear). Dodge safety tint glass. White sidewall tires.

HISTORICAL FOOTNOTES: The 1952 Dodges were introduced Nov. 10, 1951. Model year production peaked at 206,000 units. Calendar year sales of 259,519 cars were recorded. W.C. Newberg was the president of Dodge Division this year. The Meadowbrook A special series was introduced late in the calendar year, as was a new Red Ram Dodge V-8. Dodge was America's sixth largest automaker. The company reported that the number of Dodges licensed to operate on the roads this year was approximately 2.5 million cars. On a calendar year basis, Dodge made an estimated 15,613 hardtop coupes; 25,504 convertibles and 58,546 station wagons during 1952.

A well-dressed woman seems to enjoy her 1953 Dodge Coronet Diplomat two-door hardtop.

This was a big year for Dodge with its completely new, downsized body that predicted the compacts of the early-1960s, and the Red Ram V-8. The Red Ram engine and the smaller, lighter body together made the Dodge a strong performer and the most exciting Dodge ever built up to that time.

The body was smaller with no hint of any rear fender bulge. Most American cars still had a ghost of the rear fender bulge that harked back to the 1930s and 1940s when rear fenders were bolted on, but Dodge along with Plymouth and Nash pushed further into the 1950s by eliminating the bulge. The Dodge did retain its identity by keeping a grille very similar to the 1951-'52 style. The car had a one-piece curving windshield, and the rear window was a large wrap-around design. The hood was much flatter and nearly level with the front fenders, and the taillights were more natural extensions of the rear fenders. Chrysler Corporation claimed the Dodge doors opened wider. The doors featured pull-type handles.

Chairman of the board K. T. Keller, president of Chrysler Corporation through November 1950, was criticized for downsizing Dodge and Plymouth and but not changing the Chrysler and De Soto lines. Keller was trying to keep a line of practical economical cars on the road. Time would prove that Keller wasn't wrong but, rather, just several years ahead of his time.

Behind the new Red Ram V-8 was a transmission choice that was not new—Fluid Torque with Gyro-Matic. These Chrysler Corporation semi-automatics were quickly falling far behind the automatic transmissions used by the rest of the industry, especially Chevrolet's fully automatic Powerglide, accessible below Dodge's price range. Very late in the model year, the corporation began testing the fully automatic, two-speed PowerFlite on Chryslers. It became available on Dodge and De Soto in 1954.

MEADOWBROOK SERIES — (6-CYLINDER): The Meadowbrook Special was the base trim level for 1953 and was included primarily as a salesman's car. The Specials were devoid of any chrome side trim and had rubber windshield and rear window moldings. The interiors were as stark as possible. There was also a standard Meadowbrook series. Meadowbrooks featured a Dodge crest on the hood, chrome windshield and rear window moldings and chrome side steps, which began low on the body, behind the front wheel well, and ran horizontally back and swept up over the rear wheel opening. The Meadowbrook name sat at the tip of the front fenders.

A bright red 1953 Dodge Coronet Diplomat two-door hardtop set in artwork showing a polo match. *Phil Hall Collection*

Tanned bodies and the open-air freedom of Dodge's Coronet convertible were signs of the times in 1953.

Phil Hall Collection

MEADOWBROOK I.D. NUMBERS: Meadowbrook series, if assembled in Detroit, began at 32042001 and went to 32152851. If assembled in San Leandro, Calif., began at 45102001 and went to 45105772, and if assembled in Los Angeles, began at 45536001 and went to 45538622. Engine numbers began at D46-1001 and went to D46-134677.

Meadowbrook Series

Model Number	Body/Style Number	Body Type & Seating	Factory Price	Shipping Weight	Production Total
D46	Note 1	4-dr Special Sedan-6P	$2,000	3,195 lbs.	84,158
D46	Note 1	2-dr Special Sedan-6P	$1,958	3,100 lbs.	36,766
D46	Note 1	4-dr Sedan-6P	$2,000	3,175 lbs.	Note 2
D46	Note 1	2-dr Sedan-6P	$1,958	3,085 lbs.	Note 2
D47	Note 1	2-dr Suburban-6P	$2,176	3,190 lbs.	15,751

NOTE 1: *Owners seeking parts were advised: "There is no way to positively identify the type of body. When in doubt, specify the vehicle serial number and vehicle body number when ordering parts."*

NOTE 2: *There is no breakout between Meadowbrook Special models and standard Meadowbrook models. Therefore, figures given represent total Meadowbrook production for each of the body styles.*

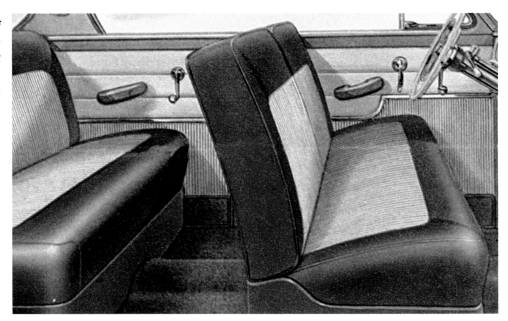

CORONET SERIES — (6-CYLINDER/V-8): The Coronet was the top trim level for 1953 and included all the Meadowbrook Series features, plus a "Jet Flow" scoop around the "Dodge V-8" emblem located beneath the Ram hood ornament. The Coronet sported a chrome gravel deflector and the Coronet name on the sides of the front fenders. The two-door hardtop was once again called the Coronet Diplomat, and they were graced with rather fancy interiors. Six-cylinder sedans appeared in March.

CORONET I.D. NUMBERS: Coronet models powered by six-cylinder engines used the same serial number sequence as the Meadowbrook series and V-8-powered Coronets. If assembled in Detroit, numbers began at 3450001 and went to 34635734. If assembled in San Leandro, Calif., began at 4250001 and went to 42507899, and if assembled in Los Angeles, began at 41500001 and went to 41504467. Engine numbers began at D44-1001 and went to D44-176412.

Coronet Series

Model Number	Body/Style Number	Body Type & Seating	Factory Price	Shipping Weight	Production Total
D46/44	Note 1	4-dr Sedan-6P	$2,111/$2,220	3,220/3,385 lbs.	Note 2
D46/44	Note 1	2-dr Sedan-6P	$2,084/$2,198	3,155/3,325 lbs.	Note 2
D48	Note 1	2-dr Diplomat Hardtop-6P	$2,361	3,310 lbs.	17,334
D48	Note 1	2-dr Convertible-6P	$2,494	3,480 lbs.	4,100
D48	Note 1	2-dr Sierra Wagon-6P	$2,503	3,425 lbs.	5,400

NOTE 1: *Owners seeking parts were advised: "There is no way to positively identify the type of body. When in doubt, specify the vehicle serial number and vehicle body number when ordering parts."*

NOTE 2: *See Note 2, 1953 Meadowbrook series. The note also applies to Coronet two-door and four-door sedans equipped with six-cylinder engines.*

NOTE 3: *The V-8 was considered a separate series, not an option. Factory prices and weights, on charts, give data for six-cylinder cars above slash and V-8 data below slash.*

ENGINES: Inline. L-head. Six-cylinder. Cast iron block. Displacement: 230 cid. Bore and stroke: 3.25 x 4.625 inches. Compression ratio: 7.1:1. Brake hp: 103 at 3600 rpm. Four main bearings. Solid valve lifters. Carburetor: Carter one-barrel Model D6H2.

All New '53 **Dodge**

HEMI HEAD OVERHEAD VALVE V-8. CAST IRON BLOCK. DISPLACEMENT: 241 cid. Bore and stroke: 3.44 x 3.25 inches. Compression ratio: 7.0:1. Brake hp: 140 at 4400 rpm. Five main bearings. Hydraulic valve lifters. Carburetor: Stromberg two-barrel Model WW3-108.

CHASSIS FEATURES: Wheelbase: (Diplomat hardtop, convertible, Suburban station wagon) 114 inches; (sedan and club coupe) 119 inches. Overall length: (Suburban and Sierra station wagons) 189.6 inches; (convertible and Diplomat) 191.3 inches; (four-door sedans and club coupes) 201.4 inches. Tires: (Meadowbrook) 6.70 x 15-inch tube-type black sidewall; (Coronet) 7.10 x 15-inch tube-type black sidewall. Three-speed manual transmission was once again the standard transmission, with Overdrive, Fluid-Drive and Gyro-Torque automatic as the optional transmissions.

CONVENIENCE OPTIONS: Electric clock. Turn signals. Mopar radio. Heater. Windshield washers. Back-up lights. Solex tinted glass. Wheel covers. Overdrive. Gyro-Matic drive (Fluid-Drive). Gyro-Torque automatic drive. White sidewall tires. Bright wheel opening trim. Chrome wire wheels. Continental spare wheel kit.

HISTORICAL FOOTNOTES: The 1953 Dodges were introduced Oct. 23, 1952, and the Coronet Six appeared in dealer showrooms March 18, 1953. Model year production peaked at 304,000 units. Calendar year sales of 293,714 cars were recorded. W.C. Newberg was the president of Dodge Division this year. The Meadowbrook Special series was introduced late in the calendar year as was a new Red Ram Dodge V-8. On Jan. 15, 1953, the 100,000th Dodge built to 1953 specifications left the factory. A general price cut took effect on March 25, 1953. Sales of a new option, air-conditioning, began April 6, 1953, during the same month the Meadowbrook Special was discontinued and the Coronet Six was announced for mid-March availability. Dodge topped all other American Eights in the Mobilgas Economy Run with a 23.4 mpg average. In September 1953, a 1954 Dodge set 196 AAA stock car speed records at the Bonneville Salt Flats in Utah including a run at 102.622 mph. On Nov. 12, 1953, the Dodge Firearrow, a futuristic sports roadster, was put on display at leading U.S. auto shows. NASCAR drivers liked the powerful Dodges and drove them to six wins in 1953, the first such victories for Dodge.

In its second year, the downsized, bulge-less 1954 Dodge had no pre-1950 design elements.

Dodges used the same body introduced in 1953 with minor changes. The new grille featured a prominent horizontal bar with a distinctive vertical post in the middle. The cars completely broke all resemblance to the 1951 and '52 models. The taillight clusters were redesigned and chrome stone shields were used on the rear fenders of the top trim level cars. The semi-automatic transmission era was finally closing, and while the Gyro-Matic was still available, mostly on six-cylinder cars, Dodge buyers could order the optional, fully automatic, PowerFlite two-speed automatic transmission.

MEADOWBROOK SERIES — (6-CYLINDER/V-8): Rubber stone shields were used on the base trim level Meadowbrook series. The Meadowbrooks also included rubber windshield and rear window moldings; the Dodge crest in the center of the hood; the Meadowbrook name, in script, on the rear fenders and a short chrome strip along the sides of the front fenders and part of the front door.

MEADOWBROOK I.D. NUMBERS: Meadowbrook series, if assembled in Detroit, began at 32152901 and went to 32189926; if assembled in San Leandro, Calif., began at 45105801 and went to 45110883. Engine numbers began at D51-1001 and went to D51-1877 and D51A-1001 and went to D51A-1877.

Meadowbrook Series

Model Number	Body/Style Number	Body Type & Seating	Factory Price	Shipping Weight	Production Total
D50/51	Note 1	4-dr Sedan-6P	$2,000/$2,151	3,195/3,390 lbs.	11,193
D50/51	Note 1	2-dr Club Coupe-6P	$1,958/$2,121	3,120/3,335 lbs.	4,251

NOTE 1: *Owners seeking parts were advised: "There is no way to positively identify the type of body. When in doubt, specify the vehicle serial number and vehicle body number when ordering parts."*

NOTE 2: *The figures to the left of slash marks represent six-cylinder models and the figures to the right represent V-8-powered models.*

CORONET SERIES — (6-CYLINDER/V-8): The Coronet was now the intermediate trim level Dodge and included all the Meadowbrook features plus chrome windshield and rear window moldings, a full-length chrome strip along the middle of the body which dipped down behind the front door to near the top of the rear wheelwell and chrome rear fender stone shields. The Coronet name, in script, appeared on the sides of the rear fenders.

CORONET I.D. NUMBERS: Coronet models powered by six-cylinder engines and assembled in Detroit began at 32160001 and went up to 32189926; if assembled in San Leandro, Calif., began at 45110001 and went up to 45110883. Coronets powered by V-8 engines and assembled in Detroit, began at 34642001 and went up to 34739536, and if assembled in San Leandro, began at 42510001 and went up to 42516879. Six-cylinder engine numbers began at D1-1001 and went to D1-35830. V-8 engine numbers began at D502-1001 and went up to D502-110857.

The Dodge hood trim let everyone know there was a ram lurking underneath.

Coronet Series

Model Number	Body/Style Number	Body Type & Seating	Factory Price	Shipping Weight	Production Total
D50/51	Note 1	4-dr Sedan-6P	$2,111/$2,220	3,235/3,405 lbs.	50,963
D50/51	Note 1	2-dr Club Coupe-6P	$2,084/$2,198	3,165/3,345 lbs.	12,499
D52/53	Note 1	2-dr Suburban-6P	$2,204/$2,492	3,185/3,400 lbs.	9,489
D52/53	Note 1	4-dr Sierra-6P	$2,694/$2,935	3,430/3,605 lbs.	1,300
D53-2	Note 1	2-dr Hardtop Coupe-6P	$2,355	3,310 lbs.	100
D53-2	Note 1	2-dr Convertible-6P	$2,489	3,505 lbs.	50

NOTE 1: *Owners seeking parts were advised: "There is no way to positively identify the type of body. When in doubt, specify the vehicle serial number and vehicle body number when ordering parts."*

NOTE 2: *The figures to the left of the slash marks represent six-cylinder models and the figures to the right represent V-8-powered models. Those models with only one set of figures were available only with V-8 power.*

In 1954, Dodge got a transmission, in the PowerFlite automatic, that matched its advanced Red Ram V-8 engine.

One could make an argument that the 1954 Dodge was the most technologically advanced heavy-hauling station wagon in North America in 1954.

ROYAL SERIES — (V-8): The Royal series was the new top trim level for 1954 and was available only with the 241-cid "Hemi" engine. The Royal models included all the Coronet features, plus chrome rocker panel moldings, a V-8 emblem, the "Jet Flow" scoop on the front of the hood, and bolt-on chrome fins along the tops of the rear fenders.

ROYAL I.D. NUMBERS: Royal models assembled in Detroit began at 34642001 and went up to 34799536. Those assembled in San Leandro, Calif., began at 42510001 and went up to 42516879. Engine numbers began at D502-1001 and went up to D502-110857.

1954 Dodge Royal Indianapolis 500 Pace Car convertible

Tom Glatch

The 1954 Dodge Royal Indianapolis 500 Pace Car convertible with its continental kit in view. Tom Glatch

The interior of this special Dodge Royal was worthy of a racing champion, circa 1954. Tom Glatch

Royal Series

Model Number	Body/Style Number	Body Type & Seating	Factory Price	Shipping Weight	Production Total
D50-3	Note 1	4-dr Sedan-6P	$2,348	3,425	50,050
D50-3	Note 1	2-dr Club Coupe-6P	$2,324	3,385	8,900
D53-3	Note 1	2-dr Hardtop Coupe-6P	$2,478	3,355	3,852
D53-3	Note 1	2-dr Convertible-6P	$2,607	3,575	2,000

NOTE 1: *See Note 1, 1947 Deluxe models.*

ENGINES: Inline. L-head. Six-cylinder. Cast iron block. Displacement: 230 cid. Bore and stroke: 3.25 x 4.625 inches. Compression ratio: 7.25:1. Brake hp: 110 at 3600 rpm. Four main bearings. Solid valve lifters. Carburetor: Carter one-barrel Model D6U1.

HEMI HEAD OVERHEAD VALVE V-8: Cast iron block. Displacement: 241 cid. Bore and stroke: 3.312 x 3.25 inches. Compression ratio: 7.5:1 (7.1:1 on Meadowbrook models). Brake hp: 150 at 4400 rpm (140 at 4400 rpm on Meadowbrook models). Five main bearings. Solid valve lifters. Carburetor: Stromberg two-barrel Model WW-3-108.

CHASSIS FEATURES: Wheelbase: (hardtop, convertible and two-door station wagon models) 114 inches; (other models) 119 inches. Overall length: (short-wheelbase models) 196 inches; (long-wheelbase models) 205.5 inches. Tires: (Meadowbrook and six-cylinder-equipped Suburbans) 6.70 x 15-inch tube-type black sidewall; (other models) 7.10 x 15-inch tube-type black sidewall. A three-speed manual was once again the standard transmission. Overdrive cost ($98); Fluid-Drive ($20) and PowerFlite automatic transmission ($189): all optional transmissions. Gyro-Matic Drive was also available ($130).

CONVENIENCE OPTIONS: Electric clock. Turn signals. Mopar radio. Power steering ($134). Back-up lights. Solex tinted glass. AirTemp air conditioning ($643). White sidewall tires ($30), Windshield washers. Power brakes ($37). Chrome wire wheels. Wire wheel covers. Continental spare tire kit.

HISTORICAL FOOTNOTES: The full-size Dodge models were introduced Oct. 8, 1953, and the four-door Dodge Sierra station wagon appeared in dealer showrooms Dec. 8, 1953. Model year production peaked at 150,930 units. Calendar year sales of 151,766 cars were recorded. W.C. Newberg was president of Dodge Division, which earned a 2.75 percent share of the total U.S. market this year, good for 8th place in the auto industry. In January 1954, Dodge Division initiated a heavy radio and television advertising campaign. On Feb. 7, 1954, an advertising contest to celebrate Dodge's 40th anniversary as a carmaker was launched. On Feb. 20, the Firearrow dream car was exhibited at the Chicago Auto Show. A new range of special spring paint colors was announced on March 22, 1954. On April 8, a Dodge equipped with overdrive transmission won out over all other low-medium priced U.S. cars in the Mobilgas Economy Run. It averaged 25.3873 mpg for the complete 1,335-mile course. On May 31,1954, a specially-trimmed Dodge convertible paced the Indianapolis 500-Mile Race, and 701 Royal 500 pace car replica convertibles were produced. The figure is included in Royal convertible production totals. Pace car engines were equipped with four-barrel carburetors and dual exhaust. On June 16, 1954, the Firearrow proved itself to be a functional dream car, as it was used to establish a woman's world speed record of 143.44 mph run at the Chrysler Proving Grounds, in Chelsea, Mich. There was only a single Dodge win in NASCAR racing this year.

Here is a period shot of the 1954 Dodge Royal preparing for its work as the Indianapolis 500 Pace Car.

Tom Glatch

All Dodge models were totally restyled in 1955. It was the dawn of the "Forward Look" at Chrysler Corporation, including at Dodge. They were more than six inches longer than the 1954 models. They were also lower and wider and were powered by a larger and more powerful V-8 engine. The six-cylinder engine also received a boost, to 123 hp, as the great performance race of the mid-1950s began. Dodge's advertising people called the new styling "Flair-Fashion." This styling was set off by the use of tri-color paint schemes. The new grille was divided into two separate openings. Each opening housed a single horizontal bar that wrapped around the fender and incorporated the parking light. All models featured a simulated hood scoop. The windshield was a wraparound affair, which Dodge referred to as a "new horizon" windshield. The new taillights were emphasized by a chrome trim piece and the higher trim levels featured dual lenses on each side (the lower of which was often replaced with back-up lights). Six-cylinder-equipped models featured the large Dodge crest in the center of the hood and trunk lid. Those models with V-8 power featured the Dodge crest over a large "V."

The 1955 Dodge Custom Royal sedan

The Dodge dash was a large, pleasing panel, and the gear selector for the PowerFlite automatic transmission was a lever that stuck out of the dash just to the right of the steering column.

CORONET SERIES — (6-CYLINDER/V-8): The Coronet was the base trim level for 1955 and featured chrome windshield and rear window moldings, chrome trim around the simulated hood scoop, chrome headlight doors and a single horizontal chrome strip running from the front fender to the rear of the front door. The Coronet name appeared, in script, along the side of the front fenders on cars with Lancer trim and just ahead of the taillights on those with standard trim. Late in the year, Lancer trim was made available on sedans and station wagons.

Dodge had a brand new look from every angle including its front grille.

The new dash was unlike anything drivers had seen in their past Dodges.

Like every 1955 Chrysler Corporation car, the Flight Control lever was mounted on the 1955 Dodge dash, the gear selector for the PowerFlite automatic transmission.

CORONET I.D. NUMBERS: Six-cylinder-powered Coronets assembled in Detroit began at 32192001 and went to 32225514 and those assembled in Los Angeles began at 48016001 and went to 48016299. V-8-powered models assembled in Detroit began with 34740001 and went to 34970679 and those assembled in Los Angeles began at 42518001 and went to 42526800. Six-cylinder engine numbers began at D56-1001 and went up to D56-34905. V-8 engine numbers began at D551-1001 and went up to D551-149857.

Coronet Series

Model Number	Body/Style Number	Body Type & Seating	Factory Price	Shipping Weight	Production Total
D55/56	Note 1	4-dr Sedan-6P	$2,068/$2,171	3,295/3,395 lbs.	46,074
D55/56	Note 1	2-dr Sedan-6P	$1,988/$2,091	3,235/3,360 lbs.	24,104
D55-1	Note 1	2-dr Lancer Hardtop-6P	$2,256	3,375 lbs.	26,727
D55/56	Note 1	2-dr Suburban-6P	$2,324/$2,427	3,410/3,550 lbs.	8,115
D55/56	Note 1	4-dr Sierra Wagon-6P	$2,438/$2,541	3,480/3,590 lbs.	5,952
D55/56	Note 1	4-dr Sierra Wagon-8P	$2,540/$2,643	3,595/3,695 lbs.	Note 2

NOTE 1: *Owners seeking parts were advised: "There is no way to positively identify the type of body. When in doubt, specify the vehicle serial number and vehicle body number when ordering parts."*

NOTE 2: *There is no breakout per six- and eight-passenger Sierra station wagon models. Production figures given under the six-passenger model represent the cumulative total for both styles.*

NOTE 3: *The figures to the left of the slash marks represent six-cylinder models and the figures to the right represent V-8 models. Those without a slash mark came only as V-8s.*

ROYAL SERIES — (V-8): The Royal was the intermediate trim level for 1955 and included all the Coronet features plus hooded, chrome headlight doors and the Royal name, in script, on the front or rear fenders. Lancer trim, standard on Lancer hardtops and convertibles, now became optional on most other models. Narrow chrome strips trailed back from the hood scoop, dropped over the side of the front fenders as they approached the windshield, dipped at the C-pillar, and continued high on the rear fenders to the taillight housings.

ROYAL I.D. NUMBERS: Royal V-8-powered models assembled in Detroit began with 34740001 and went to 34970679. Those assembled in Los Angeles began at 42518001 and went to 42526800. V-8 engine numbers began at D551-1001 and went up to D551-149857.

Royal Series

Model Number	Body/Style Number	Body Type & Seating	Factory Price	Shipping Weight	Production Total
D55-2	Note 1	4-dr Sedan-6P	$2,285	3,425 lbs.	45,323
D55-2	Note 1	2-dr Lancer Hardtop-6P	$2,370	3,425 lbs.	25,831
D55-2	Note 1	4-dr Sierra Wagon-6P	$2,634	3,655 lbs.	5,506
D55-2	Note 1	4-dr Sierra Wagon-8P	$2,736	3,730 lbs.	Note 2

A special edition of the 1955 Dodge Custom Royal Lancer was called "La Femme," French for woman.

NOTE 1: *Owners seeking parts were advised: "There is no way to positively identify the type of body. When in doubt, specify the vehicle serial number and vehicle body number when ordering parts."*

NOTE 2: *See Note 2, 1955 Coronet models.*

The interior of the 1955 Dodge "La Femme" special edition came with accessories that matched the car's interior.

CUSTOM ROYAL SERIES — (V-8): The Custom Royal was the top trim level for 1955 and included all the Royal features, plus the Royal name and medallion on the rear fenders of the sedans with standard side trim and on the front fenders of models with Lancer sweep spear trim. The Lancer hardtop and convertible models featured chrome fins on the tops of the rear fenders. In April, a Royal Lancer four-door hardtop appeared as an answer to the new four-door hardtops from General Motors. It had Lancer side trim. There was a midyear La Femme (the French word for "woman") option for the Custom Royal Lancer that featured two-tone lavender paint, a make up kit, and a matching purse and umbrella that fit into specially made pockets on the back of the front seat. The La Femme was an attempt to make the ultimate ladies' car.

The interior of the 1955 Dodge Custom Royal Lancer two-door hardtop.

Tom Glatch

The 1955 Dodge Super Red Ram V-8 produced a healthy 270 hp. Tom Glatch

CUSTOM ROYAL I.D. NUMBERS: Custom Royal V-8-powered models assembled in Detroit began with 34740001 and went to 34970679. Those assembled in Los Angeles began at 42518001 and went to 42526800. V-8 engine numbers began at D551-1001 and went up to D551-149857.

Custom Royal Series

Model Number	Body/Style Number	Body Type & Seating	Factory Price	Shipping Weight	Production Total
D55-3	Note 1	4-dr Sedan-6P	$2,448	3,485 lbs.	55,503
D55-3	Note 1	2-dr Lancer Hardtop-6P	$2,518	3,480 lbs.	30,499
D55-3	Note 1	2-dr Lancer Convertible-6P	$2,723	3,610 lbs.	3,302
D55-3	Note 1	4-dr Lancer Sedan-6P	N/A	N/A	N/A

NOTE 1: Owners seeking parts were advised: "There is no way to positively identify the type of body. When in doubt, specify the vehicle serial number and vehicle body number when ordering parts."

ENGINES: Inline. L-head. Six-cylinder. Cast iron block. Displacement: 230 cid. Bore and stroke: 3.25 x 4.625 inches. Compression ratio: 7.4:1. Brake hp: 123 at 3600 rpm. Four main bearings. Solid valve lifters. Carburetor: Stromberg two-barrel Model WW3-124.

RED RAM V-8: Overhead valve. Polysphere combustion chambers. Cast iron block. Displacement: 270 cid. Bore and stroke: 3.63 x 3.26 inches. Compression ratio: 7.6:1. Brake hp: 175 at 4400 rpm. Five main bearings. Hydraulic valve lifters. Carburetor: Stromberg two-barrel Model WW3-131.

SUPER RED RAM V-8: Overhead valve. Hemispherical combustion chambers. Cast iron block. Displacement: 270 cid. Bore and stroke: 3.63 x 3.26 inches. Compression ratio: 7.6:1. Brake hp (std..) 183 at 4400 rpm; (opt.) 193 at 4400 rpm. Five main bearings. Hydraulic valve lifters. Carburetor: (std.) Stromberg two-barrel; (opt.) Carter four-barrel.

CHASSIS FEATURES: Wheelbase: 120 inches. Overall length: 212.1 inches. Tires: (Coronet six) 6.70 x 15 tube-type black sidewall; (V-8-powered models) 7.10 x 15 black sidewall. Three-speed manual transmission was the standard transmission, with PowerFlite being the two-speed fully automatic optional transmission ($178). Overdrive was an option on standard transmission-equipped models ($108).

CONVENIENCE OPTIONS: Electric clock. Turn signals. Mopar radio ($110). Power steering ($113). Power brakes ($38). Power seats ($70). Power windows ($102). Heater. AirTemp air conditioning ($567). Windshield washers. White sidewall tires. Engine power package ($48). Spinner wheel covers. Chrome wire wheels. Tinted glass. Continental spare tire kit. Lancer trim offered a natural break for 16 two-tone and 16 three-tone color combinations.

HISTORICAL FOOTNOTES: The full-size Dodges were introduced Nov. 17, 1954, and the Coronet Sierra station wagon and Royal Lancer appeared in dealer showrooms Dec. 17, 1954. The Custom Royal Lancer four-door sedan debuted in April. Another midyear trim option, called La Femme, was the industry's first appeal to women with special Heather Rose and Sapphire White color combinations and matching cape, boots, umbrella, shoulder bag and floral upholstery fabrics. Model year production peaked at 273,286 units. Calendar year sales of 313,038 cars were recorded. W.C. Newberg was president of Dodge Division this year. The capacity of the Dodge V-8 assembly plant was greatly increased during the final months of calendar 1955, when the Plymouth V-8 plant opened. Motor Trend magazine found its Custom Royal V-8 (with PowerFlite) capable of going 0-to-60 mph in 16.2 seconds and calculated a top speed of 101.8 mph for this model. The Dodge Division began sponsoring the very popular "Lawrence Welk Show" beginning in the fall of 1955 on the ABC Television Network.

1956 Dodge
Custom Royal
sedan

Following a year of outstanding sales, Dodge wisely chose not to drastically restyle its cars for 1956. While the front end was nearly identical to the previous year, the grille's center divider jutted outward more, and this small difference altered the appearance of the front of the car quite a bit. Along with the 1956 De Soto, Dodge had some of the best two-toning of the 1950s. The rear fenders peaked higher and were a little more fin-like. On higher-trim models, the side spear swept downward toward the rear of the car, and on Custom Royals, this spear suddenly shot back upward toward the taillight. This spear played a big part in the Dodge's two-tone paint schemes. A four-door hardtop was offered for the first time in all three series. Electrical systems changed from six-volt to 12-volt.

The horsepower race was in full swing, and Dodge was right in the thick of things. The division had V-8 engines all the way up to 295 hp. The year ushered in one of Chrysler's most famous trademarks—the push-button selector for the PowerFlite automatic transmission on the left-land end of the dash. Carried over unchanged from 1955 were some of the customizer's most sought after items: the beautiful Dodge Lancer wheel covers. No chopped and channeled custom of the 1950s would be complete without a set of the Lancer spinners.

CORONET SERIES — (6-CYLINDER/V-8): The Coronet was the base trim level for 1956 and included chrome windshield and rear window moldings, chrome trim around the simulated hood scoop, chrome headlight doors, "Saddle Sweep" chrome side trim and the Coronet name, in script, along the rear fenders.

CORONET I.D. NUMBERS: Six-cylinder-powered Coronets assembled in Detroit began at 32227001 and went to 32254093. Those assembled in Los Angeles began at 48016501 and went to 48018723. V-8-powered models assembled in Detroit began at 34972001 and went to 35167854. Those assembled in Los Angeles began at 42608001 and went to 42618518. Engine numbers were D62-1001 and up for six-cylinder engines and D63-1-1001 and up for V-8 engines.

Coronet Series

Model Number	Body/Style Number	Body Type & Seating	Factory Price	Shipping Weight	Production Total
D62/63	Note 1	4-dr Sedan-6P	$2,232/$2,340	3,295/3,435 lbs.	Note 2
D62/63	Note 1	2-dr Club Sedan-6P	$2,159/$2,267	3,250/3,380 lbs.	Note 2
D63	Note 1	4-dr Lancer Hardtop-6P	$2,517	3,560 lbs.	Note 2
D63	Note 1	2-dr Lancer Hardtop-6P	$2,403	3,430 lbs.	Note 2
D63	Note 1	2-dr Convertible-6P	$2,643	3,600 lbs.	Note 2
D62/63	Note 1	2-dr Suburban-6P	$2,456/$2,564	3,455/3,605 lbs.	Note 2
D63	Note 1	4-dr Sierra Wagon-6P	$2,681	3,600 lbs.	Note 2
D63	Note 1	4-dr Sierra Wagon-8P	$2,787	3,715 lbs.	Note 2

NOTE 1: *Owners seeking parts were advised: "There is no way to positively identify the type of body. When in doubt, specify the vehicle serial number and vehicle body number when ordering parts."*

NOTE 2: *Production figures were not given for individual models and body styles. Dodge produced a total of 220,208 cars during calendar year 1956, including 142,613 Coronets. Model year production amounted to some 241,000 cars in all series.*

NOTE 3: *Prices and weights to left of slash marks are for sixes, to right for V-8s.*

1956 Dodge Custom Royal sedan

1956 Dodge Custom Royal Lancer four-door hardtop

Brad Leisure Collection

ROYAL SERIES — (V-8): The Royal was once again the intermediate trim level and included all the Coronet features plus six chrome fins on the top of the center bar in the grille, chrome rain gutters, and smooth taillight and back-up light housings. The Royal name appeared in script on the rear fenders along with the V-8 emblem.

ROYAL I.D. NUMBERS: V-8-powered models assembled in Detroit began at 34972001 and went to 35167854. Those assembled in Los Angeles began at 42608001 and went to 42618518. Engine numbers were D63-1-1001 and up on V-8 engines.

Royal Series

Model Number	Body/Style Number	Body Type & Seating	Factory Price	Shipping Weight	Production Total
D63-2	Note 1	4-dr Sedan-6P	$2,478	3,475 lbs.	Note 2
D63-2	Note 1	4-dr Lancer Hardtop-6P	$2,662	3,625 lbs.	Note 2
D63-2	Note 1	2-dr Lancer Hardtop-6P	$2,548	3,505 lbs.	Note 2
D63-2	Note 1	2-dr Custom Suburban-6P	$2,694	3,620 lbs.	Note 2
D63-2	Note 1	4-dr Custom Sierra-6P	$2,834	3,710 lbs.	Note 2
D63-2	Note 1	4-dr Custom Sierra-8P	$2,939	3,800 lbs.	Note 2

NOTE 1: *Owners seeking parts were advised: "There is no way to positively identify the type of body. When in doubt, specify the vehicle serial number and vehicle body number when ordering parts."*

NOTE 2: *See Note 2, 1956 Coronet models. A total of 48,780 Royal models were built.*

1956 Dodge Custom Sierra eight-passenger station wagon

1956 Dodge Custom Royal Lancer four-door hardtop

1956 Dodge Royal sedan *Phil Hall Collection*

The push button gear selector was new on the 1956 Dodge and all Chrysler Corporation vehicles with automatic transmissions.

Phil Hall Collection

CUSTOM ROYAL SERIES — (V-8): The Custom Royal was once again the top trim level Dodge and included all the Royal features plus hooded and painted headlight doors, grooved back-up and taillight housings, a strip of the lower body color extending up the rear edge of the rear fenders and the Custom Royal name, in script, on the rear fenders, along with the V-8 emblem. Midyear saw La Femme and Golden Lancer options for the Custom Royal Lancer two-door hardtop.

CUSTOM ROYAL I.D. NUMBERS: V-8-powered models assembled in Detroit began at 34972001 and went to 35167854. Those assembled in Los Angeles began at 42608001 and went to 42618518. Engine numbers were D63-1-1001 and up on V-8 engines.

Custom Royal Series

Model Number	Body/Style Number	Body Type & Seating	Factory Price	Shipping Weight	Production Total
D63-3	Note 1	4-dr Sedan-6P	$2,588	3,520 lbs.	Note 2
D63-3	Note 1	4-dr Lancer Hardtop-6P	$2,772	3,675 lbs.	Note 2
D63-3	Note 1	2-dr Lancer Hardtop-6P	$2,658	3,505 lbs.	Note 2
D63-3	Note 1	2-dr Convertible-6P	$2,878	3,630 lbs.	Note 2

NOTE 1: *Owners seeking parts were advised: "There is no way to positively identify the type of body. When in doubt, specify the vehicle serial number and vehicle body number when ordering parts."*

NOTE 2: *See Note 2, 1956 Coronet models. A total of 49,293 Custom Royal models were built.*

ENGINES: Inline. L-head. Six-cylinder. Cast iron block. Displacement: 230 cid. Bore and stroke: 3.25 x 4.625 inches. Compression ratio: 7.6:1. Brake hp: 131 at 3600 rpm. Four main bearings. Solid valve lifters. Carburetor: Stromberg two-barrel Model WW3-124.

RED RAM V-8: Overhead valve. Polysphere combustion chambers. Cast iron block. Displacement: 270 cid. Bore and stroke: 3.63 x 3.26 inches. Compression ratio: 7.6:1. Brake hp: 189 at 4400 rpm. Five main bearings. Hydraulic valve lifters. Carburetor: Stromberg two-barrel Model WW3-135.

SUPER RED RAM V-8: Overhead valve. Polysphere combustion chambers. Cast iron block. Displacement: 315 cid. Bore and stroke: 3.63 x 3.80 inches. Compression ratio: 8.0:1. Brake hp: 218 at 4400 rpm. Five main bearings. Hydraulic valve lifters. Carburetor: Stromberg two-barrel Model WW3-148.

SUPER RED RAM V-8: Overhead valve. Polysphere combustion chambers. Cast iron block. Displacement: 315 cid. Bore and stroke: 3.63 x 3.80 inches. Compression ratio: 8.0:1. Brake hp: 230 at 4400 rpm. Five main bearings. Hydraulic valve lifters. Carburetor: Carter four-barrel Model WCFB.

D-500 V-8: Overhead valve. Hemispherical combustion chambers. Cast iron block. Displacement: 315 cid. Bore and stroke: 3.63 x 3.80 inches. Compression ratio: 9.25:1. Brake hp: 260 at 4400 rpm. Five main bearings. Solid valve lifters. Carburetor: Carter four-barrel Type WCFB.

D-500-1 ENGINE: Same as above, but with dual Carter WCFB four-barrel carburetors and manual transmission. Brake hp: 295 at 4400 rpm. (These were midyear options.)

CHASSIS FEATURES: Wheelbase: 120 inches. Overall length: 212 inches. Tires: (six-cylinder Coronet and Suburban) 6.70 x 15 tubeless black sidewall; (Royal, Coronet and V-8 station wagons) 7.10 x 15 tubeless black sidewall; (Custom Royal) 7.60 x 15. Three-speed manual continued to be the standard transmission, with Overdrive ($102) and PowerFlite fully automatic ($184) the optional transmissions.

CONVENIENCE OPTIONS: Electric clock. Turn signals. Mopar radio. Power steering ($92). Power brakes ($38). Power seats. Power windows. Heater. Air Temp air conditioning. Hi-Way Hi-Fi automatic record player. Windshield washers. White sidewall tires.

HISTORICAL FOOTNOTES: The 1956 Dodge line was introduced on Oct. 7, 1955. Model year production peaked at exactly 233,686 units, giving the company a 3.7 percent share of the total market. Of this total (again on a model year basis) 1,687 had optional air conditioning. On a calendar year basis (Jan. 1956 to Jan. 1957), Dodge built 40,100 two-door hardtops, 10,900 four-door hardtops; 4,100 convertibles and 16,100 station wagons. These rounded off totals include 1957 models built in the fall of 1956, but 1956 models built in the fall of 1955 are not included, so this gives only a rough idea of how many of each particular body style were made. Calendar year production for Dodge totaled 205,727 cars. This was a decline of 22.4 percent over 1955. During 1956, Dodge installed automatic transmissions in 90.3 percent of all its cars; 94.8 percent had heaters; 62.6 percent had back-up lights; 60.2 percent had whitewalls; 17.3 percent had power brakes and 24.3 percent had power steering. M.C. Patterson became president and chief executive officer of Dodge Division this season. The company's address was 7900 Joseph Campau Avenue in Detroit. Some mention must be made of two special options introduced midyear in the Custom Royal series. The "La Femme" featured a lavender and white paint job and matching interior with gold flecks. It came with a matching umbrella, cap and purse hook. A Texas dealer-only promotion called the Dodge Texan caused a minor stir. The car bore the Texas flag, a symbol that was not to be used for commercial purposes. After protests to Dodge vice president William C. Newberg, the Texas flags on the Dodge were reshaped into small banners. The Golden Lancer featured a Sapphire white body and top with Gallant Saddle Gold exterior and interior trim. In September

"...the D-500 chassis represents one of the best compromises yet in a passenger car between roadability and the quality of the ride."
"It looks like Dodge is going racing in a big way... to win and show the world a rear view of the 'Flight Sweep' design."

Racer Brown, Hot Rod, May 1956

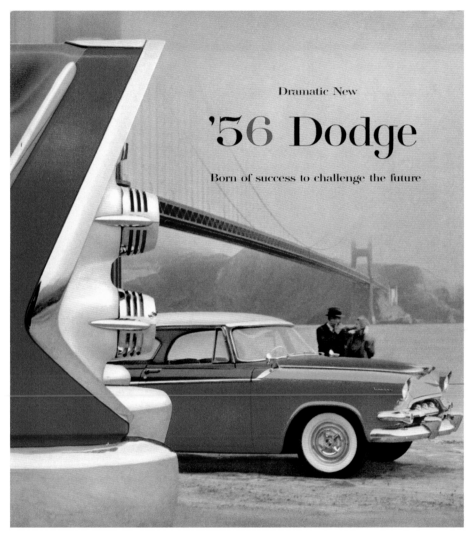

The cover of the 1956 Dodge brochure offered the "Dodge challenge." Phil Hall Collection

1955, a 1956 Dodge Custom Royal four-door sedan was driven 31,224 miles in 14 days at the Bonneville Salt Flats, Utah, and set 306 speed records. Dodges won 11 NASCAR races, a figure that wouldn't be topped until 1964.

Dodge also was the hottest car on North American drag strips during much of 1956, especially with the "dash-one," the D-500-1 engine. Dodge driver Ed Lyons went undefeated in his 1956 Dodge D-500-1 racer that year. Some, including famed drag racer and early Dodge driver, Arnie "The Farmer" Beswick, say the D-500-1 Dodges made 100+-mph runs and broke the 14 second quarter mile barrier that year. Dodge competed in both NHRA and ATAA (Automobile Timing Association of America) competitions in 1956.

The second wave of the Forward Look came to Dodge in 1957. The look was especially beautiful in the Custom Royal convertible.

The new Dodges were totally restyled from the previous year and were very much a part of the Chrysler Corporation's next step in the "Forward Look." The 1957 Dodge had the longest wheelbases in its history with the exception of special seven-passengers sedans and other special cars from the 1940s and early-1950s. The cars appeared longer, lower, wider, and the hardtops had a thin, delicate look that the factory claimed was exceptionally strong. That added to the feeling that these "Forward Look," referred to as the "Swept-Wing Dodge" in 1957 ads, appeared capable of flight. Unlike the rest of Chrysler Corporation's divisions, Dodge's fins stopped short of the rear end of the car, and had a decorative ribbed chrome end caps. Smaller 14-inch wheels helped add to the car's low profile. Front torsion bar suspension was completely new, lowering the chassis by about 5 inches, and the venerable 1940s chassis was gone. The Dodge did not have a grille, per se, but a series of bumper bars that completely covered the front of the car. The headlights were now deeply recessed below large headlight brows, and the grille featured a gull-wing-shaped horizontal bar, that dipped in the center and surrounded a large Dodge crest.

All models used a single horizontal chrome strip along the body side and chrome trim along the base of the large rear fender fins. Chrome trim surrounded the headlights and grille opening. The Dodge name, in block letters, was spaced along the front and the grille, directly below the chrome jet-styled hood ornament. Dodge offered a giant array of two-tone combinations. The roof, lower body, and fins were one color, and the second color swept from the top of the hood, down the upper body between the belt line and the top side spear, and over the top of the trunk.

Dodge shared the dash-mounted rear view mirror with the rest of the corporation. With two passengers in the car, rear vision was partially obstructed, and with four or more passengers, there was virtually no rear vision. The early examples of the dash-mounted mirror also vibrated so badly that rear vision was nearly impossible. This driver's mirror location lasted for several years, before returning to the conventional windshield mounting point. While the new Dodges were beautiful to look at, quality control problems abounded and Dodge sales suffered for the next few years.

Dodge introduced the new three-speed TorqueFlite automatic transmission, and like the rest of the car, it proved a little troublesome in its first year. Anecdotal evidence reports that it became more reliable in the following year or two.

CORONET SERIES — (6-CYLINDER/V-8): The Coronet was the base trim Dodge for 1957 and included chrome windshield and rear window moldings, chrome side trim, chrome trim along the fins and grille opening, full wheel covers, and the Coronet name on the front fenders above the chrome strip.

CORONET I.D. NUMBERS: Six-cylinder-powered Coronets assembled in Detroit began at 32255081 and went to 32292657. V-8-powered Coronets assembled in Detroit began at 35172001 and went to 35303713. Those assembled in Los Angeles began at 42620001 and went to 45547041. Six-cylinder engine numbers began at D72-1001 and went to D72-9600. After Jan. 10, 1957, engine numbers began at KDS-6-9601 and went up to KDS-6-18892. V-8 engine numbers began at KDS-1001 and went to KDS-287536.

The 1957 Dodge had its own set of fins, a look that was different from other Chrysler Corporation models.

Coronet Series

Model Number	Body/Style Number	Body Type & Seating	Factory Price	Shipping Weight	Production Total
D66/72	Note 1	4-dr Sedan-6P	$2,416/$2,524	3,470/3,620 lbs.	Note 2
D66/72	Note 1	2-dr Club Sedan-6P	$2,335/$2,443	3,400/3,530 lbs.	Note 2
D66	Note 1	4-dr Lancer Hardtop-6P	$2,630	3,665 lbs.	Note 2
D66	Note 1	2-dr Lancer Hardtop-6P	$2,545	3,570 lbs.	Note 2
D66	Note 1	2-dr Lancer Convertible-6P	$2,807	3,815 lbs.	Note 2

NOTE 1: *Owners seeking parts were advised: "There is no way to positively identify the type of body. When in doubt, specify the vehicle serial number and vehicle body number when ordering parts."*

NOTE 2: *Production figures were not given for individual models and body styles. Dodge produced a total of 257,488 cars during calendar year 1957, including 160,979 Coronets. Coronet model year output, in round figures, was 160,500 cars.*

NOTE 3: *Prices and weights to left of slash marks are for sixes, to right for V-8s.*

ROYAL SERIES — (V-8): The Royal was once again the intermediate trim level and included all the Coronet features plus chrome headlight doors and a "V" medallion on the rear deck lid. The Royal name appeared on the front fender above the chrome trim strip.

ROYAL I.D. NUMBERS: Royal models assembled in Detroit began at 37240001 and went to 37321614. Those assembled in Los Angeles began at 45540001 and went to 45631610. V-8 engine numbers began at KDS-1001 and went to KDS-287538.

Royal Series

Model Number	Body/Style Number	Body Type & Seating	Factory Price	Shipping Weight	Production Total
D67-1	Note 1	4-dr Sedan-6P	$2,677	3,620 lbs.	Note 2
D67-1	Note 1	4-dr Lancer Hardtop-6P	$2,783	3,690 lbs.	Note 2
D67-1	Note 1	2-dr Lancer Hardtop-6P	$2,734	3,585 lbs.	Note 2
D67-1	Note 1	2-dr Lancer Convertible-6P	$2,996	3,830 lbs.	Note 2

NOTE 1: *Owners seeking parts were advised: "There is no way to positively identify the type of body. When in doubt, specify the vehicle serial number and vehicle body number when ordering parts."*

NOTE 2: *Production figures were not given for individual models and body styles. Dodge produced a total of 257,488 cars during calendar year 1957. A total of 40,999 Royal models were built on a calendar year basis. Royal series model year output, in rounded off figures, was 41,000 cars.*

CUSTOM ROYAL SERIES — (V-8): The Custom Royal was once again the top trim level Dodge and included all the Royal features plus six vertical bumper teeth between the bumper and the horizontal grille bar, the gold Dodge name on the hood and the trunk lid, and the Custom Royal name on the sides of the front fenders, above the chrome trim strip.

Another look at the 1957 Dodge fins that were unlike any of the other Chrysler Corporation cars.

CUSTOM ROYAL I.D. NUMBERS: Custom Royal models assembled in Detroit began at 37240001 and went to 37321614. Those assembled in Los Angeles began at 45540001 and went to 45631610. V-8 engine numbers began at KDS-1001 and went to KDS-287536.

Custom Royal Series

Model Number	Body/Style Number	Body Type & Seating	Factory Price	Shipping Weight	Production Total
D67-2	Note 1	4-dr Sedan-6P	$2,846	3,690 lbs.	Note 2
D67-2	Note 1	4-dr Lancer Hardtop-6P	$2,956	3,750 lbs.	Note 2
D67-2	Note 1	2-dr Lancer Hardtop-6P	$2,885	3,670 lbs.	Note 2
D67-2	Note 1	2-dr Convertible-6P	$3,111	3,810 lbs.	Note 2

NOTE 1: *Owners seeking parts were advised: "There is no way to positively identify the type of body. When in doubt, specify the vehicle serial number and vehicle body number when ordering parts."*

NOTE 2: *See Note 2, 1957 Coronet models. A total of 55,149 Custom Royal models were built on a calendar year basis. Custom Royal series output, on a model year basis, in round figures, was 47,000 units.*

Even in its base Coronet form, the 1957 Dodge was a dressy package. Its second-wave Forward Look design responded well to two-toning.

There was plenty of room in the 1957 Dodge station wagon. John Lee

The 1957 version of the Forward Look added futuristic styling to the utilitarian Dodge station wagon. John Lee

STATION WAGON SERIES — (V-8): For the first time, station wagons were included in their own series. The two-door Suburban and four-door Sierra models were the base trim level and compared to the Coronet series of conventional cars. The Custom Sierra was the top trim level and compared to the Royal series of conventional cars. An interesting feature of the 1957 Dodge station wagons was the location of the spare tire. It was mounted behind the right rear wheel and was accessible from a removable fender skirt located behind the rear wheelwell. This feature was borrowed from the earlier Plainsman, a stylish Chrysler Corporation show car station wagon from the mid-1950s.

STATION WAGON I.D. NUMBERS: Station wagon models were assembled only in Detroit and began at 38001001 and went to 38022513 for the Suburban and Sierra models, or began at 38535001 and went to 38542217 for the Custom Sierra. Engine numbers corresponded to the Royal series of conventional cars.

Station Wagon Series

Model Number	Body/Style Number	Body Type & Seating	Factory Price	Shipping Weight	Production Total
D70	Note 1	2-dr Suburban-6P	$2,826	3,830 lbs.	Note 2
D70	Note 1	4-dr Sierra-6P	$2,911	3,930 lbs.	Note 2
D70	Note 1	4-dr Sierra-9P	$3,038	4,015 lbs.	Note 2
D71	Note 1	4-dr Custom Sierra-6P	$3,052	3,960 lbs.	Note 2
D71	Note 1	4-dr Custom Sierra-9P	$3,180	4,030 lbs.	Note 2

NOTE 1: *Owners seeking parts were advised: "There is no way to positively identify the type of body. When in doubt, specify the vehicle serial number and vehicle body number when ordering parts."*

NOTE 2: *See Note 2, 1957 Coronet models. A total of 30,481 station wagons were built on a calendar year basis. Station wagon model year output, in round figures, was 32,000 units.*

D-500 SERIES— (V-8): The D-500 was actually a high-performance engine option for all series. However, in this edition, we are listing it in series format, because of its importance to collectors. The representative prices and weights shown are based on adding the option to a pair of Custom Royal models. Dodge D-500s included all features of the base series models, plus the high-performance 285-, 310- or 340-hp V-8 engines.

D-500 I.D. NUMBERS: See Dodge V-8 model I.D. numbers above. Engine numbers began at KD-501-1001 and went to KD-501-1102.

D-500 Series

Model Number	Body/Style Number	Body Type & Seating	Factory Price	Shipping Weight	Production Total
D501	Note 1	2-dr Club Sedan-6P	$3,279	3,885 lbs.	Note 2
D501	Note 1	2-dr Convertible-6P	$3,635	3,975 lbs.	Note 2

NOTE 1: *Owners seeking parts were advised: "There is no way to positively identify the type of body. When in doubt, specify the vehicle serial number and vehicle body number when ordering parts."*

NOTE 2: *Production of 500 Dodge D-500s was scheduled. Approximately 101 cars were fitted with D-501 engines.*

ENGINES: Inline. L-head. Six-cylinder. Cast iron block. Displacement: 230 cid. Bore and stroke: 3.25 x 4.625 inches. Compression ratio: 8.0:1. Brake hp: 138 at 4000 rpm. Four main bearings. Solid valve lifters. Carburetor: Stromberg one-barrel Model WW3-159.

RED RAM V-8: Overhead valve. Cast iron block. Displacement: 325 cid. Bore and stroke: 3.69 x 3.80 inches. Compression ratio: 8.5:1. Brake hp: 245 at 4400 rpm in Coronet and Royal series, 260 at 4400 rpm in Custom Royal series. Five main bearings. Hydraulic valve lifters. Carburetor: (245 hp) Stromberg two-barrel Model WW3-149; (260 hp) Carter WCFB-2532S.

The 1957 Dodge did not have a grille, per se, since its front was all bumper. The Royal series had six teeth on top of the bumper that stuck up into the lowest grille slot.

D-500 V-8: Overhead valve. Cast iron block. Displacement: 325 cid. Bore and stroke: 3.69 x 3.80 inches. Compression ratio: 10.0:1. Hemispherical heads. Brake hp: 285 at 5200 rpm. Solid valve lifters. Carburetor: Carter four-barrel Type WCFB.

SUPER D-500 ENGINE: same as above but with dual Carter WCFB four-barrel carburetors. Brake hp: 310 at 5200 rpm.

D-501 V-8: Overhead valve. Cast iron block. Displacement: 354 cid. Bore and stroke: 3.94 x 3.63 inches. Compression ratio: 10.0:1. Hemispherical heads. Brake horsepower: 340 at 5200 rpm. Hydraulic valve lifters. Carburetor: Two Carter WCFB four-barrel (midyear offering).

CHASSIS FEATURES: Wheelbase: 122 inches. Overall length: (station wagon) 214.4 inches; (other models) 212.2 inches. Tires: (Coronet) 7.50 x 14 tubeless black sidewall; (D-500) 7.60 x 15 tubeless black sidewall; (Royal, Custom Royal, station wagons and convertibles) 8.00 x 14 tubeless black sidewall.

CONVENIENCE OPTIONS: Electric clock. Turn signals. Mopar radio. PowerFlite or TorqueFlite automatic transmissions. Power steering. Power brakes. Power windows. Power seats. Heater. Air Temp air conditioning. Hi-Way Hi-Fi automatic record player. Windshield washers. White sidewall tires.

HISTORICAL FOOTNOTES: This year saw the introduction of the famous torsion bar front suspension, called "Torsion-Aire," that Chrysler used from 1957 on. The 1957 Dodge lineup was introduced Oct. 30, 1958, the same day that all other Chrysler products debuted that season. The division's total model year production peaked at 281,359 cars, which gave Dodge a 4.5 percent market share. On a 1957 calendar year basis, Dodge manufactured 82,220 two-door hardtops; 6,960 two-door convertibles; 8,100 two-door station wagons and 34,210 four-door station wagons. This does not include 1957 models built in the fall of 1956 but it does include 1958 models built in calendar 1957. Therefore it can only be used as an indication of body style popularity in calendar 1957. On a model year basis, 96.5 percent of all 1957 Dodges had automatic transmissions; 25.9 percent had power brakes; 2.2 percent had power seats; 2.1 percent had power windows; 53.7 percent had radios; 15.1 percent had dual exhaust and 93.4 percent had V-8 engines. M.C. Patterson was president of the division again this year.

The 1957 Dodge sedans didn't have the compound-curve windshield. Their windshields did not curve back at the top to meet the plane of the roof.

*1958 Dodge
Custom Royal
Lancer four-door
hardtop*

Phil Hall Collection

The 1958 Dodges continued to use the 1957 body shell with only minor restyling. Dodge now had a true grille and quad headlights. The grille had abbreviated horizontal center bars, which housed the parking lights at their inside edge. A major concentration at Dodge in 1958 was power. All engines were of the "wedge" single rocker head design. The ultimate, an electronically fuel-injected 361-cid version, put out 333 hp, but the fuel-injected models were troublesome, and some sources say Chrysler recalled all, or nearly all, of them. The Bendix Corporation, the company that made the "Electrojector" unit, recorded that a dozen Dodges were originally equipped with their pioneering, if flawed, fuel injection system. Anecdotal evidence suggests that the general quality problems improved through 1958 and '59, and the TorqueFlite became more reliable.

Coronet Series — (6-cylinder/V-8): The Coronet was the base trim level for 1958 and included chrome windshield and rear window moldings, chrome trim around the grille opening and headlights, a single chrome strip along the body-side and base of the rear fender fins and the Coronet name, in script, along the back of the side chrome strip. The Dodge name, in block letters, was spaced along the front edge of the hood.

CORONET I.D. NUMBERS: Six-cylinder-powered Coronets assembled in Detroit were numbered LD1-1001 and up. Those assembled in Newark were numbered LD1N-1001 and up. V-8 Coronets assembled in Detroit were numbered LD2-1001 and up. Those assembled in Los Angeles were numbered LD2L-1001 and up. Those assembled at Newark were numbered LD2N-1001 and up. Engine numbers were L230-1001 and up for sixes and L325-1001 and up for V-8s.

*1958 Dodge
Coronet Royal
Lancer sedan*

Phil Hall Collection

Coronet two-door sedan, V-8, Coronet Series

Model Number	Body/Style Number	Body Type & Seating	Factory Price	Shipping Weight	Production Total
LD½	Note 1	4-dr Sedan-6P	$2,495/$2,602	3,410/3,555 lbs.	Note 2
LD½	Note 1	2-dr Sedan-6P	$2,414/$2,521	3,360/3,505 lbs.	Note 2
LD2-L1	Note 1	4-dr Lancer Hardtop-6P	$2,729	3,605 lbs.	Note 2
LD2-L1	Note 1	2-dr Lancer Hardtop-6P	$2,644	3,540 lbs.	Note 2
LD2-L1	Note 1	2-dr Convertible-6P	$2,907	3,725 lbs.	Note 2

NOTE 1: *Owners seeking parts were advised: "There is no way to positively identify the type of body. When in doubt, specify the vehicle serial number and vehicle body number when ordering parts."*

NOTE 2: *Production figures were not given for individual models and body styles. Dodge produced a total of 135,505 cars during calendar year 1958, including 77,388 Coronets. Dodge model year output peaked at 133,953 units. In rounded figures, 77,000 of these cars were Coronets.*

NOTE 3: *Prices and weights to left of slash marks are for sixes, to right for V-8s.*

ROYAL SERIES — (V-8): The Royal was once again the intermediate trim level and included all the Coronet features. On this series, the chrome trim at the base of the rear fender fin flared out to a pointed dip, before angling up to the top of the fin. Twin chrome hood ornaments were another distinction.

ROYAL I.D. NUMBERS: V-8 Royals assembled in Detroit were numbered LD2-1001 and up. Those assembled in Los Angeles were numbered LD2L-1001 and up. Those assembled at Newark were numbered LD2N-1001 and up. Engine numbers were L325-1001 and up.

Royal Series

Model Number	Body/Style Number	Body Type & Seating	Factory Price	Shipping Weight	Production Total
LD2M	Note 1	4-dr Sedan-6P	$2,757	3,570 lbs.	Note 2
LD2M	Note 1	4-dr Lancer Hardtop-6P	$2,875	3,640 lbs.	Note 2
LD2M	Note 1	2-dr Lancer Hardtop-6P	$2,814	3,565 lbs.	Note 2

NOTE 1: *Owners seeking parts were advised: "There is no way to positively identify the type of body. When in doubt, specify the vehicle serial number and vehicle body number when ordering parts."*

NOTE 2: *Total Royal models built on a calendar year basis N/A. On a model year basis, using rounded off figures, Royal output was counted as 15,500 units.*

CUSTOM ROYAL SERIES — (V-8): The Custom Royal was once again the top trim level Dodge and included all the Royal features plus "knight's head" emblems on the front fenders, a gold Dodge name on the hood and trunk, and chrome rain gutter moldings. Dodge introduced the additional Regal Lancer two-door hardtop early in the 1958 model run and also offered a Spring Special trim package later in the model run. The Spring Special included a special grille medallion, blackout headlights, new side molding, rear fin trim, and license box trim.

CUSTOM ROYAL I.D. NUMBERS: Custom Royal models assembled in Detroit were numbered LD3-1001 and up. Those assembled in Los Angeles were numbered LD3L-1001 and up. Those assembled in Newark were numbered LD3N-1001 and up. Engine numbers were L350-1001 and up.

Custom Royal Series

Model Number	Body/Style Number	Body Type & Seating	Factory Price	Shipping Weight	Production Total
LD3H	Note 1	4-dr Sedan-6P	$2,985	3,640 lbs.	Note 2
LD3H	Note 1	4-dr Lancer Hardtop-6P	$3,097	3,670 lbs.	Note 2
LD3H	Note 1	2-dr Lancer Hardtop-6P	$3,026	3,610 lbs.	Note 2
LD3H	Note 1	2-dr Convertible-6P	$3,253	3,785 lbs.	Note 2
LD3H	Note 1	2-dr Regal Lancer-6P	$3,200	3,655 lbs.	Note 2

NOTE 1: *Owners seeking parts were advised: "There is no way to positively identify the type of body. When in doubt, specify the vehicle serial number and vehicle body number when ordering parts."*

NOTE 2: *A total of 23,949 Custom Royal models were built on a calendar year basis. On a model year basis, Custom Royal output was 21,000 units in rounded off figures.*

STATION WAGON SERIES — (V-8): For 1958, station wagons continued to be in their own series. As in 1957, the two-door Suburban was the base trim level and was comparable to the Coronet series of conventional cars. The Sierra was the intermediate trim level station wagon and was comparable to the Royal series of conventional cars. The Custom Sierra was the top trim level and was comparable to the Custom Royal series of conventional cars.

STATION WAGON I.D. NUMBERS: Station wagon models used the same serial number sequence as the Custom Royal series.

Station Wagon Series

Model Number	Body/Style Number	Body Type & Seating	Factory Price	Shipping Weight	Production Total
LD3L	Note 1	2-dr Suburban-6P	$2,930	3,875 lbs.	Note 2
LD3L	Note 1	4-dr Sierra-6P	$2,995	3,930 lbs.	Note 2
LD3L	Note 1	4-dr Sierra-9P	$3,137	3,990 lbs.	Note 2
LD3H	Note 1	4-dr Custom Sierra-6P	$3,172	3,955 lbs.	Note 2
LD3H	Note 1	4-dr Custom Sierra-9P	$3,314	4,035 lbs.	Note 2

NOTE 1: *Owners seeking parts were advised: "There is no way to positively identify the type of body. When in doubt, specify the vehicle serial number and vehicle body number when ordering parts."*

NOTE 2: *A total of 30,481 station wagons were built in the calendar year. On a model year basis, 20,000 station wagons were built (rounded off figures).*

ENGINES: Inline. L-head. Six-cylinder. Cast iron block. Displacement: 230 cid. Bore and stroke: 3.25 x 4.825 inches. Compression ratio: 8.0:1. Brake hp: 138 at 4000 rpm. Four main bearings. Solid valve lifters. Carburetor: Stromberg one-barrel Model WW3-159.

RED RAM V-8: Overhead valve. Cast iron block. Displacement: 325 cid. Bore and stroke: 3.69 x 3.80 inches. Compression ratio: 8.0:1. Brake hp: 245 at 4400 rpm (265 at 4600 rpm in Royal models). Five main bearings. Hydraulic valve lifters. Carburetor: (Coronet V-8) Stromberg Model WW3-163 two-barrel; (Royal V-8) Carter WCFB-2660S two-barrel.

RAM FIRE V-8: Overhead valve. Cast iron block. Displacement: 350 cid. Bore and stroke: 4.05 x 3.38 inches. Compression ratio: 10.0:1. Brake hp: 295 at 4600 rpm. Five main bearings. Hydraulic valve lifters. Carburetor: Carter four-barrel.

1958 Dodge Custom Royal sedan Phil Hall Collection

D-500 V-8: Overhead valve. Cast iron block. Displacement: 361 cid. Bore and stroke: 4.12 x 3.38 inches. Compression ratio: 10.0:1. Brake hp: 305 at 4600 rpm. Five main bearings. Hydraulic valve lifters. Carburetor: Carter four-barrel Model WCFB.

SUPER D-500 V-8: Overhead valve. Cast iron block. Displacement: 361 cid. Bore and stroke: 4.12 x 3.38 inches. Compression ratio: 10.0:1. Brake hp: 320 at 4600 rpm. Carburetor: Two Carter four-barrel Model WCFB.

ELECTRONIC FUEL LNJECTION V-8: Overhead valve. Cast iron block. Displacement: 361 cid. Bore and stroke: 4.12 x 3.38 inches. Compression ratio: 10.0:1. Brake hp: 333 at 4800 rpm. Five main bearings. Hydraulic valve lifters. Fuel system: Bendix electronic fuel injection.

CHASSIS FEATURES: Wheelbase: 122 inches. Overall length: (station wagons) 214.4 inches; (other models) 212.2 inches. Tires: (Coronet) 7.50 x 14; (Royal, Custom Royal and station wagons) 8.00 x 14 tubeless black sidewall.

CONVENIENCE OPTIONS: Electric clock. Turn signals. Mopar radio. PowerFlite ($180). TorqueFlite ($220). Power steering ($92). Power brakes ($38). Power windows. Power seats. Heater. Air Temp air conditioning ($381). Hi-Way Hi-Fi automatic record player. Windshield washer. White sidewall tires. Seat belts.

HISTORICAL FOOTNOTES: The 1958 Dodges were introduced on Nov. 1, 1957. Model year production peaked at 133,953 units. Calendar year sales of 114,206 cars were recorded. M.C. Patterson was president of the Dodge division this year. The demand for Dodge sixes increased during 1958, rising from 4.6 percent to 9.7 percent. On a model year basis, 96.4 percent of all Dodges had automatic transmission; 62.5 percent had power steering; 34 percent had power brakes; 2.5 percent had power windows; 44.7 percent had radios; 23.4 percent had tinted glass; 4.4 percent had air conditioning and 7.2 percent had dual exhaust. The 1958 Regal Lancer was a limited edition Dodge two-door hardtop with special paint, trim and interior. It came only in bronze finish, combined with either black or white. Approximately 12 Dodges were built with the new Bendix EFI (electronic fuel injection) system. This option was later deleted and these cars were officially recalled for conversion to normal carburetion.

"Prior to Torsion-Aire suspension Chrysler cars were… wallowing, nosediving and squatting but no so today."

James Potter, Motor Trend, March 1958

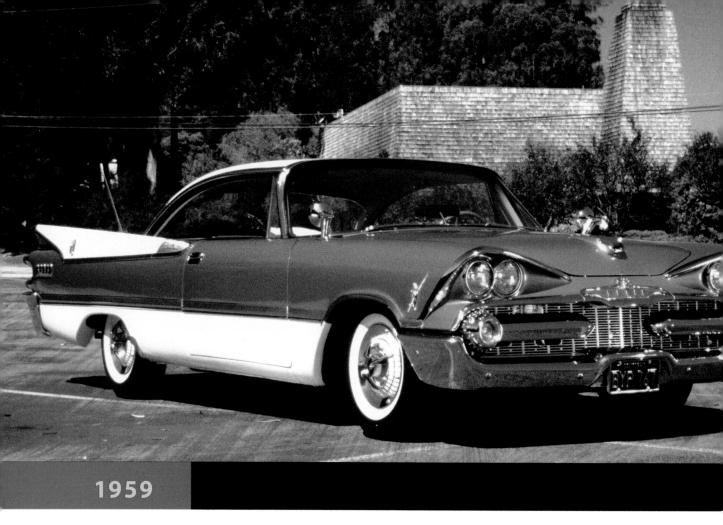

The 1959 Dodge Custom Royal Lancer showed the Forward Look still in full swing but the cars were becoming heavier looking and less delicate.

The new Dodges were easily recognizable, though the styling used on the 1957 and 1958 models was exaggerated in 1959. While the Chryslers and De Sotos took on a squarer look, Dodge went the other way with a broad oval grille. The grille still had the abbreviated bars of 1958 containing the parking lights, but was made of a tough-looking mesh. The fins didn't seem to rise as high, possibly because the rear fenders were already a bit higher. The huge headlight brows were no longer flattened on the top, and they continued downward toward the grille and made more of a scowling face. The fins still ended short of the rear of the car, but the taillights extended well beyond the end of the car, ensconced in long, tube-like housings that clearly imitated jet engine nozzles.

The great horsepower race of the 1950s was easing, but Dodge continued to build high-performance cars. This year's offering in the high horsepower category was the first of the famous 383-cid V-8 engines, which Chrysler used for more than a decade. The 383 boasted 345 hp in its Super D-500 format. Also new for 1959 was the Swivel-Seat option. With a simple motion of a lever at the side of the seat, the unit swung out to meet the occupant. Dodge also experimented with an optional, self-leveling rear air suspension, called LevelFlite.

CORONET SERIES — (6-CYLINDER/V-8): The Coronet continued to be the base trim level and included chrome windshield and rear window moldings, a single horizontal chrome strip along the body side and chrome trim at the lower edge of the fender fin. The Dodge name, in block letters, appeared on the trunk lid (directly below a combination Dodge crest and trunk handle). The Coronet name, in script, appeared on the front fender. At midyear, a "Silver Challenger" option was available on the two-door sedan.

CORONET I.D. NUMBERS: Six-cylinder-powered Coronets assembled in Detroit were numbered M302100001 and up. Those assembled in Newark were numbered M305100001 and up. V-8-powered models assembled in Detroit were numbered M312100001 and up. Those assembled in Newark were numbered M315100001 and up. V-8 models assembled in California were numbered M314100001 and up.

The 1959 Dodge Custom Royal Lancer convertible stands out near a flowing fountain. The car always left a great impression.

In 1959, Dodge offered optional swivel seats, a style designed to help people enter and exit cars more comfortably.

Coronet Series

Model Number	Body/Style Number	Body Type & Seating	Factory Price	Shipping Weight	Production Total
MD½L	41	4-dr Sedan-6P	$2,537/$2,657	3,425/3,615 lbs.	8,103
MD½L	21	2-dr Club Sedan-6P	$2,466/$2,586	3,375/3,565 lbs.	5,432
MD½L	23	2-dr Lancer Hardtop-6P	$2,594/$2,714	3,395/3,590 lbs.	2,151
MD2L	43	4-dr Lancer Hardtop-6P	$2,792	3,620 lbs.	8,946
MD2L	27	2-dr Convertible-6P	$3,039	3,775 lbs.	1,840

NOTE 1: *A total of 96,782 Coronet models were produced during calendar year 1959. Exactly 151,851 Dodges were built for the 1959 model year. In slightly rounded off figures, the model year output of Coronets was counted at 96,900 units.*

NOTE 2: *Prices and weights to left of slash marks are for sixes, to right for V-8s.*

ROYAL SERIES — (V-8): The Royal continued to be the intermediate trim level and included all Coronet features, plus a long horizontal chrome strip (from the front wheelwell to the rear of the car), which is wider than the trim used on the Coronet. Royals also featured horizontal scoring on this strip. A stylized V-8 emblem appeared on the front fenders and the Royal name appeared on a wide molding at the front of the rear fender fins.

ROYAL I.D. NUMBERS: Royal models assembled in Detroit were numbered M332100001 and up. Those assembled in Newark were numbered M335100001 and up and those assembled in California were numbered M334100001 and up.

Royal Series

Model Number	Body/Style Number	Body Type & Seating	Factory Price	Shipping Weight	Production Total
MD3M	41	4-dr Sedan-6P	$2,884	3,640 lbs.	8,389
MD3M	43	4-dr Lancer Hardtop-6P	$3,019	3,690 lbs.	2,935
MD3M	23	2-dr Lancer Hardtop-6P	$2,940	3,625 lbs.	3,483

NOTE 1: *A total of 14,807 Royal models were produced during calendar year 1959. In slightly rounded off figures, the model year output of Royals was counted at 14,900 units.*

CUSTOM ROYAL SERIES — (V-8): The Custom Royal continued to be the top trim level and included all the Royal features, plus the Custom Royal name on the wide molding at the front of the rear fender fins.

CUSTOM ROYAL I.D. NUMBERS: Custom Royal models assembled in Detroit were numbered M352100001 and up. Those assembled in Newark were numbered M355100001 and up and those assembled in California were numbered M354100001 and up.

Custom Royal Series

Model Number	Body/Style Number	Body Type & Seating	Factory Price	Shipping Weight	Production Total
MD3H	41	4-dr Sedan-6P	$3,095	3,660 lbs.	8,925
MD3H	43	4-dr Lancer Hardtop-6P	$3,229	3,745 lbs.	5,019
MD3H	23	2-dr Lancer Hardtop-6P	$3,151	3,675 lbs.	6,278
MD3H	27	2-dr Convertible-6P	$3,372	3,820 lbs.	984

NOTE 1: *A total of 21,206 Custom Royal models were produced during calendar year 1959. In slightly rounded off figures, the model year output of Custom Royals was counted at 16,500 units.*

STATION WAGON SERIES — (V-8): Station wagons continued to have their own series for 1959. The two-door Suburban was dropped, and the four-door Sierra replaced the Suburban as the base trim level. The Custom Sierra continued in the top trim level, equaling the Royal series of conventional cars in trim.

STATION WAGON I.D. NUMBERS: Station wagon models assembled in Detroit were numbered 372100001 and up. Those assembled in Newark were numbered 375100001 and up and those assembled in California were numbered 374100001 and up.

Swept fins, canted dual antennas, bright two-tone paint and more make this 1959 Dodge Custom Royal Lancer convertible unforgettable.

David Lyon

The 1959 Dodge convertibles and hardtops had the familiar Chrysler Corporation compound-curve windshield. GM caught up with this look in the 1959 model year.

Station Wagon Series

Model Number	Body/Style Number	Body Type & Seating	Factory Price	Shipping Weight	Production Total
MD3-L	45A	4-dr Sierra-6P	$3,053	3,940 lbs.	11,069
MD3-L	45B	4-dr Sierra-9P	$3,174	4,015 lbs.	6,650
MD3-H	45A	4-dr Custom Sierra-6P	$3,268	3,980 lbs.	2,434
MD3-H	45B	4-dr Custom Sierra-9P	$3,389	4,020 lbs.	3,437

NOTE 1: *A total of 23,590 station wagons were produced during calendar year 1959. In slightly rounded off figures, the model year output of Dodge station wagons was 23,500.*

Chrysler, De Soto and Dodge station wagons had unique taillights they didn't share with sedans. The Dodge version had two taillights.

ENGINES: L-head. Inline. Six-cylinder. Cast iron block. Displacement: 230 cid. Bore and stroke: 3.25 x 4.38 inches. Compression ratio: 8.0:1. Brake hp: 135 at 3600 rpm. Four main bearings. Solid valve lifters. Carburetor: Stromberg one-barrel.

RED RAM V-8. OVERHEAD VALVE. CAST IRON BLOCK. DISPLACEMENT: 326 cid. Bore and stroke: 3.95 x 3.31 inches. Compression ratio: 9.2:1. Brake hp: 255 at 4400 rpm. Five main bearings. Hydraulic valve lifters. Carburetor: Carter two-barrel.

RAM FIRE V-8. OVERHEAD VALVE. CAST IRON BLOCK. DISPLACEMENT: 361 cid. Bore and stroke: 4.12 x 3.38 inches. Compression ratio: 10.1:1. Brake hp: 295 at 4600 rpm on Royal and Sierra models, 305 at 4600 rpm on Custom Royal and Custom Sierra models. Five main bearings. Hydraulic valve lifters. Carburetor: (295 hp) Carter two-barrel; (305 hp) Carter four-barrel.

D-500 V-8. OVERHEAD VALVE. CAST IRON BLOCK. DISPLACEMENT: 383 cid. Bore and stroke: 4.25 x 3.38 inches. Compression ratio: 10.1:1. Brake hp: 320 at 4600 rpm. Five main bearings. Hydraulic valve lifters. Carburetor: Carter four-barrel.

SUPER D-500 V-8. OVERHEAD VALVE. CAST IRON BLOCK. DISPLACEMENT: 383 cid. Bore and stroke: 4.25 x 3.38 inches. Compression ratio: 10.0:1. Brake hp: 345 at 5000 rpm. Five main bearings. Hydraulic valve lifters. Carburetor: Two Carter four-barrel.

CHASSIS FEATURES: Wheelbase: 122 inches. Overall length: 217.4 inches (216.4 inches on station wagons). Tires: (Coronet) 7.50 x 14; (all others) 8.00 x 14-inch tubeless black sidewalls.

CONVENIENCE OPTIONS: TorqueFlite transmission, all V-8 models ($226.90). PowerFlite transmission, Coronet and Royal ($189.10). Power steering, V-8 only ($92.15). Power brakes ($42.60). Power window lifts ($102.30). Power tailgate window, two-seat wagons ($34.10). Six-Way power seat ($95.70). Dual exhaust ($30.90). Push-button radio ($86.50). Rear speaker ($14.95). Radio with dual antenna ($14.05). Heater and defroster ($93.55). Tires: white sidewall 7.50 x 14, Coronet except convertible ($33.35); 8.00 x 14, other models ($41.75). Two-tone paint standard colors ($18.55); Deluxe colors ($34.10). Solex glass ($42.60); windshield only ($18.55). Back-up lights ($10.70). Wheel covers ($14.30); Deluxe ($30.50). Electric clock ($15.95). Windshield washer ($11.80). Variable speed windshield wipers ($6.60). Windshield washer and Vari-speed wipers ($18.25). Front and rear Air Foam seat ($10.70). Undercoating ($12.85). Air conditioning with heater, V-8s only ($468.55); wagons ($662.95). Carpets ($11.80). Rear window defroster ($20.60). Sure-Grip differential, all except convertible ($49.70). Padded instrument panel ($20.00). Padded sun visors ($8.00). Automatic headlight beam changer ($49.70). Heavy-duty 70-amp battery ($8.60). Custom trim package, Coronet except convertible ($56.00). D-500 383 cid/320 hp four-barrel carb engine with dual exhaust and TorqueFlite transmission, Coronet convertible ($368.00); Coronet V-8 except convertible ($398.90); Royal and Sierra station wagons ($328.10); Custom Royal convertible ($273.35); Custom Royal and Custom station wagons ($304.15). Super D-500 345 hp engine, Coronet V-8 except convertible ($540.45); Coronet convertible ($509.60); Royal and Sierra station wagons ($469.65); Custom Royal convertible ($414.95); Custom Royal and Custom station wagons ($445.75). LevelFlite, V-8s only ($127.55). Outside rearview mirror ($6.45). Remote control left outside rearview mirror ($17.75); right ($8.60). Co-Pilot speed warning device ($12.85). Storage compartment with lock, two-seat station wagons ($28.20). Swivel seat ($70.95).

HISTORICAL FOOTNOTES: The 1959 Dodges were introduced on Oct. 10, 1958. Model year production peaked at 151,851 units, of which approximately 15,600 were sixes and 136,200 were V-8 powered. Dodge assembled 13,515 two-door sedans; 65,752 four-door sedans; 29,610 two-door hardtops; 16,704 four-door hardtops; 2,733 convertibles; 13,515 four-door two-seat station wagons and 10,022 four-door three-seat station wagons in the 1959 model year. Dodge Division's calendar year output was 192,798 units this year, accounting for a 3.44 percent share of the total market. M.C. Patterson continued as president and general manager of Dodge Division this season. For the model run, about 94 percent of all Dodges had automatic transmissions; 68.9 percent had power steering; 27.4 percent had power brakes; 23.2 percent had windshield washers; 84.7 percent had back-up lights; 4.5 percent had air conditioning and only 0.7 percent had the rare LevelFlite air suspension, an option that did not last long.

In 1959, the well-styled Dodge Sierra station wagon was a lot of workhorse for the money.

IMPERIAL

Top to bottom: The elegant 1950 Chrysler Imperial sedan

The 1950 Chrysler New Yorker and Imperial models look the same but the Imperial was quietly styled and had its own three-piece back window.

The Chrysler Imperial had its own identifying chrome script in 1950.

The Chrysler New Yorker had a plush interior, but the Imperial's was ultra-plush, extra-cushy and thickly upholstered befitting its quiet elegance.

1950-1959

Introduction

The Imperial was only a Chrysler up through 1954, and in 1955, the corporation bestowed upon the luxurious model line the distinction of its own division. After 1955, it was simply Imperial. The 1950 through 1954 examples are Chrysler Imperials.

A rare choice was the 1950 Chrysler Crown Imperial limousine.

This 1950 Chrysler Imperial sedan offers several visual clues about its upscale identity.

The 1950 through 1954 Chrysler Imperials are Chryslers in every sense of the name, and mostly, the Imperial's distinction surrounded the passengers on the interior of the car where dignified colors, sculpted door panels, and even cushier upholstery than the New Yorker cradled the passengers. The New Yorker interior's "cush-factor" is hard to beat, but the Chrysler Imperial did it. Where 1950-'52 New Yorkers had chrome bright metal on the dash, the Chrysler Imperial had a softer, non-mirror-like, brushed finish that lacked the glitz factor and allowed the passengers to feel more dignified. The Chrysler Imperial line is where the limousines resided.

The 1955 Imperial is a big, impressive automobile with all of Chrysler's engineering and mechanical integrity. It had its own grille, similar to the Chrysler 300, and its own much-longer version of Chrysler "100 Million Dollar Look" body, but the public never quite accepted the Imperial as being a separate make, competing directly with Cadillac. The 1955 and '56 Imperials shared their dashboard with the Chrysler New Yorker. Maybe if the Imperial had its own dash, it might have seemed like something other than a Chrysler from behind the wheel. Even the low-line Chrysler Windsor used the same dash, though with fewer colors. It may have been acceptable for the Chrysler Imperial to share a dash with the low-line Chrysler Royal in the early-'50s, but when creating a separate division, the '55 Imperial should have had its own dash.

The "Forward Look" swept through Chrysler Corporation in 1957, and the Imperial came into its own as a truly unique car from the rest of the corporation. The 1957 through '59 Imperials share almost nothing with Chrysler New Yorkers styling-wise. The Imperial's fins were higher and longer, the grille completely its own, and the dash had two giant round instrument clusters for 1957 and '58. The Imperial was finally a car worthy of its own division, and so it would be into the 1970s.

IMPERIAL SERIES — SERIES C49N: The new Imperial was essentially a New Yorker with custom interior. It had a Cadillac-style grille treatment that included circular signal lights enclosed in a wraparound, ribbed chrome piece. Side trim was similar to last year's model, but the front fender strip ended at the front doors and the rear fender molding was at tire-top level and integrated into the stone guard.

IMPERIAL I.D. NUMBER: The serial number was located on a plate on the left front door hinge pillar post. Engine number was on top front center of engine block. Serial numbers 7146001 to 7156654 were used only on Series C49 Imperials. Serial numbers 7813501 to 7813916 were used on Series C50 Crown Imperials. Engine numbers on regular Imperials were shared with the other 1950 Chrysler Eights. They fell within the range C49-1001 to 43041. The engine numbers used on Crown Imperials were distinct and ranged from C50-1001 to 1433.

Imperial Series

Series Number	Body/Style Number	Body Type & Seating	Factory Price	Shipping Weight	Production Total
C49-N	Note 1	4-dr Sedan-6P	$3,055	4,245 lbs.	9,500
C49-N	Note 1	4-dr Deluxe Sedan-6P	$3,176	4,250 lbs.	1,150

CROWN IMPERIAL SERIES — SERIES C50: Unlike the standard Imperial, the Crown had a side trim treatment in which the rear fender molding and stone guard were separate. Body sill moldings were used on all Imperials, but were of a less massive type on the more massive Crown models. A special version of the limousine was available. It featured a unique leather interior and a leather-covered top that blacked out the rear quarter windows. Power windows were standard.

Crown Imperial Series

Series Number	Body/Style Number	Body Type & Seating	Factory Price	Shipping Weight	Production Total
C50	Note 1	4-dr Sedan-8P	$5,229	5,235 lbs.	209
C50	Note 1	4-dr Limousine-8P	$5,334	5,305 lbs.	205

ENGINE: Inline. L-head 8. Cast iron block. Displacement: 323.5 cid. Bore and stroke: 3.25 x 4.87 inches. Compression ratio: 7.25:1. Brake hp: 135 at 3200 rpm. Five main bearings. Solid valve lifters. Carburetor: Carter one-barrel Model BB-E7J4.

CHASSIS FEATURES: Wheelbase: (Imperial) 131.5 inches; (Crown Imperial) 145.5 inches. Overall length: (Imperial) 214 inches; (Crown Imperial) 230.25 inches. Front tread: (Imperial) 57 inches; (Crown Imperial) 57 inches. Rear tread: (Imperial) 58 inches; (Crown Imperial) 64 inches. Tires: (Imperial) 8.20 x 15; (Crown Imperial) 8.90 x 15. The industry's first disc brakes, Ausco-Lambert "self-energizing" disc brakes, were standard in Crown Imperial series.

OPTIONS: White sidewall tires. Wing vent deflectors. Exhaust deflector. Mopar radio. Mopar heater. Locking gas cap. Weatherproof ignition. Mopar auto compass. Windshield washer. Spare tire valve extension. A brand new option (also available on Chrysler Eights) was electrically operated power windows. Prestomatic transmission with Fluid Drive was standard. Heavy-duty oil bath air cleaner. Vacuum booster fuel pump.

HISTORICAL FOOTNOTES: The 1950 Chrysler Imperial models were introduced in January 1950. Model year production began in December 1949. D.A. Wallace was president of the Chrysler Division of Chrysler Corp., with offices at 12200 East Jefferson Avenue in Detroit. The Derham custom body company, of Rosemont, Pa., continued to create some beautiful vehicles on the Imperial chassis.

Its unique wheel covers and understated trim are keys to this car's identity as a 1951 Chrysler Imperial convertible.

IMPERIAL SERIES — SERIES C54: In an unusual move for the 1950s, the Imperial had less chrome than the lower-priced New Yorker that it was based on. It had three horizontal grille bars (one across the center), parking lights between the bars, and a chrome vertical center piece. Aside from its front fender nameplate, side body trim was limited to moldings below the windows; rocker panel moldings; bright metal stone shields and a heavy, horizontal molding strip running across the fender skirts. This may have been another attempt to make the Imperial a dignified, less flashy model that gave the owner more luxury but in a very quiet way.

Secretly, through, under the hood, the Chrysler Imperial now carried the hemispherical V-8, and the quiet, dignified Imperial shared components with what would become some of NASCAR's most brutal racing cars.

IMPERIAL L.D. NUMBERS: The serial number was located on a plate on the left front door hinge pillar post. Engine number was on top front center of engine block. Series C54 Imperial Eights had serial numbers 7736501 to 7753512. Engine numbers used on these cars were in the same range of numbers (C51-8-1001 to 67967) used on other 1951 Chrysler Eights, with the engines in mixed production sequence. Series C53 Crown Imperials had serial numbers 7814501-7815000. Engine numbers on these cars were also in the same range as for other Chrysler Eights.

Imperial Series

Series Number	Body/Style Number	Body Type & Seating	Factory Price	Shipping Weight	Production Total
C54	Note 1	4-dr Sedan-8P	$3,699	4,350 lbs.	21,711
C54	Note 1	2-dr Club Coupe-6P	$3,687	4,230 lbs.	1,189
C54	Note 1	2-dr Hardtop-6P	$4,067	4,380 lbs.	3,450
C54	Note 1	2-dr Convertible-6P	$4,427	4,570 lbs.	650

NOTE 1: *N/A.*

NOTE 2: *Production Totals include 1952 models.*

"It has abundant power and performance with extreme ease of driving and reasonable fuel economy."

"…this latest V-8 from Chrysler can be reckoned as one of the finest examples of the modern American car."

The Motor, Nov. 14, 1951

CROWN IMPERIAL SERIES — SERIES C53: In addition to its size and increased passenger capacity, center-opening rear doors, and a concealed gas filler cap were a couple of distinguishing features for the Crown Imperial. The hood ornament had a crown medallion in the center of the "V" on the car's nose. Imperial models did not have lower front fender belt moldings. Power steering and Fluid Torque Drive were standard in Crown Imperials.

Crown Imperial Series

Model Number	Body/Style Number	Body Type & Seating	Factory Price	Shipping Weight	Production Total
C53	Note 1	4-dr Sedan-8P	$6,623	5,360 lbs.	360
C53	Note 1	4-dr Limousine-8P	$6,740	5,450 lbs.	338

NOTE 1: N/A.
NOTE 2: Production Total includes 1952 models.

ENGINE: V-8. Overhead valve. Cast iron block. Displacement: 331.1 cid. Bore and stroke: 3.81 x 3.62 inches. Compression ratio: 7.5:1. Brake hp: 180 at 4000 rpm. Five main bearings. Hydraulic valve lifters. Carburetor: Carter two-barrel Model WCD-830S.

CHASSIS FEATURES: Wheelbase: (Imperial) 131.5 inches; (Crown Imperial) 145.5 inches. Front tread: (Imperial) 56 inches; (Crown Imperial) 60 inches. Rear tread: (Imperial) 58 inches; (Crown Imperial) 66 inches. Tires: (Imperial) 8.20 x 15; (Crown Imperial) 8.90 x 15.

OPTIONS: Hydraguide power steering, in Imperial Eight ($226); standard in Crown Imperial Eight. Power brakes. Power disc brakes standard on Crown Imperial. Power steering. Air conditioning. All Weather Comfort System. Electric lift windows. Mopar radio. White sidewall tires. External sun visor. Fog lights. Spotlights. Exhaust deflector. Outside rearview mirror.

HISTORICAL FOOTNOTES: The 1951 Chrysler line (including Imperials) was introduced to the public on Feb. 9, 1951. On May 28, 1951, the Economic Stabilization Agency permitted the company to change its prices, to cover increased costs of the new V-8s. The increases were $251.19 for New Yorkers and Imperial Eights and $261.38 for the Crown Imperials. New features of this year included the Firepower V-8 engine (with hemispherical-segment cylinder heads); Hydraguide power steering and Oriflow shock absorbers. Assemblies of 1951 models began in December 1950 and the model year ran until November 1951. In this time span an estimated 156,000 units were built to 1951 specifications (Chrysler and Imperials together). A total of three special "parade phaetons" were built on the Crown Imperial chassis and used by the cities of Los Angeles, New York and Detroit. These cars were later updated with mid-1950s styling. The "Imperial Rose" was a special C54 series show car custom-made by the factory this year.

1952

IMPERIAL SERIES — SERIES C54: If you liked the 1951 Imperial, you'd feel the same way about the 1952 models, since they were practically identical. The best way to separate cars of both years is through reference to serial numbers. The convertible body style was dropped. Unlike the other Chryslers, the Imperial's taillights were not changed. Power steering was standard.

IMPERIAL I.D. NUMBERS: The serial number was located on a plate on the left front door hinge pillar post. Engine number was on top front center of engine block. Serial numbers for C54 Imperials built as 1952 models were recorded as C-7753601 to 7763596. Engine numbers C52-8-1001 to 59631 were used in this series, as well as in other Chrysler Eights, with engines built in mixed production sequence. Crown Imperials had serial numbers 7815101 to 7815306. Engine numbers, however, were shared with Chrysler V-8s.

Imperial Series

Series Number	Body/Style Number	Body Type & Seating	Factory Price	Shipping Weight	Production Total
C54	Note 1	4-dr Sedan-6P	$3,884	4,350 lbs.	Note 2
C54	Note 1	2-dr Club Coupe-6P	$3,851	4,230 lbs.	Note 2
C54	Note 1	2-dr Hardtop-6P	$4,249	4,380 lbs.	Note 2

NOTE 1: *N/A.*

NOTE 2: *See 1951 Production Total.*

CROWN IMPERIAL SERIES — SERIES C53: The "new" Crown Imperial was unchanged for 1952. Only 338 of these cars were made in the 1951-1952 model run and serial numbers indicate that 205 were registered as 1952 automobiles. A minor change was a one-inch reduction in front tread measurement.

Crown Imperial Series

Series Number	Body/Style Number	Body Type & Seating	Factory Price	Shipping Weight	Production Total
C53	Note 1	4-dr Sedan-8P	$6,922	5,360 lbs.	Note 2
C53	Note 1	4-dr Limousine-8P	$7,044	5,450 lbs.	Note 2

NOTE 1: *N/A.*

NOTE 2: *See 1951 Production Total.*

ENGINE: V-8. Overhead valve. Cast iron block. Displacement: 331.1 cid. Bore and stroke: 3.81 x 3.62 inches. Compression ratio: 7.5:1. Brake hp: 180 at 4000 rpm. Five main bearings. Hydraulic valve lifters. Carburetor: Carter two-barrel Model WCD-884S.

CHASSIS FEATURES: Wheelbase: (Imperial) 131.5 inches; (Crown Imperial) 145.5 inches. Overall length: (Imperial) 213-⅛ inches; (Crown Imperial) 145-½ inches. Front tread: (Imperial) 57 inches; (Crown Imperial) 57 inches. Rear tread: (Imperial) 58 inches; (Crown Imperial) 66 inches. Tires: (Imperial) 8.20 x 15-inch; (Crown Imperial) 8.90 x 15-inch. Ausco-Lambert "self-energizing" disc brakes standard in Crown Imperial series.

OPTIONS: Power brakes. (Power disc brakes standard on Crown Imperial.) Power steering, on C54 ($199); on C53 (standard equipment). Air conditioning. Solex glass (new option). White sidewall tires. Electric window lids. Sun visor. Radio. Heater and defroster. Exhaust deflector. Spare tire valve extension. Locking gas cap. Windshield washer. Fog lamps. Spotlights. Outside rearview mirror. Vanity mirror. Fluid-Torque drive was $167 extra on C54 Imperials and standard equipment on C53 Crown Imperials. Heavy-duty oil bath air cleaner. Vacuum booster fuel pump. Oil filter.

HISTORICAL FOOTNOTES: The 1952 Chrysler models, including Imperials, were introduced on Dec. 14, 1951. The Office of Price Stabilization (OPS), which set pricing policies during the Korean War, allowed Chrysler to make an across-the-board increase in retail prices on Feb. 11, 1952. On August 23, the OPS abandoned the policy of placing ceilings on new car prices and Chrysler again boosted its tags from $18 to $30. D.A. Wallace remained as president of the division. Model year production for all Chryslers was estimated at 91,253 units. The Imperial convertible, introduced only one year earlier, was dropped and not replaced until 1957.

Literature showed the 1952 Chrysler Crown Imperial limousine, complete with logo.

Phil Hall Collection

The spacious interior of the 1952 Chrysler Crown Imperial limousine.

Phil Hall Collection

Wire wheels, tinted glass and chrome against black all work to highlight the 1953 Chrysler Imperial sedan.

John Lee

CUSTOM IMPERIAL SERIES — SERIES C58: Although the Custom Imperial resembled the New Yorker, it had a different wheelbase, taillights and side trim. Clean front fenders and a higher rear fender stone shield set it apart from the "ordinary" Chryslers. This was the first year for the stylized eagle hood ornament. Power brakes, power windows, center folding armrests (front and rear) and a padded dash were standard. Parking lights on all Imperials were positioned between the top and center grille moldings, a variation from the design used on other Chrysler cars. The Custom Imperial six-passenger limousine had, as standard equipment, electric windows; electric division window; floor level courtesy lamps; rear compartment heater; fold-up footrests; seatback mounted clock and special, luxury cloth or leather interiors. On March 10, 1953, the Custom Imperial Newport hardtop was added to the Imperial line at $325 over the price of the eight-passenger sedan. However, Chrysler instituted a general price cut on March 25, and the new model was then reduced $45. A week later, the delivery and handling charges for Imperials were raised $10, so the customer came out $35 ahead in the long run.

IMPERIAL I.D. NUMBERS: The serial number was located on a plate on the left front door hinge pillar post. Engine number was on top of engine block at front water outlet elbow. Serial numbers C58-7765001 to 7773869 were used on 1953 Custom Imperials. Engine numbers fell in the range C53-8-1001 to 86292, which were shared with other Chrysler V-8 series. Crown Imperials had serial numbers C59-7816001 to 7816162. Engine numbers were in the same range used for Custom Imperials, as well as other Chrysler V-8s.

Custom Imperial Series

Series Number	Body/Style Number	Body Type & Seating	Factory Price	Shipping Weight	Production Total
C58	Note 1	4-dr Sedan-8P	$4,260	4,305 lbs.	7,793
C58	Note 1	4-dr Limousine-6P	$4,797	4,525 lbs.	243
C58	Note 1	2-dr Hardtop-6P	$4,560	4,290 lbs	823

NOTE 1: *N/A.*

CROWN IMPERIAL SERIES — SERIES C59: The eagle hood ornament was about the only thing new on the 1953 Crown Imperial. The nameplate was changed slightly and the limousine featured moldings on top of rear fenders. It had a 12-volt electrical system (the Custom had a six-volt system). Power steering was standard and PowerFlite fully-automatic transmission was installed in a small number of late-in-the-year cars for testing and evaluation.

Crown Imperial Series

Series Number	Body/Style Number	Body Type & Seating	Factory Price	Shipping Weight	Production Total
C59	Note 1	4-dr Sedan-8P	$6,922	5,235 lbs.	48
C59	Note 1	4-dr Limousine-8P	$7,044	5,275 lbs.	111

NOTE 1: N/A.

ENGINE: V-8. Overhead valve. Cast iron block. Displacement: 331.1 cid. Bore and stroke: 3.81 x 3.62 inches. Compression ratio: 7.5:1. Brake hp: 180 at 4000 rpm. Five main bearings. Hydraulic valve lifters. Carburetor: Carter WCD-935S.

CHASSIS FEATURES: Wheelbase: (Custom Imperial hardtop) 131.5 inches; (sedan and limousine) 133.5 inches; (Crown Imperial) 145.5 inches. Overall length: (Custom Imperial) 219 inches; (Crown Imperial) 229 inches. Front tread: (Custom Imperial) 57 inches; (Crown Imperial) 57 inches. Rear tread: (Custom Imperial) 57 inches, (Crown Imperial) 66 inches. Tires: (Custom Imperial) 8.20 x 15; (Crown Imperial) 8.90 x 15. Ausco-Lambert "self-energizing" disc brakes standard in Crown Imperial series.

OPTIONS: Power disc brakes were standard on C59 Crown Imperials. Power steering was optional on Custom Imperials ($177) and standard in Crown Imperials. Air conditioning. Power windows. At the start of the model year, Fluid-Torque transmission was standard equipment on all Imperials. In June 1953, PowerFlite fully-automatic transmission was selectively introduced and was subsequently made standard equipment in all 1954 Imperials.

HISTORICAL FOOTNOTES: The 1953 Chrysler line, including Imperials, was introduced Oct. 30, 1952. The Custom Imperial Newport hardtop was introduced on March 18, 1953. E.C. Quinn became president of Chrysler Division this year. Chrysler Corp. unveiled its PowerFlite transmission early in the summer. At that time, it had been under "road test" by a number of specially-selected customers whose use of the fully-automatic transmission was monitored. By the time the production go-ahead was given, assembly of 1953 Imperials had ended. It is possible to find 1953 Imperials with PowerFlite, although the first general-sales installations were made in 1954 models. It was made standard in Imperials and optional in other Chrysler cars.

The 1953 Chrysler Imperial sedan looked great going as well as coming.

John Lee

"It will keep up with anything on the road and probably will walk away from 95 percent."

George Aitchison, Man's Day, 1952

The 1954 Chrysler Imperial was the height of luxury available from Chrysler Corporation.

CUSTOM IMPERIAL SERIES — SERIES C64: The new Custom Imperial had a grille consisting of a heavy, wraparound horizontal center bar (with five ridges on top) and integrated circular signal lights. Its front fender nameplate was above a chrome strip, which ran the length of the front door to the front wheel opening. The rear fender stone guard was larger than in 1953, but the rocker panel molding and rear fender chrome strip style were still the same. The back-up lights were now located directly below the taillights, rather than dividing the lights as in the previous year's model.

IMPERIAL I.D. NUMBERS: The serial number was located on a plate on the left front door hinge pillar post. Engine number was on top of engine block at front water outlet elbow. Serial numbers C64-7775001 to 7780767 were found on Custom Imperials. Serial numbers C64-7817001 to 7817100 were used on 1954 Crown Imperials. The engine numbers C542-8-1001 to 40478 were used on all 1954 Chrysler Eights.

Custom Imperial Series

Series Number	Body/Style Number	Body Type & Seating	Factory Price	Shipping Weight	Production Total
C64	Note 1	4-dr Sedan-6P	$4,260	4,355 lbs.	4,324
C64	Note 1	2-dr Hardtop-6P	$4,560	4,345 lbs.	1,249
C64	Note 1	4-dr Limousine-6P	$4,797	4,465 lbs.	85

NOTE 1: N/A.

CROWN IMPERIAL SERIES — SERIES C66: The Crown Imperial shared basic styling with the Custom. However, it had center-opening rear doors and Cadillac-like rear fender taillights. Air conditioning was standard.

Crown Imperial Series

Series Number	Body/Style Number	Body Type & Seating	Factory Price	Shipping Weight	Production Total
C66	Note 1	4-dr Sedan-8P	$6,922	5,220 lbs.	23
C66	Note 1	4-dr Limousine-8P	$7,044	5,295 lbs.	77

NOTE 1: N/A.

In 1954, all Chrysler models, including the Imperial, got an entirely new dash for the first time since 1949.

The 1954 Chrysler Imperial came with factory air conditioning and even the AirTemp air intake near the car's back window got a stylish promotion.

ENGINE: V-8. Overhead valve. Cast iron block. Displacement: 331.1 cid. Bore and stroke: 3.81 x 3.62 inches. Compression ratio: 7.5:1. Brake hp: 235 at 4400 rpm. Five main bearings. Hydraulic valve lifters. Carburetor: Carter four-barrel Model WCFB-2041S.

CHASSIS FEATURES: Wheelbase: (Custom Imperial hardtop) 131.5 inches; (Custom Imperial sedan and hardtop) 133.5 inches; (Crown Imperial) 145.5 inches. Overall length: (C64 Newport) 221.75 inches; (C64) 223.75 inches; (C66) 236-⅜ inches. Tires: (Custom Imperial) 8.20 x 15-inch; (Crown Imperial) 8.90 x 15-inch. Ausco-Lambert "self-energizing" disc brakes were standard in the Crown Imperial series.

OPTIONS: Power disc brakes were standard on the Crown Imperial. Power drum brakes were optional on Custom Imperial. Power steering was standard on the Crown Imperial and optional on the Custom Imperial. Air conditioning. Electric lift windows.

HISTORICAL FOOTNOTES: Derham Custom Body Co. built a special Custom Imperial Landau Victoria this year, with a Victoria-style half-roof and open driver's compartment. This Contessa show car was seen at the 1954 automobile shows. It was based on the Custom Imperial Newport hardtop with modifications including a vinyl-and-plexiglas roof, continental tire extension kit, chromed Kelsey-Hayes wire wheels plus a custom pink and white interior and exterior finish.

The 1955 Imperial styling was a combination of quiet and flashy in the same car. The Lincoln was probably a closer comparison than Cadillac to its looks.

A memorable feature was the stand-up taillights on the '55 Imperial. They appeared first on the K310 and C-200 concept cars designed by Virgil Exner.

IMPERIAL SERIES — SERIES C69: Imperial, like all Chrysler Corp. cars, was completely restyled for 1955. It had bumper-integrated signal lights. Each section of the two-piece split grille consisted of two large vertical bars, crossed by like-size horizontal ones. The Imperial eagle crest was placed between the sections. Side trim consisted of fender-to-fender mid-body molding and full-length lower body trim. Unique to the make were free-standing rear fender-mounted taillights. Many styling cues for the new Imperial were taken from the successful "parade car" Imperials, also designed by Virgil Exner.

IMPERIAL I.D. NUMBERS: The serial number was located on a plate on the left front door hinge pillar post. Engine number was on top of engine block at front water outlet elbow. Imperials and Crown Imperials were numbered C55-1001 to 12464. Engine numbers CE55-1001 to 12490 were used in mixed series production.

Imperial Series

Series Number	Body/Style Number	Body Type & Seating	Factory Price	Shipping Weight	Production Total
C69	Note 1	4-dr Sedan-6P	$4,483	4,565 lbs.	7,840
C69	Note 1	2-dr Hardtop-6P	$4,720	4,490 lbs.	3,418

NOTE 1: *N/A.*

CROWN IMPERIAL SERIES — SERIES C70: The center-opening rear doors of previous Crown sedans and limousines were replaced by conventional ones in 1955. It shared the same basic styling as the standard Imperial but had a different roof with a smaller, rectangular rear window. New features included power disc brakes and a 12-volt electrical system.

Crown Imperial Series

Series Number	Body/Style Number	Body Type & Seating	Factory Price	Shipping Weight	Production Total
C70	Note 1	4-dr Sedan-8P	$7,603	5,145 lbs.	45
C70	Note 1	4-dr Limousine-8P	$7,737	5,205 lbs.	127

NOTE 1: *N/A.*

The Chrysler name does not appear anywhere on the exterior of the 1955 Imperials.

The 1955 Imperial had a very plush interior but it shared its dash with the rest of the Chrysler line.

ENGINE: V-8. Overhead valve. Cast iron block. Displacement: 331.1 cid. Bore and stroke: 3.81 x 3.82 inches. Compression ratio: 8.50:1. Brake hp: 250 at 4600 rpm. Carburetor: Carter four-barrel Model WCFB-2126S.

CHASSIS FEATURES: Wheelbase: (Imperial) 130 inches; (Crown Imperial) 149.5 inches; Tires: (Imperial) 8.20 x 15-inch and (Crown Imperial) 8.90 x 15-inch.

OPTIONS: Power brakes and power steering were standard with all Imperials. A four-way power seat was standard in eight-passenger styles. Extra-cost options: Air conditioning. Power windows. Signal-seeking radio.

HISTORICAL FOOTNOTES: The Custom Imperial Town Limousine was dropped for 1955. Model year introductions were scheduled on Nov. 17, 1954. E.C. Quinn was president of Chrysler Division this year. Beginning this season, Chrysler considered the Imperial to be a separate marque or make and duly registered it as such with the U.S. Government. Imperial production figures were broken out from the totals for the rest of the Chrysler line. Chrysler Division's New Yorker and Imperial series climbed to second rank in the high-priced field, with 84,330 new car registrations in calendar 1955. This total included some 1954 Chrysler-lmperials and could be a misleading figure to some degree. The Imperial/New Yorker Division competed with Cadillac, Lincoln and Packard, and Packard was the only one of those companies the Imperial "outsold" by itself (New Yorkers were targeted against senior Buicks). Genuine leather interior trims were offered in the front seat of Crown Imperial Limousines and eight-passenger sedans and in combinations for the Imperial Southampton four-door. In 1955, Imperial production was moved to the Jefferson Ave. plant in Detroit.

Imperial was clearly Chrysler Corporation's most luxurious model, but this two-door hardtop hints at a future trend, the personal luxury car.

IMPERIAL SERIES — SERIES C73: Front end styling resembled last year's model, but the rear fenders were taller and the full-length mid-body side molding wrapped around them. The rear bumpers were attractively redesigned and seemed integrated into the rear fenders. Taillights were once again mounted on the fenders.

IMPERIAL I.D. NUMBERS: The serial number was located on a plate on the left front door hinge pillar post. Engine number was on top of engine block at front water outlet elbow. Serial numbers for C73 series models were C56-1001 to 11715. Serial numbers for C70 models were C56-1001 to 9826. Engine numbers CE56-1001 to 11750 were used in cars of both series.

Imperial Series

Series Number	Body/Style Number	Body Type & Seating	Factory Price	Shipping Weight	Production Total
C73	Note 1	4-dr Sedan-6P	$4,832	4,575 lbs.	6,821
C73	Note 1	4-dr Hardtop-6P	$5,225	4,680 lbs.	1,543
C73	Note 1	2-dr Hardtop-6P	$5,094	4,555 lbs.	2,094

NOTE 1: *N/A.*

One giveaway that the car was cooled was the 1956 Imperial air intake.

Giant eagles adorned the front and rear of the 1956 Imperial so there was no need for the Chrysler New Yorker/Windsor-like eagle hood ornament.

The giant eagle continued to be the Imperial's logo in 1956 and it appeared as large emblems and in upholstery patterns.

CROWN IMPERIAL SERIES — SERIES C70: Styling changes were minimal. About the only difference between the 1956 and last year's Crown was the side trim. The new version had mid-body moldings that extended only from the tip of the front fender to slightly beyond the beginning of the rear fender. There were five slanted slashes and a chrome outline of the tailfin on the rear fenders.

Crown Imperial Series

Series Number	Body/Style Number	Body Type & Seating	Factory Price	Shipping Weight	Production Total
C70	Note 1	4-dr Sedan-8P	$7,603	5,145 lbs.	51
C70	Note 1	4-dr Limousine-8P	$7,737	5,205 lbs.	119

NOTE 1: *N/A.*

In 1956, Imperial introduced a four-door hardtop to its offerings.

An endearing trait on the 1956 Imperial four-door hardtop was its well-engineered, scissor action when the windows were rolled down.

"In hard turns and bends I found it biting in and holding on like a bat in a wind tunnel."

"These Imperials, when properly tuned, will get up to 120 mph and will cruise at 80 with no more effort than it takes to down a milkshake."

Tom McCahill, Mechanix Illustrated, August 1956

ENGINE: V-8. Overhead valve. Cast iron block. Displacement: 353.1 cid. Bore and stroke: 3.94 x 3.63 inches. Compression ratio: 9.0:1. Brake hp: 280 at 4600 rpm. Carburetor: Carter four-barrel Model WCFB-2314S.

A well-preserved 1956 Imperial two-door hardtop enters a Michigan auto show area.

David Lyon

CHASSIS FEATURES: Wheelbase: (Imperial) 133 inches; (Crown Imperial) 149.5 inches. Tires: (Imperial) 8.20 x 15; (Crown Imperial) 8.90 x 15.

OPTIONS: Power steering, power brakes and Four-Way power seats were standard equipment. Options included power windows and air conditioning. PowerFlite automatic transmission, now with push-button control, was standard in all Imperials when the model year started. A new three-speed TorqueFlite automatic transmission became available on all Imperials in the spring.

HISTORICAL FOOTNOTES: The 1956 Imperials were introduced Oct. 21, 1955. Model year production peaked at 10,685 cars. Calendar year production was counted as 12,130 units. This was the first calendar year that Imperial production records were recorded separate from Chrysler figures for the entire 12 months. E.C. Quinn was president of the Chrysler Division this year. Imperial was emerging as a strong selling luxury car in this period. Separate production lines for Imperials were set up at Chrysler's Kercheval and Jefferson plants in Detroit. The 1956 Imperial could go from 0-to-60 mph in 12.8 seconds. It had a top speed of over 104 mph.

In spite of being a sportier, less formal car, the 1956 Imperial was still a large, long, luxurious car that didn't let the passenger forget its class, especially inside.

The eagle icon turned heads, as if the dramatic 1957 Imperial sedan needed more attention.

IMPERIAL SERIES — SERIES IM-1: Imperial styling moved further away from that of other Chrysler Corporation cars in 1957. Hardtop models featured a distinctive "overlapping" rear-section roof. The taillights were now integrated into the tips of the tailfins. Wraparound "eyebrow" trim above the headlights extended half the length of the front fenders. Mid-body chrome trim ran from the rear deck panel to the front tire well. The grille looked like a mesh of chrome pieces. Signal lights were sandwiched between the two horizontal bumpers. A simulated spare-tire cover trunk lid was optional on all 1957 Imperials.

IMPERIAL L.D. NUMBERS: The serial number was located on a plate on the left front door hinge pillar post. Engine number was on top of engine block at front water outlet elbow. Imperial, Imperial Crown, LeBaron and Crown Imperial serial numbers were C57-1001 to 36890. Engine numbers were CE57-1001 to 36950.

Imperial Series

Series Number	Body/Style Number	Body Type & Seating	Factory Price	Shipping Weight	Production Total
IM1-1	Note 1	4-dr Sedan-8P	$4,838	4,640 lbs.	5,654
IM1-1	Note 1	4-dr Hardtop-6P	$4,838	4,780 lbs.	7,527
IM1-1	Note 1	2-dr Hardtop-6P	$4,736	4,640 lbs.	4,885

IMPERIAL CROWN SERIES — SERIES IM1-2: Like all Imperial series, the Imperial Crown (not to be confused with the plusher Crown Imperial, of course) had recessed door handles. Exterior styling was basically the same as that used on the standard Imperial. However, Imperial Crowns had a tiny crown emblem above the second "I" in the Imperial nameplate. A convertible was offered for the first time since 1951.

Imperial Crown Series

Series Number	Body/Style Number	Body Type & Seating	Factory Price	Shipping Weight	Production Total
IM1-2	Note 1	4-dr Sedan-6P	$5,406	4,740 lbs.	3,642
IM1-2	Note 1	4-dr Hardtop-6P	$5,406	4,920 lbs.	7,843
IM1-2	Note 1	2-dr Hardtop-6P	$5,269	4,755 lbs.	4,199
IM1-2	Note 1	2-dr Convertible-6P	$5,598	4,830 lbs.	1,167

IMPERIAL LEBARON SERIES — SERIES IM1-4: A distinctive front-fender emblem in place of the Imperial signature was the easiest way to tell the plush LeBaron from other Imperials.

The 1957 Imperial Crown Southampton is dominated by the Imperial eagle logo.

Few cars expressed 1950s elegance better than the 1957 Imperial Crown convertible.

A press photo shows an attractive view of the 1957 Imperial four-door hardtop Southampton

Phil Hall Collection

Imperial LeBaron Series

Series Number	Body/Style Number	Body Type & Seating	Factory Price	Shipping Weight	Production Total
IM1-4	Note 1	4-dr Sedan-6P	$5,743	4,765 lbs.	1,729
IM1-4	Note 1	4-dr Hardtop-6P	$5,743	4,900 lbs.	911

CROWN IMPERIAL SERIES: The 1957 Crown Imperials were custom-built by Ghia in Turin, Italy. Several coats of blue, maroon, black or green lacquer were applied to them for an unsurpassed finish. The Crown Imperials had 1958-style grilles and their doors extended into the roof. Carpeting, air conditioning and power windows were just a few of the standard features.

Crown Imperial Series

Series Number	Body/Style Number	Body Type & Seating	Factory Price	Shipping Weight	Production Total
Note 1	Note 2	4-dr Limousine-8P	$12,000	5,960 lbs.	36

ENGINE: V-8. Overhead valve. Cast iron block. Displacement: 392.7 cid. Bore and stroke: 4.0 x 3.9 inches. Compression ratio: 9.25:1. Brake hp: 325 at 4600 rpm. Carburetor: Carter Type four-barrel Model WCFB-2590S.

CHASSIS FEATURES: Wheelbase: (Imperial, Crown and LeBaron) 129 inches; (Crown Imperial) 149.5 inches. Tires: 9.50 x 14-inch.

OPTIONS: Power brakes (standard). Power steering (standard). Four-Way power seat. Air conditioning ($590). Radio ($176). Solex glass ($50). Power windows ($125). TorqueFlite automatic transmission with push-button shift control was standard equipment.

HISTORICAL FOOTNOTES: The new Imperials were introduced, with other Chryslers, on Oct. 30, 1956. Quad headlights were offered on all Imperials sold in states where this setup was legal. The Ghia-built Crown Imperial limousine was announced on Jan. 2, 1957. Originally programmed for production of 75 units, the car sold less than half that amount. Model year output for Imperial peaked at 35,734 cars including, in rounded figures, 17,500 Imperials; 16,000 Crown Imperials and 2,500 LeBarons. Calendar year production was recorded as 37,946 units. E.C. Quinn was again president of Chrysler Division this year. "Chrysler in 1957 aggressively established Imperial as a volume automobile line," said Chrysler president L.L. "Tex" Colbert.

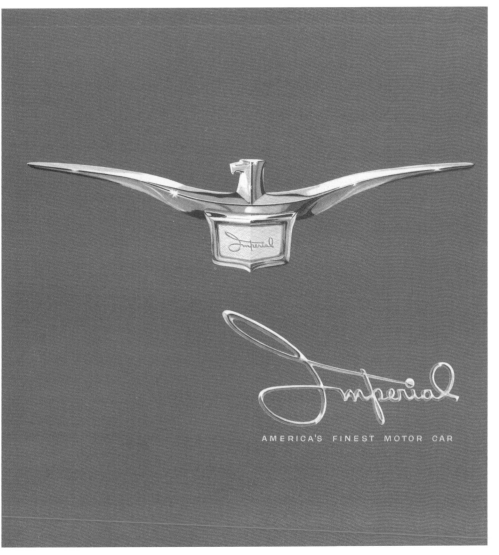

Modern art combined with modern auto styling with this 1957 Imperial convertible press photo.

The bright red color and the giant golden eagle show off the dramatic 1958 Imperial Crown convertible at its finest.

IMPERIAL SERIES — SERIES LY1-L: "America's most distinctive fine car" is how advertisements described the new Imperial. Styling changes were confined primarily to the grille. The mesh pattern of 1957 was replaced by four "stacks" of horizontal bars. The front bumper was now one solid piece with circular signal light pods extending from its lower section. Standard equipment included power brakes, power steering, back-up lights, windshield washer, and quad headlights. A simulated spare-tire-cover trunk lid was optional on all 1958 Imperials.

IMPERIAL L.D. NUMBERS: The serial number was located on a plate on the left front door hinge pillar post. Engine number was on top of engine block at front water outlet elbow. Serial numbers were LY1-1001 to 17325 for Imperial, Imperial Crown and Imperial LeBaron models. Engine numbers 58C-1001 and up were used in these series. Crown Imperial limousines were numbered C57-1001 and up and had engine numbers CE57-1001 and up.

Imperial Series

Series Number	Body/Style Number	Body Type & Seating	Factory Price	Shipping Weight	Production Total
LY1-L	Note 1	4-dr Sedan-6P	$4,945	4,950 lbs.	1,926
LY1-L	Note 1	4-dr Hardtop-6P	$4,839	4,795 lbs.	3,336
LY1-L	Note 1	2-dr Hardtop-6P	$4,945	4,640 lbs.	1,901

IMPERIAL CROWN SERIES — SERIES LY1-M: A tiny crown emblem above the second "I" in the Imperial nameplate remained the easiest way to tell the Imperial Crown from the standard Imperial. It came with a Six-Way power seat, power windows and an outside rearview mirror.

Imperial Crown Series

Series Number	Body/Style Number	Body Type & Seating	Factory Price	Shipping Weight	Production Total
LY1-M	Note 1	4-dr Sedan-6P	$5,632	4,755 lbs.	1,240
LY1-M	Note 1	4-dr Hardtop-6P	$5,632	4,915 lbs.	4,146
LY1-M	Note 1	2-dr Hardtop-6P	$5,388	4,730 lbs.	1,939
LY1-M	Note 1	2-dr Convertible-6P	$5,759	4,820 lbs.	675

1958 Imperial Crown two-door Southampton (two-door hardtop)   Phil Hall Collection

1958 Imperial Crown four-door Southampton (four-door hardtop)

"Chrysler's Torsion-Aire suspension is miles ahead in every respect."

"The car… is quiet as Gimbel's basement on Christmas morn. In four words — it's America's finest car."

Tom McCahill, Mechanix Illustrated, July 1958

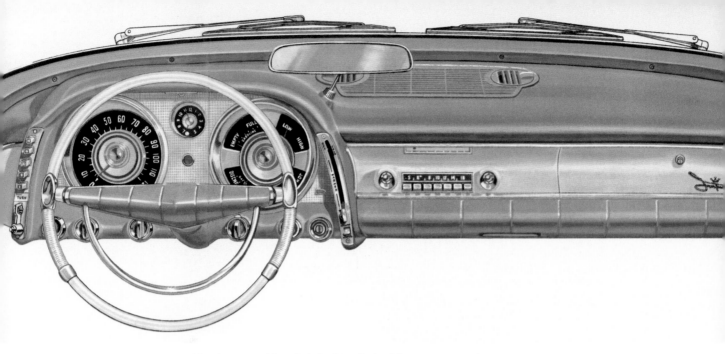

The elegant and futuristic-looking dash of the 1958 Imperial. Phil Hall Collection

The plush interior of the 1958 Imperial Crown was portrayed for potential buyers.

Phil Hall Collection

IMPERIAL LEBARON SERIES — SERIES LY1-H: LeBarons had a distinctive emblem on the front fenders, instead of the Imperial name in script.

Imperial LeBaron Series

Series Number	Body/Style Number	Body Type & Seating	Factory Price	Shipping Weight	Production Total
LY1-H	Note 1	4-dr Sedan-6P	$5,969	4,780 lbs.	501
LY1-H	Note 1	4-dr Hardtop-6P	$5,969	4,940 lbs.	538

CROWN IMPERIAL SERIES: Because of its late introduction in 1957, the "new" custom-built Crown Imperial was the same as last year's model. Great care was taken in the construction of this car. In fact, reportedly as many as 17 hours were spent on every auto just to make sure the doors fit perfectly. Carpeting, air conditioning, power steering, power windows and power brakes were only some of the many standard features.

Crown Imperial Series

Series Number	Body/Style Number	Body Type & Seating	Factory Price	Shipping Weight	Production Total
Note 1	Note 2	4-dr Limousine-8P	$15,075	5,960 lbs.	31

ENGINE: V-8. Overhead valve. Cast iron block. Displacement: 392.7 cid. Bore and stroke: 4.0 x 3.9 inches. Compression ratio: 10.0:1. Brake hp: 345 at 4600 rpm. Carburetor: Carter four-barrel Model AFB-2651S.

CHASSIS FEATURES: Wheelbase: (Imperial, Crown and LeBaron) 129 inches: (Crown Imperial) 149.5 inches. Tires: 9.50 x 14-inch.

OPTIONS: Power brakes. Power steering. Air conditioning ($590.20). Rear window defogger ($21.45). Custom heater ($140.60). Instant heater ($177.50). Six-Way power seat ($118.30). Power windows ($125.00). Electric touch radio with rear speaker and power antenna ($76.00). Solex glass ($50.40). White sidewall rayon tires, 9.50 x 14 ($55.10). Standard two-tone paint ($20.45). Auto pilot ($88.70). Electric door locks (two-door hardtop) with power windows ($40.70). Electric door locks (four-door models) with power windows ($65.80).

HISTORICAL FOOTNOTE: The 1958 Imperial line was introduced to the public Nov. 1, 1957. Most 1958 Imperials, 93.6 percent, had power seats; 92.9 percent had power windows; 86 percent had whitewall tires and 33.3 percent had air conditioning. The 1958 Imperial line received extra attention befitting custom cars. Body seams were finished and soldered by hand. Workers did custom wet sanding between paint coats. The seat bolsters and convertible tops also were painstakingly fitted. According to author Jeffrey Godshall, each 1958 Imperial was road tested before being shipped.

The 1958 Imperial Crown sedan was shown in a demure green in product literature.

Phil Hall Collection

The elegant 1958 Imperial LeBaron four-door Southampton had a stately bearing.

Phil Hall Collection

The three-year-old Imperial design still looked sharp in 1959, especially in comparison to the extreme styles from Buick, Cadillac and Lincoln.

IMPERIAL CUSTOM SERIES — SERIES MY1-L: The front-end treatment was jazzed up for 1959. Chrome-encased headlight pods were linked by a large, center grille bar with five curved vertical pieces. Side trim, roof designs and the protruding tailfin taillight resembled the previous year's model's. A lower rear-quarter panel stone shield and the Imperial name printed on the front fenders were two other changes. Buyers had their choice of three optional hardtop roof treatments. The Landau had a simulated rear canopy. The Silvercrest featured a stainless steel section covering the front half of the roof. The Silvercrest Landau was a combination of the first two. All 1959 Imperials came with power brakes, power steering, dual exhaust, electric clock, windshield washer and undercoating.

IMPERIAL I.D. NUMBERS: The serial number was located on a plate on the left front door hinge pillar post. Engine number was stamped behind water pump on engine. Serial numbers took the form: M617100001 and up. The first symbol designated year ("M" = 1959). The second symbol designated make ("6"= Imperial). The third symbol designated series ("1" = Custom, "3" = Crown, "5" = LeBaron). The fourth symbol designated manufacturing plant ("7" = Detroit). The fifth to tenth symbols designated production numbers. Body number plates located below the hood, in various locations, indicate schedule date, body production number, and body series (see column two in charts below), plus trim, paint and accessories data.

Imperial dropped its headlights to grille level and they became part of the grille's theme in 1959 instead of floating above as they had in the previous two years.

Imperial Custom Series

Series Number	Body/Style Number	Body Type & Seating	Factory Price	Shipping Weight	Production Total
MY1-L	613	4-dr Sedan-6P	$5,016	4,735 lbs.	2,071
MY1-L	614	4-dr Hardtop-6P	$5,016	4,745 lbs.	3,984
MY1-L	612	2-dr Hardtop-6P	$4,910	4,675 lbs.	1,743

The 1959 Imperial had a new instrument panel but retained the entire dash from the previous two years including the push-button gear selector and flipper-style turn signals.

This 1959 Imperial had the optional automatic day-night mirror that changed to the night position when bright lights shined on its sensor.

The white home and coating of snow bring out the elegance of this 1959 Crown Imperial limousine.

IMPERIAL CROWN SERIES — SERIES MY1-M: Crown emblems on the front fenders were about the only way to distinguish the exterior of a Crown from a Custom. Standard features included Six-Way power seat, power windows, outside rearview mirror, vanity mirror and license plate frame.

Imperial Crown Series

Series Number	Body/Style Number	Body Type & Seating	Factory Price	Shipping Weight	Production Total
MY1-M	633	4-dr Sedan-6P	$5,647	4,830 lbs.	1,335
MY1-M	634	4-dr Hardtop-6P	$5,647	4,840 lbs.	4,714
MY1-M	632	2-dr Hardtop-6P	$5,403	4,810 lbs.	1,728
MY1-M	635	2-dr Convertible-6P	$5,774	4,850 lbs.	555

IMPERIAL LEBARON SERIES — SERIES MY1-H: Its nameplate on the front fenders and special emblem on the chrome rear quarter panels were exterior features of the LeBaron. In addition to the standard equipment found on the other series, LeBarons had two-tone paint and whitewall tires.

Imperial LeBaron Series

Series Number	Body/Style Number	Body Type & Seating	Factory Price	Shipping Weight	Production Total
MY1-H	653	4-dr Sedan-6P	$6,103	4,865 lbs.	510
MY1-H	654	4-dr Hardtop-6P	$6,103	4,875 lbs.	622

CROWN IMPERIAL SERIES: Custom-built by Ghia of Italy, the Crown Imperial remained one of the finest custom-built luxury cars in the world. Basic styling was like that used on the standard Imperials. It came with air conditioning, power windows, carpeting, and many other features.

Crown Imperial Series

Series Number	Body/Style Number	Body Type & Seating	Factory Price	Shipping Weight	Production Total
Note 1	Note 2	4-dr Limousine-8P	$16,000	5,960 lbs.	7

ENGINE: V-8. Overhead valve. Cast iron block. Displacement: 413.2 cid. Bore and stroke: 4.18 x 3.75 inches. Compression ratio: 10.0:1. Brake hp: 350 at 4600 rpm. Carburetor: Carter four-barrel Model AFB-2797S.

CHASSIS FEATURES: Wheelbase: (Custom, Crown and LeBaron) 129 inches; (Crown Imperial) 149.5 inches. Tires: (all models) 9.50 x 14.

OPTIONS: Power brakes, standard. Power steering. Air conditioning ($590.20). Air suspension ($156). Rear window defogger ($21.45). Custom conditioned heater ($136.30). Instant heater ($164.95). Six-Way power seat ($124.80). Power windows ($125). Electric Touch radio, plus speaker and power antenna ($168.80). Electric Touch radio, plus speaker and power antenna for convertibles ($153.40). Solex glass ($53.75). Whitewall rayon tires ($55.10). Whitewall nylon tires ($76.55). Whitewall nylon tires on LeBaron ($27.50). Two-tone paint ($20.45). Landau two-tone paint ($31.20). Auto pilot ($96.80). Electric door locks on two doors with power windows ($47.40). Electric door locks on four-doors with power windows ($72.50). Automatic beam changer ($54.90). Flitesweep deck lid ($55.45). Extra heavy-duty 40-amp generator ($42.60). Mirror-matic on Imperial Custom ($22.20); on Crown and LeBaron ($18.20). Outside remote control mirror on custom ($18.75); on Crown and LeBaron ($11. 90). Outside manual mirror ($6.85). Power swivel seat on Custom ($226.15); on Crown and LeBaron ($101.35). Stainless steel roof, hardtops ($139.80). Sure-grip differential ($57.45). True-level ride ($159.90). Leather trim Crown hardtops and convertible ($52.70).

The famous "gunsight" taillight used by the Exner design team at Chrysler appeared in a lightly altered form on the 1959 Imperials.

HISTORICAL FOOTNOTES: The vast majority of 1959 Imperials, 97.1 percent, had radios; 37.5 percent had air conditioning and 81.1 percent came with tinted glass.

PLYMOUTH

Clockwise: The 1950 Plymouth had a fancy dash, yet was the lowest-priced car in the Chrysler Corporation stable.

In coupe form, the 1950 Plymouth had a less boxy appearance.

The 1950 Plymouth three-window business coupe is dressed in period accessories including visor and wide-stripe whitewalls.

In 1928, Walter P. Chrysler called his new low-price car Plymouth, where the Pilgrims landed, and used the Mayflower ship logo.

1950-1959

Introduction

The 1949 to '52 Chrysler products, especially four-door sedans, are often criticized for being too boxy at a time when General Motors' fastback bodies were getting sleeker and lower in keeping with the Jet Age. The good news was that DeSoto and Chrysler had the hood length and size to offset some of the boxiness, and to an extent, so did the full-size Dodge. The styling was more cruel to Plymouth because the car was as tall and squarely styled as the big cars, but its shorter length and proportions made it look top-heavy and ungainly. The good news was that the Plymouth was by far the most comfortable low-priced car on the road, and it had the same "chair-high" seats as its big sisters within Chrysler Corporation. That was coupled with Chrysler's characteristic good braking, easy steering, high-pressure engine oiling, and silent gears and made Plymouth was one of the most enjoyable cars on the road from behind the wheel.

The rear treatment on the 1950 Plymouth gave it a wider, more proportioned look than it had in 1949.

In 1949, Plymouth had the same rear treatment as the rest of the corporation with bolt-on rear fenders that narrowed toward the rear of the car and had rear bumpers that did not extend beyond the width of the car. This exaggerated Plymouth's narrow, tall rear profile. For 1950, the rear fenders were widened and the rear bumpers extended beyond the width of the rear fenders. This treatment greatly helped the looks of the Plymouth from the rear. The bumpers were no longer ribbed as they had been in 1949.

Plymouth eliminated the elaborate multi-purpose trunk lid piece that served as a trunk handle/license plate frame/brake light/back-up light and license plate light housing. They replaced it with a simple trunk handle, and the taillights did double-duty as the brake and signal lights as other brands did.

The Plymouth grille simplified into an easy-on-the-eye cross of two bars that met in the middle of the grille, and the opening was trimmed in heavy-looking bright-metal. The Mayflower sailed the highways as the Plymouth hood ornament once again.

The combination of these styling elements made the Plymouth simpler, cleaner, and more modern than the more ornate, Art Deco 1940 models, but Plymouth did keep the darkly woodgrained dash with the big, chrome radio housing and speaker grille in the middle of the dash. The dash was handsome for a car of its price range.

DELUXE (SHORT WHEELBASE) SIX — (6-CYLINDER) — SERIES P-19: The short-wheelbase Deluxe was a very small car, and it only came in two body styles – three-passenger coupe and turtle-back two-door sedan. Horizontal spears decorated both the front and rear fender sides and chrome headlamp rings and vertical bumper guards were seen once more. The side of the front fender earned a Deluxe script. At the rear, smaller trunk emblems, handles and taillights were featured. Deluxe models did not have rear gravel guards and used rubber windshield and rear window surrounds. Rear windows were made slightly larger. In September 1950, a fancy Special Suburban was offered. It had bright metal gravel guards and window frames, fancier upholstery and Special Suburban front fender script. Both Suburbans continued to use 1949-style rear fenders.

PLYMOUTH L.D. NUMBERS: The serial number plate on the left front door post is the only code used for identification/registration purposes. It consists of a Plymouth prefix "P" and two symbol series number (P-19, P-20). The four or more symbols following this are the production sequence number starting with 1001 at each factory. Engine number near front upper left side of block between first and second cylinders takes same format as serial number, but may not match. Engine numbers should not be used for identification. Engine numbers sometimes had suffixes: A = .020 inch cylinder overbore; B = .010 inch undersize journals; and diamond-shaped symbol = .008 inch oversize tappet bore. Plymouth factory codes are: M=Detroit, Mich.; LA=Los Angeles, Calif.; E=Evansville, Ind.; and SL=San Leandro, Calif. These codes do not appear in the serial number. Chrysler did not use body/style numbers at this time. Serial numbers for 1950 at each factory were as follows: P-19 Deluxe: (M) 18041001-18119094; (E) 24012001-24035538; (LA) 28004001-28009848 and (SL) 28503501-28511177. P-20 Deluxe: (M) 15359501-15456084; (E) 22097001-22125803; (LA) 26030501-26035870 and (SL) 26504001-26510569. P-20 Special Deluxe: (M) 12384501-12627867; (E) 20367001-22125803; (LA) 26030501-26035870 and (SL) 26504001-26510569. Engine numbers for the three series were: P20-1001-P204.

Deluxe Six Series

Series Number	Body/Style Number	Body Type & Seating	Factory Price	Shipping Weight	Production Total
P-19	N/A	2-dr Sedan-6P	$1,492	2,946 lbs.	67,584
P-19	N/A	2-dr Coupe-3P	$1,371	2,872 lbs.	16,861
P-19	N/A	2-dr Suburban-5P	$1,840	3,116 lbs.	34,457

Special Deluxe

Series Number	Body/Style Number	Body Type & Seating	Factory Price	Shipping Weight	Production Total
P-19	N/A	2-dr Suburban-5P	$1,946	3,155 lbs.	Note 1

NOTE 1: *Special Deluxe Suburban Production Total included in the 34,457 Suburbans built.*

DELUXE SIX — (6-CYLINDER) — SERIES P-20: The Deluxe series were full-size Plymouths. They were still smallish cars, but they were large enough to come in four-door sedan and two-door club coupe bodies. Styling changes for 1950 Plymouth P-20 models paralleled those of the lower-priced cars, although, some of the parts, such as grille members, were actually larger. They looked the same, but were not interchangeable between both series. Two models continued to be offered in the low-level Deluxe trim line. Standard features included Deluxe front fender script, black rubber windshield and rear window moldings, painted dashboard and garnish moldings, and plainer upholstery fabrics. In base form, no rear fender gravel shields were provided. Unlike many other makers, Plymouth did not use black rubber stone guards on its cheaper models. However, chrome shields could be ordered as an option on all Plymouths. To increase rear vision, the rear window glass area was enlarged and now extended to the rear deck region. Small hubcaps were standard equipment on Plymouth Deluxe automobiles.

Deluxe Six Series

Series Number	Body/Style Number	Body Type & Seating	Factory Price	Shipping Weight	Production Total
P-20	N/A	4-dr Sedan-6P	$1,551	3,068 lbs.	87,871
P-20	N/A	2-dr Club Coupe-6P	$1,519	3,040 lbs.	53,890

SPECIAL DELUXE — (6-CYLINDER) — SERIES P-20: The Special Deluxe P-20 series was Plymouth's high-dollar range. These cars had, as standard equipment, bright metal windshield and rear window frames, richer interior fabric choices, woodgrain finish on metal interior panels, and Special Deluxe front fender script. The convertible was officially described as a convertible club coupe, and it used leather upholstery and a power top riser mechanism and came with a simulated leather snap-on boot. The station wagon had the same features outlined for comparable 1949 models, although, its rear fenders and taillights were of the 1949 style. Factory photographs indicate Special Deluxes came with larger hubcaps, but not full wheel covers, and most of these cars seem to have small hubcaps with trim rings. Also, as in 1949, the large cars had slightly bigger tires. Other features found as regular equipment in the Special Deluxe models were armrests on both front doors, cigar lighter, and clock.

Special Deluxe Six Series

Series Number	Body/Style Number	Body Type & Seating	Factory Price	Shipping Weight	Production Total
P-20	N/A	4-dr Sedan-6P	$1,629	3,072 lbs.	234,084
P-20	N/A	2-dr Club Coupe-6P	$1,603	3,041 lbs.	99,361
P-20	N/A	2-dr Convertible-6P	$1,982	3,295 lbs.	12,697
P-20	N/A	4-dr Station Wagon-8P	$2,372	3,353 lbs.	2,057
P-20	N/A	Chassis only	N/A	N/A	2,091

The '51 Plymouth Cambridge club coupe may not be as sleek and graceful as the comparable Fleetline sedan, but it was an example of comfort over styling.

The 1950 Plymouth had improved upon 1949's boxy design and created a slightly sleeker, more modern-looking car. The 1951 Plymouth continued this trend. The hood contour was lower, flatter, smoother and broader, and the front fenders sloped downward at the front. The grille had a full-width, bow-shaped upper bar and a horizontal center blade, which was also slightly bowed. A trio of vertical elements looked more like misplaced bumper guards. The bowed grille bars created a frowning face, something like Hudson had at the same time.

Horizontal parking lights were set into vertical extensions of the upper bar. The full wraparound bumper was of more massive design and had two vertical guards. A plate, with the word "Plymouth" stamped into it, stretched above the grille. Mayflower nose emblems and hood mascots appeared. The Deluxe and Special Deluxe names were gone and replaced with three new names.

Plymouth got a new dash which was plainer but less tied to the art deco 1930s and, therefore, a little more modern.

CONCORD — (6-CYLINDER) — SERIES P-22: The new Concord P-22 series played the same role in the Plymouth lineup as the short-wheelbase Deluxe had in the past. Additional trim included front and rear fender moldings, rocker sill strips, black rubber windshield frame, new hubcaps, upper beltline trim, and Concord fender script. The Concord Suburban was now a two-seat economy station wagon with spare tire carried inside. The Concord Savoy replaced the Special Deluxe Suburban and came with large hubcaps, chrome gravel guards, bright metal window frames, extra trim moldings, and special two-tone luxury upholstery. Standard equipment for the Concord Savoy included front and rear armrests, rear passenger assist straps, rear seat side storage compartments, and sliding central windows. Savoy nameplates were seen on the front fenders. This was now the company's fanciest station wagon-type vehicle, since the woodie was dropped from the P-23 series.

PLYMOUTH I.D. NUMBERS: The serial number on plate on left front door post is the only code used for identification/registration purposes. It consists of a Plymouth prefix "P" and two symbol series number (P-22, P-23). The four or more symbols following this are the production sequence number starting with 1001 at each factory. Engine number near front upper left side of block between first and second cylinders takes same format as serial number, but may not match. Engine number should not be used for identification. Engine numbers sometimes had suffixes: A = .020 inch cylinder overbore; B = .010 inch undersize journals; and diamond-shaped symbol = .008 inch oversize tappet bore. Plymouth factory codes are: M=Detroit, Mich.; LA=Los Angeles, Calif.; E=Evansville, Ind.; and SL=San Leandro, Calif. These codes do not appear in serial number. Chrysler did not use body/style numbers at this time. Serial numbers for 1951 at each factory were as follows: P-22 Deluxe Concord: (M) 18126001-18192309; (E) 24042001-24056628; (LA) 28011001-28015486 and (SL) 28513001-28518903. P-23 Deluxe Cambridge: (M) 15460001-15577561; (E) 22132001-22159468; (LA) 26040001-26045476 and (SL) 26512001-26517909. P-23 Special Deluxe Cranbrook: (M) 12635001-12906467; (E) 20435001-20482924; (LA) 25112001-25124987; (SL) 25531001-25545618. Engine numbers for all three series were P23-1001 and up.

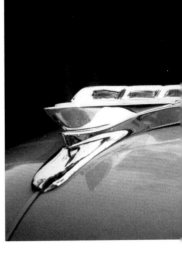

The Mayflower logo looked more like a steamship than a sailing ship in 1951.

Concord Series

Series Number	Body/Style Number	Body Type & Seating	Factory Price	Shipping Weight	Production Total
Deluxe Trim					
P-22	N/A	2-dr Sedan-6P	$1,673	2,969 lbs.	49,139
P-22	N/A	2-dr Coupe-3P	$1,537	2,919 lbs.	14,255
P-22	N/A	2-dr Suburban-5P	$2,064	3,124 lbs.	76,520
Special Savoy Trim					
P-22	N/A	2-dr Suburban-5P	$2,182	3,184 lbs.	Note 1

NOTE 1: *Production Total of Savoy Special Suburban included in Suburban 76,520 total.*

NOTE 2: *Production Total covers both 1951 and 1952 Series P-22 Plymouths.*

CAMBRIDGE — (6-CYLINDER) — SERIES P-23: The new Cambridge models played the same role in the Plymouth lineup as the former standard wheelbase Deluxes with comparable body styles.

The word "Cambridge" appeared on fender-sides, above the horizontal trim spear. All 1951 Plymouths came with interior colors selected to match the exterior finish. The Cambridge could be ordered with more options.

Cambridge

Series Number	Body/Style Number	Body Type & Seating	Factory Price	Shipping Weight	Production Total
P-23	N/A	4-dr Sedan-6P	$1,739	3,104 lbs.	179,417
P-23	N/A	2-dr Club Coupe-6P	$1,703	3,059 lbs.	101,784

NOTE 1: *Production Total covers both 1951 and 1952 Plymouth P-23 series.*

CRANBROOK — (6-CYLINDER) — SERIES P-23: The 1951 Cranbrook models played the starring role in the annual Plymouth revue. They replaced the former Special Deluxe line and embodied similar attributes. Block letters spelled out the model designation at the upper, trailing front fender area. The new Belvedere two-door hardtop had the fashionable pillarless, airy look that was growing in popularity at the time. It featured a smoothly wrapped-around three-piece backlight, wedge-shaped rear side windows, cloth and simulated leather upholstery and special Belvedere nameplates on the front fendersides. A convertible was another exclusive offering in Cranbrook level trim, but the station wagon was gone. Plymouth's classiest utility model this season was the Savoy in the short wheelbase P-22 series.

The 1952 Plymouth Cambridge sedan appeared in sales literature with blackwall tires because of the Korean War shortages.

Phil Hall Collection

Due to the outbreak of war in Korea, Plymouth continued its 1951 models into 1952 with only surface changes. The emblem on the nose of the cars was slightly redesigned. Signature style chrome script plates were used to adorn the front fenders as model identification trim. At the rear, the manufacturer's nameplate was repositioned from above the trunk emblem to a relief cut into the top of the emblem. Prices were increased with permission from government agencies, but the series nomenclature didn't change. Consequently, output figures for 1951 and 1952 Plymouths are recorded as a single total. Overdrive transmission was a Plymouth technical addition this season. America's number three maker had not offered this feature on previous postwar models. By the end of the run, nearly 51,670 cars had this option installed. Neither automatic nor semi-automatic transmissions were yet available in Plymouth automobiles.

It was also hard to buy a Plymouth equipped with optional whitewall tires this year. Raw material supplies were greatly diminished, due to restrictions imposed during the Korean conflict. Despite National Production Administration (NPA) ceilings on auto manufacturing during the Korean War, Plymouth continued as the output leader among Chrysler Corp. divisions. The company produced approximately 50 percent of all Chrysler automobiles built this year.

Solex tinted glass appeared on the options list for all Plymouths.

CONCORD — (6 CYLINDER) — SERIES P-22: Very few Concords came off the assembly line for the 1952 model year. The short wheelbase Concord was dropped from production in October, 1952.

PLYMOUTH I.D. NUMBERS: The serial number plate on the left front door post is the only code used for identification/registration purposes. It consists of a Plymouth prefix "P" and two symbol series number (P-22, P-23). The four or more symbols following this are the production sequence number starting with 1001 at each factory. Engine number near front upper left side of block between first and second cylinders takes same format as serial number, but may not match. Engine number should not be used for identification. Engine numbers sometimes had suffixes: A = .020 inch cylinder overbore; B = .010 inch undersize journals; and diamond-shaped symbol = .008 inch oversize tappet bore. Plymouth factory codes are: M=Detroit, Mich.; LA=Los Angeles, Calif.; E=Evansville, Ind.; and SL=San Leandro, Calif. These codes do not appear in serial number. Chrysler did not use body style numbers at this time. Serial numbers for 1952 at each factory changed as follows: Concord: (M) 18192501-18223600; (E) 24056701-24063833; (LA) 28015701-2801555 and (SL) 28519101-28522352. Cambridge: (MA) 15577801-1566660; (E) 22159601-22181520; (LA) 26045701-26049991 and (SL) 26518201-26523546. Cranbrook: (M) 12906701-13066238; (E) 20485001-20516075; (LA) 25125301-25134190 and (SL) 25546101-25555957. Engine numbers for all series were P23-1001 and up.

Concord Series

Series Number	Body/Style Number	Body Type & Seating	Factory Price	Shipping Weight	Production Total
Deluxe Trim					
P-22	N/A	2-dr Sedan-6P	$1,753	2,959 lbs.	Note 1
P-22	N/A	2-dr Coupe-3P	$1,610	2,893 lbs.	Note 1
P-22	N/A	2-dr Suburban-5P	$2,163	3,145 lbs.	Note 1
Special Savoy Trim					
P-22	N/A	2-dr Suburban-5P	$2,287	3,165 lbs.	Note 1

NOTE 1: *See 1951 Plymouth production totals. Figures for both years are lumped together with no annual breakout available.*

CAMBRIDGE — (6-CYLINDER) — SERIES P-23: The 1952 Cambridge was a mildly face-lifted version of the previous comparable model. The only variations between both years were number codes, prices and redesigned nameplates plus new hood and trunk emblems.

Cambridge Series

Series Number	Body/Style Number	Body Type & Seating	Factory Price	Shipping Weight	Production Total
P-23	N/A	4-dr Sedan-6P	$1,822	3,068 lbs.	Note 1
P-23	N/A	2-dr Club Coupe-6P	$1,784	3,030 lbs.	Note 1

NOTE 1: *See 1951 Plymouth production totals. Figures for both years are lumped together with no annual breakout available.*

CRANBROOK — (6-CYLINDER) — SERIES P-23: As is the case with other 1952 Plymouths, the Cranbrook models were merely a continuation of the basic 1951 product for another year. The only annual changes were new model identification script, redesigned hood mascots and slightly revised trim at the front and rear. Even the P-23 series designation was carried through again. The Belvedere received some extra attention in that its identification badge was repositioned to the rear roof pillar, and the car employed a different type of two-tone finish. The top color with this paint scheme extended onto the rear quarter sheet metal. While the front and sides of the body were done in one tone, the roof, rear deck lid and deck lid surrounding area were painted a second shade that contrasted with the main color.

Two-tone colors were attractive on the sporty 1952 Plymouth Cranbrook Belvedere two-door hardtop

Phil Hall Collection

Cranbrook Series

Series Number	Body/Style Number	Body Type & Seating	Factory Price	Shipping Weight	Production Total
P-23	N/A	4-dr Sedan-6P	$1,914	3,088 lbs.	Note 1
P-23	N/A	2-dr Club Coupe-6P	$1,883	3,046 lbs.	Note 1
P-23	N/A	2-dr Hardtop Coupe-6P	$2,216	3,105 lbs.	Note 1
P-23	N/A	2-dr Convertible-6P	$2,329	3,256 lbs.	Note 1

NOTE 1: See 1951 Plymouth production totals. Figures for both years are lumped together with no annual breakout available.

Engine:

PLYMOUTH SIX: Inline. L head. Cast iron block. Displacement: 217.8 cid. Bore and stroke: 3.25 x 4.375 inches. Compression ratio: 7.0:1. Brake hp: 97 at 3600 rpm. Four main bearings. Solid valve lifters. Carburetor: Carter Type BB one-barrel Model D6H2

CHASSIS FEATURES: Wheelbase: (Concord) 111 inches; (Cambridge, Cranbrook) 118-½ inches. Overall length: (Concord) 188-½ inches; (Cambridge, Cranbrook) 193-⅞ inches. Front tread: (all models) 55-⅞ inches. Rear tread: (all models) 58-7/16 inches. Tires: (Concord sedan and coupe) 6.40 x 15-inch; (Cranbrook) 6.70 x 15-inch.

OPTIONS: Heater and defroster. Radio and antenna. Wheel trim rings. Full disc wheel covers. Solex tinted safety glass. Bumper guards. Grille guards. Spotlight. Fog light. Outside rearview mirror. White sidewall tires. External sun shade. Traffic light viewer. Rear fender chrome gravel shields. License plate frames. Seat covers. Rear seat speaker. Glove compartment lock. Electric clock. Special body colors. Mudguard flaps. Three-speed manual transmission was standard. Overdrive transmission ($102). Heavy-duty air cleaner was available at extra cost. Available rear axle gear ratios: (P-22) 3.73:1 or 3.90:1; (P-23) 3.90:1 or 4.10:1.

HISTORICAL FOOTNOTES: The 1952 Plymouths were introduced on Jan. 4, 1952. Sales went down 23.74 percent, largely due to the outbreak of fighting in Korea. Model year production peaked at 368,000 units. Calendar year sales of 474,836 cars were recorded. D.S. Eddins was the chief executive officer of the company this year. On a calendar year basis, Plymouth manufactured 21,290 Belvederes, 4,269 convertibles and 35,885 Suburbans between Jan. 1, 1952, and the same date a year later. Some of these were 1953 models that entered production in the fall of 1952, earlier than usual. Overdrive transmission was a new option this year and was installed in 61,710 Plymouths built to 1952 specifications. The 111-inch wheelbase Concord line was dropped in October 1952. Plymouth bodies were built by Briggs Manufacturing Co. Plymouths were assembled at Detroit, Mich.; Evansville, Ind. and Los Angeles and San Leandro, Calif. The Detroit plant had 1,393,497 square feet under one roof and was one-half mile long. The National Production Administration (NPA) established production quotas this year, based on Korean war materials allotments. Aircraft hulls were constructed, under government contract, in the Evansville factory with the first one delivered late in 1952.

"The 'chair-height' seats give yielding but solid support. Our test crew was as fresh after three days of cross country driving as the start."
"The Plymouth is *inexpensively* but not *cheaply* made."

Motor Trend, April 1952

Plymouth celebrated its 25th anniversary this season with all-new styling. Plymouth had a more modern body with a one-piece windshield. Detachable rear fenders were finally abandoned, and there was no hint of a rear fender bulge that harked back to the 1930s when rear fenders were bolted on. Plymouth decorated the front fenders and rear quarters with wide, horizontal, stamped body lines that gave some shape to an otherwise rather plain body. The main grille bar and parking lights formed a horizontal V-shape, Plymouth and De Soto had the advantage of having truly new grilles to go with their new body designs. Chrysler and Dodge grilles resembled their 1951 and '52 grille a little too much and didn't match the new car. The "Mayflower" hood ornament was fully redesigned. A new hood emblem incorporated the name Plymouth and the glove compartment was placed in the center of the instrument panel. The fuel filler pipe was located below the deck lid on the left side. This was the greatest resemblance Plymouth had to arch-rival Chevrolet since before World War II, and Plymouth's design was much more competitive.

The 1953 Plymouths were downsized, along with the Dodges, by former president, and then chairman of the board K. T. Keller. The design was criticized at that time.

The Plymouth was a decidedly small car because Chrysler Corporation executive K.T. Keller tried to limit the size of the economy cars. The "smaller on the outside and bigger on the inside" strategy had iffy results. Keller wasn't wrong, but he was several years too early.

Plymouth introduced its first automatic transmissions ever. Hy-Drive put a modern torque converter between the engine and the three-speed manual transmissions, much like Chrysler had before World War II with Fluid Drive. The driver could shift the Plymouth through the gears with, theoretically, some torque multiplication from the torque converter. Plymouth suggested the gearshift should stay in third gear where the steering column-mounted gear selector denoted drive. In high gear, the torque converter would make all the ratio changes, and the Plymouth would drive more like a Buick Dynaflow or non-shifting 1950 to '52 Chevrolet Powerglide. Yet, Hy-Drive was a disappointment because of two quirks – one mechanical quirk and one marketing quirk. The mechanical quirk was that the torque converter shared oil with the engine and made a very complicated system. The marketing quirk was just when Plymouth brought out the non-shifting Hy-Drive, Chevrolet installed a valve body that made the Powerglide a fully automatic, self-shifting transmission. So Plymouth was again behind the Chevrolet transmission curve.

CAMBRIDGE — (6-CYLINDER) — SERIES P24-1: The Cambridge line was the base offering and used the same wheelbase as the more expensive Plymouths. Cambridge identification features included black rubber windshield frames, Cambridge front fender script on passenger cars, and Suburban front fender script on station wagons. These cars had no side spears, no gravel shields, no tail ornaments and stationary rear vent windows. Small hubcaps were standard equipment. A new feature was a "one-third/two-third" type front seat, which was used in all two-door models. New equipment features included splay-mounted rear leaf springs, Oriflow shock absorbers, cyclebond brake linings and floating engine oil intake.

The 1953 Plymouth station wagon was the perfect choice for the people who lived in a growing American phenomenon, the suburbs.

PLYMOUTH I.D. NUMBERS: The serial number plate was located on the left door post. Serial number starts with prefix (P=Plymouth) and three digit series code: 24-1; 24-2, followed by sequential production number starting at 1001 at each factory. Factory codes: M=Detroit, Mich.; LA=Los Angeles, Calif.; E=Evansville, Ind.; and SL=San Leandro, Calif. These codes do not appear in serial number. Engine numbers near front upper left of block between cylinders one and two. Engine number resembles serial number, but may not match. Engine numbers should not be used for identification. Prefix symbols changed to P24-1=Cambridge and P24-2=Cranbrook. Serial numbers at each factory were: Cambridge: (M) 13070001-13505308; (E) 2052001-20657000; (LA) 25136001-25161846; and (SL) 25560001-25588345. Cranbrook: same number range as Cambridge. Engine numbers for both series were P24-1001 through P24-628721.

Cambridge Series

Series Number	Body/Style Number	Body Type & Seating	Factory Price	Shipping Weight	Production Total
P24-1	N/A	4-dr Sedan-6P	$1,745	2,983 lbs.	93,585
P24-1	N/A	2-dr Club Cpe-6P	$1,707	2,943 lbs.	1,050
P24-1	N/A	2-dr Bus Coupe-3P	$1,598	2,888 lbs.	6,975
P24-1	N/A	2-dr Suburban-6P	$2,044	3,129 lbs.	43,545
P24-1	N/A	2-dr Sedan-6P	—	—	56,800

CRANBROOK — (6-CYLINDER) — SERIES P24-2: Cranbrooks shared all 1953 styling changes but had a higher level of trim and appointments. Identification points included chrome windshield moldings, chrome sweep spears on front and rear fenders, chrome gravel shields, chrome "fishtail" ornaments, operable vent wings in all doors, and special front fender nameplates. The signature script on passenger cars read Cranbrook or Belvedere, while those on the Suburban station wagon read Savoy. The Belvedere was marketed as a luxury level, two-door pillarless hardtop. Its special features included a band of chrome and medallions on the rear roof pillar, higher grade interior trim, and fancier interior colors coordinated with the exterior color. The Savoy also had special upholstery and interior appointments to set it apart from the basic Suburban. The convertible, as usual, had leather grained trim, power top riser, special door panels and a new, zip-out pliable plastic rear window.

Cranbrook Series

Series Number	Body/Style Number	Body Type & Seating	Factory Price	Shipping Weight	Production Total
P-24-2	N/A	4-dr Sedan-6P	$1,853	3,023 lbs.	298,976
P-24-2	N/A	2-dr Club Coupe-6P	$1,823	2,971 lbs.	92,102
P-24-2	N/A	2-dr Belvedere Hardtop-6P	$2,044	3,027 lbs.	35,185
P-24-2	N/A	2-dr Savoy Suburban-6P	$2,187	3,170 lbs.	12,089
P-24-2	N/A	2-dr Convertible Coupe-6P	$2,200	3,193 lbs.	6,301
P2402	N/A	Chassis only	—	—	843

NOTE 1: *2,250 Belvedere sedans were built in addition to the above total.*

NOTE 2: *760 Belvedere sport coupes were built in addition to the above total.*

Engine:

PLYMOUTH SIX: Inline. L-head. Cast iron block. Displacement: 217.8 cid. Bore and stroke: 3.24 x 4.375 inches. Compression ratio: 7.1:1. Brake hp: 100 at 3600 rpm. Four main bearings. Solid valve lifters. Carburetor: Carter Type BB one-barrel Model D6H2.

CHASSIS FEATURES: Wheelbase (all models) 114 inches. Overall length: (all models) 189-⅛ inches. Front tread: (all models) 55-⅞ inches. Rear tread: (all models) 58-7/16 inches. Tires: (all models) 6.70 x 15-inch.

OPTIONS: Heater and defroster ($45). Radio ($100). Tinted glass ($31). Directional signals ($17). Windshield washer ($11). Back-up lights. Chrome wheel discs. Chrome wire wheels ($293). Painted wire wheels. Wire spoke wheel covers, set ($99). White sidewall tires. Grille guard. Bumper wing guards. Front fender molding, Cambridge. Rear fender molding, Cambridge. Chrome grille molding, Cambridge. Chrome gravel shields. Chrome exhaust extension. Taxicab package. Wheel trim rings. Outside sun shade. Traffic light viewer. Spotlight. Fog lamps. Seat covers. License plate frames. Three-speed manual transmission was standard. Overdrive transmission ($98). Semi-automatic transmission ($146). Available rear axle gear ratios: (standard) 3.73:1; (overdrive) 4.10:1.

HISTORICAL FOOTNOTES: The 1953 Plymouths were introduced Nov. 20, 1952, and the Ghia-built XX-500 prototype appeared in dealer auto shows from March 14 through 22, 1953. Sales increased 39.5 percent during Plymouth's 25th anniversary year and the eight-millionth Plymouth was made in September. Model year production peaked at 636,000 units. Calendar year sales of 662,515 cars were recorded. J. P. Mansfield was the chief executive officer of the company this year. Hy-Drive transmission and Synchro Silent Drive were introduced. A total of 600,447 Plymouths were registered in calendar 1953. On March 23, 1953, Plymouth reduced prices on its models by an average of $100. The 1953 production totals marked a new, all-time high for Plymouth Division. Chrysler purchased the Briggs Manufacturing Co. on Dec. 29, 1953. Hy-Drive was first introduced in March 1953. By July, 25 percent of all Plymouths produced were ordered with Hy-Drive. The Detroit factory accounted for 70 percent of Plymouth's total production. During the calendar year, 9,900 Plymouths were built with power steering (most likely all being 1954 models). For the model year, 109,300 Plymouths had overdrive attachments. Plymouth built its last Grumman Albatross. On March 23, 1953, prices on all models were slashed an average of $100. This helped spur an all-time sales record for the model year.

The 1953 Plymouth Mayflower hood ornament was back to looking like a sailing ship after a few years of looking more like a steam ship.

Despite being new on the outside, the 1953 Plymouth offered an option that continued a traditional offering from the 1930s, overdrive.

The premier Plymouth sedan in 1954 was this Belvedere model.

Annual styling revisions amounted to a minor face lift over the previous season, although model offerings were substantially rearranged. The Plymouth name now appeared at the center of the main horizontal grille bar with wraparound chrome moldings on each side. The headlights took on a recessed look by widening the chrome-plated surrounds. Circular front parking lamps were used and mounted at the outboard ends of the lower horizontal grille bar.

On Feb. 26, 1954, fully-automatic PowerFlite transmission was added to the optional equipment list. Plymouth buyers could order cars with three-speed manual overdrive, semi-automatic, or automatic transmission. A total of about 75,000 of all 1954 Plymouths came with the latter unit attached.

PLAZA — (6-CYLINDER) — SERIES P25-1: The Plaza line was the base Plymouth series for 1954. Plaza models used black rubber gravel shields and had Plaza front fender script. Power steering was introduced as a new option, but was used in only about 20,000 cars built in this calendar year, but some of these were 1955 models manufactured in the fall of 1954. The Plaza four-door sedan had stationary rear vent panes. Two-door styles featured the "one-third/two-thirds"-type front seat.

PLYMOUTH I.D. NUMBERS: The serial number plate was located on the left door post. Serial number started with prefix (P=Plymouth) and two symbol series code (P25-1=Plaza; P25-2=Savoy and P25-3=Belvedere) followed by sequential production number starting at 1001 at each factory. Factory codes: M=Detroit, Mich.; LA=Los Angeles, Calif.; E=Evansville, Ind.; and SL=San Leandro, Calif. These codes do not appear in the serial number. Engine numbers were near the front upper left of the block between cylinders one and two. The engine number resembles the serial number, but may not match. Engine numbers should not be used for identification. Serial numbers at each factory were: (M) 13506001-13829336; (E) 20658001-20739829; (LA) 25163001-25175377; (SL) 25590001-25606284. Engine numbers P25-1001 through P25-243000 were used until Feb. 25, 1954. Engine numbers past this date were P25-243001 to P25-454271. The three series were manufactured in mixed production fashion and used the same range of serial and engine numbers.

"The clutch-assisted Hy Drive… teams up with power steering, good vision and the car's short overhang to provide some of the easiest city-type driving to be found in any class."

Motor Trend, January 1954

Plaza Series

Series Number	Body/Style Number	Body Type & Seating	Factory Price	Shipping Weight	Production Total
P25-1	N/A	4-dr Sedan-6P	$1,745	3,004 lbs.	43,077
P25-1	N/A	2-dr Club Coupe-6P	$1,707	2,943 lbs.	27,976
P25-1	N/A	2-dr Business Coupe-3P	$1,598	2,889 lbs.	5,000
P25-1	N/A	2-dr Suburban-6P	$2,044	3,122 lbs.	35,937
P25-1	N/A	Chassis only	—	—	1
P25-1	N/A	2-dr Club Coupe-6P	—	—	1,275

SAVOY — (6-CYLINDER) — SERIES P25-2: The Savoy nameplate changed from a model to a series designation this year. It was used to identify Plymouth's middle-priced line and also signified a higher level of trim and appointments. Identification features of the Savoy included full-length side body moldings, newly designed chrome gravel shields and Savoy signatures placed on the cowl side area of front fenders. Bright metal windshield frames replaced the black rubber-type used with Plazas. The Savoy interior was a bit fancier, too, but most of its extras qualified as exterior trim. The highest grade fabrics and furnishings were reserved for Belvederes. A surprise was the Suburbans were not normally provided with Savoy level trim, even though the name had been taken from the fancy all-steel station wagon model. The Chrysler Historical Archives indicate that a small number of Savoy Suburbans were manufactured.

Savoy Series

Series Number	Body/Style Number	Body Type & Seating	Factory Price	Shipping Weight	Production Total
P25-2	N/A	4-dr Sedan-6P	$1,853	3,036 lbs.	139,383
P25-2	N/A	2-dr Club Sedan-6P	$1,815	2,986 lbs.	25,396
P25-2	N/A	2-dr Club Coupe-6P	$1,823	2,982 lbs.	30,700
P25-2	N/A	2-dr Suburban	—	—	450
P25-2	N/A	Chassis only	—	—	3,588

BELVEDERE — (6-CYLINDER) — SERIES P25-3: The Belvedere nameplate no longer identified only the two-door pillarless hardtop. This designation now labeled a four-model lineup including the hardtop, a sedan, a convertible, and a fancy all-steel Suburban station wagon. Identification points included all extras found on Savoys plus full wheel discs, chrome "fishtail" rear fender top fins, full-length rocker sill moldings and Belvedere front fender script. The hardtop and sedan also featured roof pillar medallions. The convertible had similar medallions behind the gravel shields and the station wagon (Suburban) had fin-less rear fenders, making each model slightly distinctive. Dressier interior furnishings were used on all of these cars. They included richer combinations of fabrics, extra armrests, special dashboard trim, Deluxe steering wheel, clock, and fancier garnish moldings. In the spring, a special trim option was released for Belvedere hardtops and convertibles. It added a narrow, fin-shaped chrome molding below the side window openings, with the area above finished in contrasting color. When the production of 1954 Plymouths ended, on Aug. 20, 1954, Plymouth dropped the Hy-Drive semi-automatic transmission.

Belvedere Series

Series Number	Body/Style Number	Body Type & Seating	Factory Price	Shipping Weight	Production Total
P25-3	N/A	4-dr Sedan-6P	$1,933	3,050 lbs.	106,601
P25-3	N/A	2-dr Hardtop Coupe-6P	$2,125	3,038 lbs.	25,592
P25-3	N/A	2-dr Convertible Coupe-6P	$2,281	3,273 lbs.	6,900
P25-3	N/A	2-dr Suburban-6P	$2,268	3,186 lbs.	9,241
P25-3	N/A	Chassis only	—	—	2,031

Engines:

PLYMOUTH SIX: Inline. L-head. Cast iron block. Displacement: 217.8 cid. Bore and stroke: 3.24 x 4.375 inches. Compression ratio: 7.1:1. Brake hp: 100 at 3600 rpm. Four main bearings. Solid valve lifters. Carburetor: Carter Type BB one-barrel Model D6H2.

OPTIONAL PLYMOUTH SIX: Inline. L-head. Cast iron block. Displacement: 230.2 cid. Bore and stroke: 3.25 x 4.625 inches. Compression ratio: 7.25:1. Brake hp: 110 at 3600 rpm. Four main bearings. Solid valve lifters. Carburetor: Carter Type BB one-barrel Model BB-D6H2. (This "high head" engine was optional on cars late in 1954.)

CHASSIS FEATURES: Wheelbase: (all models) 114 inches. Overall length: (Suburban) 190-¼ inches; (passenger cars) 193-½ inches. Front tread: (all models) 55-⅞ inches. Rear tread: (all models) 58-7/16 inches. Tires: (all models) 6.70 x 15.

OPTIONS: Power steering ($139.75). Radio ($82.50). Heater ($56.25). Directional signals ($13.30). Whitewall tires, exchange ($26.65). "Egg Cup" electric clock. Wire wheel covers ($59.15). Full wheel discs ($14). Wire wheels, chrome ($279.50). Wire wheels, painted ($102.15). Two-tone paint. Back-up lights. Bumper wing guards. Grille guard. Wheel trim rings. Seat covers. Vent-A-Shades. Solex tinted glass ($21). Wood weave door trim, convertible and sport coupe ($37.65). Continental spare wheel mount ($129). Outside sun visor. Traffic lamp viewer. Deluxe trim, four-door ($108). Custom trim, four-door ($188). Power brakes ($37). Three-speed manual transmission was standard. Overdrive transmission ($99.55). Semi-automatic transmission ($145.80); PowerFlite fully automatic transmission ($189). Six-cylinder 230.2 cid/110 hp "high head" engine. Available rear axle gear ratios: (standard) 3.73:1; (overdrive) 4.10:1 and (Hy-Drive) 3.73:1.

HISTORICAL FOOTNOTES: The 1954 Plymouths were introduced Oct. 15, 1953, and the Belvedere appeared in dealer showrooms on the same date. Model year production peaked at 433,000 units. Calendar year sales of 399,900 cars were recorded. J.P. Mansfield was the chief executive officer of the company this year. Robert Anderson, who later became Chrysler Division head officer, was Plymouth's chief engineer. Chrysler's Chelsea, Michigan, proving grounds opened this year. When the proving grounds were dedicated in June, one of the special cars seen was a Plymouth Belvedere hardtop with a gas turbine engine. On March 15, 1954, power brakes were introduced as a Plymouth option at $36.55. A total of 61,000 1954 models had PowerFlite fully automatic transmission and 75,000 had Hy-Drive semi-automatic attachments. Hy-Drive was dropped at the end of the 1954 model run. Production of 1954 models stopped on Aug. 13, 1954. Factory dream cars seen this year included the Plymouth-Ghia Explorer.

The 1955 Plymouths were completely restyled with new longer, lower bodies. All sheet metal was new and more modern. The upper edge of the body line ran in a straight line from front to rear. A sweeping roofline was supported by wraparound glass at both ends. The side panels were slab shaped. Hood and deck were flatter. At the front, the fenders hooded the single headlamps. The grille cavity was highlighted by two wing-shaped, horizontal blades that were joined at the center by a ribbed horizontal tie-bar. Chrysler Corporation brake and clutch pedals no longer went through the floor but were suspended under the dash. That change conveniently moved the master cylinder to the firewall from under the floor where it had been since the 1920s.

The 1955 Belvedere two-door hardtop marked a new era for Plymouth.

The Plymouth dash was perfectly symmetrical – maybe a little too symmetrical. On the left end of the dash, the large round speedometer was accompanied by two gauges, and on the right-hand end of the dash, the large round radio speaker was accompanied by two gauges – placing two of the dash gauges in front of the passenger and nearly out of sight of the driver. The gear selector for the PowerFlite automatic transmission was a lever, called the "Flite lever." It stuck out of the dash to the right of the steering column.

This was one of the most exciting years in the history of the American auto industry, and some General Motors dealers set records in 1955 that still stand into the 21st century. The GM publicity machine made such a big deal out of the new Chevrolet V-8 that many collectors forget Plymouth not only went V-8 in 1955, but Plymouth brought out two V-8s. Chevrolet printed a pocket-sized booklet called "Fingertip Facts for the 1955 Chevrolet" for salesman to carry with them as they dazzled customers with the new Chevrolet. The booklet denegrated the new Plymouth V-8 as just being a "modified truck engine," forgetting to mention that the 241-cid Hemi-V-8 had performed magnificently on the Pikes Peak race the year before. The larger Plymouth V-8 would have performed even better hooked to the PowerFlite, and both engines were far more technologically advanced than the Chevrolet V-8. If only Chrysler's publicity machine had been as enthusiastic as the GM machine. The memories of the 1955 Plymouths might rival the Chevrolets.

"The only effort you have to expend in this car is pointing it in the direction you want to go, pushing down on the throttle and, for all intents and purposes, you are there."

"All this adds up to a product that's going to satisfy a lot of people."

Walt Moron, Motor Trend, February 1955

Plymouth received the fully automatic PowerFlite automatic transmission in 1955 and a Flight Selector lever on the dash.

PLAZA — (6-CYLINDER/V-8) — SERIES P26/P27: The Plaza represented the low-priced line, but could be had with either six-cylinder or V-8 power plants. No extraneous trim appeared on this series. Chrome ornamentation was limited to a large signature script, placed ahead of the front wheel opening. A fin-shaped hood ornament was used. Windshield framing was in black rubber. Cars with V-8 power had V-shaped emblems attached to the hood and trunk. A Plymouth badge occupied the hood. At the rear, vertical taillights were set into the reversed fender tips. Buyers were able to order side spear moldings as optional equipment after mid year. These moldings ran from below the taillight to the middle of the front door and then slanted forward, hitting the rocker sill at the door's front lower corner. Sales features included many new items such as tubeless tires, follow-through starter, and push-button door handles. Plainer-looking cloth upholstery was standard in the Plaza, but vinyl combinations were available at a slightly extra cost. A business coupe was still provided in this model range. It used the two-door sedan body shell with only a front seat and storage space in the rear compartment.

PLYMOUTH I.D. NUMBERS: The serial number plate was located on the left door post. The serial number started with the prefix (P=Plymouth) and series code (P26=six-cylinder; P27=V-8) followed by sequential production number starting at 1001 at each factory. Factory codes: M=Detroit, Mich.; LA=Los Angeles, Calif.; E=Evansville, Ind.; and SL=San Leandro, Calif. These codes do not appear in the serial number. Six-cylinder engine numbers near front upper left of block between cylinders one and two. V-8 engine numbers on flat surface at front of block between two cylinder heads. The engine number resembled the serial number, but may not match. Engine numbers should not be used for identification. Serial numbers at each factory were kept according to the type of engine and changed as follows: P26 six-cylinder: (M) 13835001-14119261; (E) 20745001-20819358 and (LA) 25180001-25200109. P27 V-8: (M) 15630001-15871476; (E) 22118201-22244749 and (LA) 26524001-26549993 and 26500000-26500290. Engine numbers were as follows: P26-1001 to P26-378770, P27-1001 to P27-60200 and P27-60201 to P27-298919.

Plaza Series

Series Number	Body/Style Number	Body Type & Seating	Factory Price	Shipping Weight	Production Total
P26/27	N/A	4-dr Sedan	$1,756/$1,859	3,129/3,246	84,156
P26/27	N/A	2-dr Club Sedan-6P	$1,713/$1,816	3,089/3,202	53,610
P26	N/A	2-dr Business Coupe-3P	$1,614	3,025	4,882
P26/27	N/A	2-dr Suburban-6P	$2,052/$2,155	3,261/3,389	31,788
P26/27	N/A	4-dr Suburban-6P	$2,133/$2,237	3,282/3,408	15,442

NOTE 1: *Data above slash for six-cylinder/below slash for V-8.*

NOTE 2: *The three-passenger business coupe came only with six-cylinder power.*

ALL-NEW PLYMOUTH '55

See it...drive it...today at your Plymouth dealer's. A great new car for the YOUNG IN HEART

Plymouth stressed a "Young at Heart" image in 1955 attempting to reach a younger audience.

SAVOY — (6-CYLINDER/V-8) — SERIES P26/P27: The Savoy was Plymouth's mid-priced model range in 1955. Standard equipment included slightly dressier interiors, chrome windshield frames, a bright metal roof gutter rail, chrome trim on the rear deck overhang, a horizontal sweep spear molding high on front fenders and doors, and Savoy front fender signature script. A Sport Tone trim option was available on the Savoy after mid year at slight extra cost. General styling features are the same as those outlined for 1955 Plazas. Cars with V-8 power had V-shaped hood and deck insignia. Sixes of all trim levels were designated as part of the P26 series, while V-8s were P27 models.

Savoy Series

Series Number	Body/Style Number	Body Type & Seating	Factory Price	Shipping Weight	Production Total
P26/27	N/A	4-dr Sedan-6P	$1,855/$1,958	3,154/3,265 lbs.	162,741
P26/27	N/A	2-dr Club Sedan-6P	$1,812/$1,915	3,109/3,224 lbs.	74,880

NOTE 1: Data above slash for six-cylinder/below slash for V-8.

BELVEDERE — (6-CYLINDER/V-8) — SERIES P26/P27: The Belvedere was the high-priced Plymouth line. It had the same general styling features described for other models, with richer interior and exterior finish. All body styles had the Belvedere front fender script, chrome windshield and rear window moldings, chrome trim on the rear deck lid overhang, chrome trim inside the headlight hoods, moldings decorating the tail lamps, and bright metal highlights on the rear roof pillar. Sedans and station wagons had full-length chrome sweep spears on their sides. The sport coupe and convertible had special contrasting color sweep panels as standard equipment. The panel was formed by the side molding arrangement and two-tone paint treatment. A horizontal spear ran from the headlamp hood to the mid-door area. A second horizontal spear ran from above the tail lamp to the middle of the door. Forward slanting moldings intersected the front spear below the front vent window and below the windshield post. The shorter one, below the vent window, also intersected the lower horizontal piece. The longer one dropped to the rocker sill at the mid-door point. Panels underneath the lower horizontal molding and between the slanting pieces were finished in a contrasting color, usually matching the roof color. A small crest-type emblem was placed between the slanting moldings on the door. Belvedere upholstery came in especially rich combinations, such as Jacquard "Black Magic" Boucle. Deluxe steering wheels, dual ashtrays, armrests, clock, and special courtesy lights were included as regular attributes.

Belvedere Series

Series Number	Body/Style Number	Body Type & Seating	Factory Price	Shipping Weight	Production Total
P26/27	N/A	4-dr Sedan-6P	$1,954/$2,057	3,159/3,267	160,984
P26/27	N/A	2-dr Club Sedan-6P	$1,911/$2,014	3,129/3,228	41,645
P26/27	N/A	2-dr Hardtop Coupe-6P	$2,088/$2,192	3,149/3,261	47,375
P27	N/A	2-dr Convertible-6P	$2,326	3,409	8,473
P26/27	N/A	4-dr Suburban-6P	$2,297/$2,400	3,330/3,475	18,488

NOTE 1: *Data above slash for six/below slash for V-8.*

NOTE 2: *Belvedere convertible came only as a V-8.*

NOTE 3: *786 Belvedere four-door sedans; 100 club coupes; 93 hardtops and 21 Suburbans were built for Canada.*

NOTE 4: *Plymouth made 10 Savoy chassis-only and one Belvedere chassis-only.*

Engines:

SIX: Inline. L-head. Cast iron block. Displacement: 230.2 cid. Bore and stroke: 3.25 x 4.625 inches. Compression ratio: 7.4:1. Brake hp: 117 at 3600 rpm. Four main bearings. Solid valve lifters. Carburetor: Carter Type BB one-barrel Model 2063SA.

HY-FIRE V-8: Overhead valve. Cast iron block. Displacement: 241 cid. Bore and stroke: 3.44 x 3.25 inches. Compression ratio: 7.6:1. Brake hp: 157 at 4400 rpm. Five main bearings. Hydraulic (non-adjustable) valve lifters. Carburetor: Carter Type BBD two-barrel Model 2262S.

OPTIONAL V-8: Overhead valve. Cast iron block. Displacement: 259.2 cid. Bore and stroke: 3.563 x 3.25 inches. Compression ratio: 7.6:1. Brake hp: 167 (optional 177) at 4400 rpm. Five main bearings. Hydraulic (non-adjustable) valve lifters. Carburetor: Carter Type BBD two-barrel Model 2155S (optional Carter four-barrel Model WCFB-2253S).

CHASSIS FEATURES: Wheelbase: (all models) 115 inches. Overall length: (all models) 203.8 inches. Front tread: (all models) 58-13/32 inches. Rear tread: (all models) 58-½ inches. Tires: (all models) 6.70 x 15-inch.

Plymouth was an important ingredient in the first wave of Virgil Exner's Forward Look in 1955.

OPTIONS: Power brakes ($35). Power steering ($90). Air conditioning ($525). Power seat ($42). Power windows ($95). Radio ($83). Standard heater ($45). Deluxe heater ($70). Whitewalls, exchange ($25). Full wheel discs. Wire wheel discs. Grille guard. Seat covers. Dual exhaust. Oil filter. Rear seat speaker. Two-tone paint. Tinted Solex glass. Bumper guards. Variable speed electric wipers. Windshield washer. Three-speed manual transmission was standard. Overdrive transmission ($100). Automatic transmission ($165). V-8 240 cid/157 hp two-barrel engine. V-8 260 cid/167 hp two-barrel engine. V-8 260 cid/177 hp four-barrel engine. Available rear axle gear ratios: (standard) 3.73:1; (automatic) 3.54:1; (overdrive) 4.00:1.

Plymouth's Savoy sedan attracted buyers seeking both style and value in 1955.

HISTORICAL FOOTNOTES: The 1955 Plymouths were introduced Nov. 17, 1954, and the Suburbans appeared in dealer showrooms Dec. 22, 1954. Model year production peaked at 672,100 units. Calendar year sales of 742,991 cars were recorded. J.P. Mansfield was the chief executive officer this year. Plymouth created a new fleet sales department during 1955. The club coupe was dropped. Four-door Suburbans and Belvedere two-door sedans were new Plymouth styles. Detroit area dealers were shown the new models on Nov. 4, 1954, as the cars had entered actual production during September. Production lines at the Detroit factory were made 67 feet longer because the 1955 models were larger than past Plymouth products. On a calendar year basis, 35,664 Plymouths had power brakes; 33,000 had power steering; 348,771 (46 percent) had automatic transmission; 30,791 had overdrive and 60.8 percent had V-8 engines. The 157-hp V-8 was dropped (except for Canadian and export models) by the end of 1954 so Plymouth could advertise the highest standard horsepower V-8 ($167) in the low-priced field. Chevy and Ford both offered 162-hp V-8s.

For 1956, Plymouth face lifted the body introduced the previous season. Styling changes included fin-type rear fenders and a new grille with a grid pattern center piece decorated with a gold V-shaped emblem on V-8 models. Full-length taillights extended from the tip of the rear fins to the back-up lamp housing. Plymouth block lettering stretched across the edge of the hood, and a wide jet airplane-type hood mascot in keeping with that year's theme for Chrysler Corporation, "Flightsweep Styling." The side trim on two-toned models became a little more complicated, and the model name was included on a chrome sign where all the side trim met in the middle of the front door.

The exciting 1956 Plymouth Fury two-door hardtop

Tom Glatch

PLAZA/DELUXE SUBURBAN — (6-CYLINDER/V-8) — SERIES P28/P29-1: The Plaza range included the economy offerings. Identification features included rubber windshield and rear window gaskets, painted taillight trim, Plaza rear fender side script, painted back-up light housings, small hubcaps, single horizontal front fender spears, and painted roof gutter rails. This year the Plymouth Suburban station wagons were actually grouped in their own, separate four model series. However the Deluxe Suburban was trimmed in Plaza fashion and will be included as such in this catalog.

PLYMOUTH I.D. NUMBERS: The serial number plate was located on the left door post. Serial numbers started with the prefix (P=Plymouth) and series code (P28=six-cylinder; P29=V-8) followed by sequential production number starting at 1001 at each factory. Factory codes: M=Detroit, Mich.; LA=Los Angeles, Calif.; E=Evansville, Ind.; and SL=San Leandro, Calif. These codes do not appear in serial numbers. Six-cylinder engine numbers were near the front upper left of block between cylinders one and two. The V-8 engine number was on the flat surface near the front of the block between two cylinder heads. The engine numbers resembled serial number, but may not match. Engine numbers should not be used for identification. Prefix symbols changed as follows: P28-1 = Plaza six; P28-2 = Savoy six and P28-3 = Belvedere six; P29-1 = Plaza V-8; P29-2 = Savoy V-8 and P29-3 = Belvedere V-8 and Fury. Serial numbers at each factory were changed as follows: Six-cylinder: (M) 14120001-14272723; (E) 20820001-20857927 and (LA) 25202001-25212960. V-8: (M) 15873001-16080450; (E) 22247001-22325907 and (LA) 26552001-26590897. Fury V-8: (M) 15873001-16080450; (E) 22247001-22325907 and (LA) 26552001-26590897. Engine numbers were: P28-1001 to P28-204591 (six); P29-40001 to P29-80000 (187 hp V-8); P29-250001 to P29-274000 (187 hp V-8): P29-1001 to P29-40000 (180 hp V-8); P29-80001 to P29-250000 (180 hp V-8) and P29-1001 to P29-329132 (Fury V-8).

"This Plymouth is no 'rock.' It is, in fact, the bestest yet in Plymouths."

Racer Brown, Hot Rod, May 1956

Plaza Series/Deluxe Suburban

Series Number	Body/Style Number	Body Type & Seating	Factory Price	Shipping Weight	Production Total
P28/29-1	N/A	4-dr Sedan-6P	$1,868/$1,971	3,145/3,275 lbs.	60,197
P28/29-1	N/A	2-dr Club Sedan-6P	$1,825/$1,928	3,100/3,250 lbs.	43,022
P28/29-1	N/A	2-dr Business Coupe-6P	$1,726/$1,829	3,030/3,170 lbs.	3,728
P28/29	N/A	2-dr Deluxe Suburban-6P	$2,138/$2,241	3,285/3,460 lbs.	23,866

SAVOY/CUSTOM SUBURBAN — **(6-CYLINDER/V-8)** — **P28/P29-2:** The Savoy line was the mid-range 1956 Plymouth offering and shared annual styling changes with other models. Standard equipment included, front fender horizontal sweep spear molding, chrome taillight molding, chrome headlight trim, painted back-up lamp housing, bright metal windshield and rear window frames, small hubcaps, and Savoy rear fender script. Although actually part of a separate series, two custom Suburbans came with Savoy-type features and trim, except for the rear fender script, which read "Custom Suburban." One of these six-passenger station wagons was a two-door model and the other had four-doors. As usual, the interiors on the mid-priced Plymouths earned a few extra rich appointments. Buyers could also dress-up the exterior of Savoys (and Plazas) with the optional "Sport Tone" molding treatment.

Savoy Series/Custom Suburban

Series Number	Body/Style Number	Body Type & Seating	Factory Price	Shipping Weight	Production Total
P28/29-2	N/A	4-dr Sedan-6P	$1967/$2,070	3,160/3,295 lbs.	51,762
P28/29-2	N/A	2-dr Club Sedan-6P	$1,924/$2,027	3,125/3,255 lbs.	57,927
P28/29-2	N/A	2-dr Sport Coupe-6P	$2,071/$2,174	3,155/3,275 lbs.	16,473
P28/29	N/A	4-dr Custom Suburban-6P	$2,255/$2,358	3,375/3,565 lbs.	33,333
P28/29	N/A	2-dr Custom Suburban-6P	$2,209/$2,312	3,355/3,500 lbs.	9,489

NOTE 1: *Data above slash for six/below slash for V-8.*

The 1956 Plymouth Belvedere sedan was strikingly stylish, yet tasteful.

BELVEDERE/SPORT SUBURBAN/FURY — (6-CYLINDER/V-8) — SERIES P28/P29-3: The Belvedere was again Plymouth's high trim level car. The four-door Sport Wagon, in the Suburban series, also had Belvedere features. A new body style was the four-door hardtop Sport Sedan. Identifiers for these models included front door model nameplates, chrome back-up lamp housings, "Forward Look" medallions; armrests; clock; Deluxe steering wheel; dressier interior trappings, and bright metal moldings on the windshield, rear window, headlights and taillights, rear deck lid overhang and front edge of the hood. Belvederes and Sport Suburbans came standard with "Sport Tone" side trim of a distinct, angled-back pattern. The Sport Suburban also had "Forward Look" medallions on the rear fenders and tweed pattern seat cushions and backs plus a rooftop luggage carrier. Introduced as a midyear model, the Plymouth Fury high-performance sport coupe was actually part of the Belvedere V-8 series. Its custom features included an off-white exterior finish, tapering gold anodized aluminum side trim, gold-finished aluminum grille, directional signals, back-up lights, variable-speed wipers, dual exhaust system with chrome deflectors, windshield washers, dual outside rearview mirrors, prismatic inside rearview mirror, special tires, gold anodized spoke-style wheel covers and a 240-hp V-8. There was also a Fury rear fender script.

Belvedere/Fury Series/ Sport Suburban

Series Number	Body/Style Number	Body Type & Seating	Factory Price	Shipping Weight	Production Total
P28/29-3	N/A	4-dr Sedan-6P	$2,051/$2,154	3,170/3,325 lbs.	84,218
P28/29-3	N/A	4-dr Sport Sedan-6P	$2,223/$2,326	3,270/3,415 lbs.	17,515
P28/29-3	N/A	2-dr Club Sedan-6P	$2,008/$2,111	3,125/3,285 lbs.	19,057
P28/29-3	N/A	2-dr Sport Coupe-6P	$2,155/$2,258	3,165/3,320 lbs.	24,723
P29-3	N/A	2-dr Convertible-6P	$2,478	3,435 lbs.	6,735
P28/29	N/A	4-dr Sport Suburban-6P	$2,425/$2,528	3,420/3,605 lbs.	15,104
Fury Sub-series					
P29-3	N/A	2-dr Sport Coupe-6P	$2,807	3,650 lbs.	4,485

1956 Plymouth Suburban two-door station wagon

John Lee

Engines:

SIX: Inline. L-head. Cast iron block. Displacement: 230.2 cid. Bore and stroke: 3.25 x 4.625 inches. Compression ratio: 7.6:1. Brake hp: 125 (optional 131) at 3600 rpm. Four main bearings. Solid valve lifters. Carter Type BB one-barrel Model 2063SA (optional Carter Type BBS two-barrel Model 2293S).

V-8: Overhead valve. Cast iron block. Displacement: 268.8 cid. Bore and stroke: 3.63 x 3.256 inches. Compression ratio: 8.0:1. Brake hp: 180 at 4400 rpm. Five main bearings. Hydraulic valve lifters. Carburetor: Carter Type BBD two-barrel Model 2259SB. Base V-8 for all except Fury.

FURY V-8: Overhead valve. Cast iron block. Displacement: 303 cid. Bore and stroke: 3.81 x 3.31 inches. Compression ratio: 9.25:1. Brake hp: 240 at 4800 rpm. Five main bearings. Solid valve lifters. Carburetor: Carter Type WCFB four-barrel Model 2442S.

OPTIONAL V-8: Overhead valve. Cast iron block. Displacement: 276.1 cid. Bore and stroke: 3.75 x 3.125 inches. Compression ratio: 8.0:1. Brake hp: 187 at 4400 rpm. Five main bearings. Hydraulic or solid valve lifters. Carburetor: Carter Type BBD two-barrel Model 2407S. NOTE: This is called the "277 engine" and came with solid valve lifters when the optional four-barrel "Power Pack" was installed.

CHASSIS FEATURES: Wheelbase: (all models) 115 inches. Overall length: (all models) 204.8 inches. Front tread: (all models) 58-13/32 inches. Rear tread: (Fury) 58-29/32 inches; (all other models) 58-½ inches. Tires: (Fury) 7.10 x 15-inch; (all other models) 6.70 x 15-inch.

OPTIONS: Power brakes ($40). Power steering ($81). Air conditioning, V-8 club sedan/sport coupe/four-door sedan/sport sedan only ($427). Power windows ($102). Power seat ($45). Standard radio ($90). Deluxe radio ($107). Heater ($75). Full wheel discs. Wheel trim rings. Wire wheel covers. White sidewall tires. Front safety belts. Rear safety belts. Hi-Way Hi-Fi. Undercoating. Padded dashboard. Outside rearview mirror. "Sport Tone" moldings. Two-tone paint. Bumper guards. Station wagon rooftop luggage rack. Back-up lights. Directional signals. Windshield washer. Solex tinted glass. Three-speed manual transmission was standard. Overdrive transmission ($108). Automatic transmission ($184). V-8 268.8 cid/180 hp two-barrel engine. A V-8 276.1 cid/187 hp two-barrel engine. A V-8 276.1 cid/200 hp four-barrel engine. A V-8 303 cid/240 hp Fury four-barrel engine. Four-barrel carburetor was standard with the Fury V-8 and available as "Power Pack" equipment on the 276.1-cid V-8 (Carter WCFB-2442). Positive traction rear axle. Available rear axle gear ratios: (standard) 3.73:1; (automatic) 3.73:1; (overdrive) 4.11:1.

HISTORICAL FOOTNOTES: The 1956 Plymouths were introduced Oct. 21, 1955, and the Fury sport coupe appeared in dealer showrooms Jan. 7, 1956. Model year production peaked at 521,000 units. Calendar year sales of 452,958 cars were recorded. J. P. Mansfield was the chief executive officer this year. Push-button PowerFlite automatic transmission controls were introduced. The Plainsman station wagon, a futuristic show car powered by a Plymouth engine and riding on a Plymouth chassis, appeared at the Chicago Auto Show. An experimental turbine-powered Fury sport coupe was also constructed. Optional equipment installed on 1956 Plymouth models, by percentage, included automatic transmission (61.7 percent); power steering (61 percent); power brakes (6.0 percent); power seat (0.6 percent); power windows (0.6 percent); radio (34.3 percent); heater (94.8 percent); whitewalls (44.9 percent); overdrive (3.3 percent); tinted glass (19.2 percent); windshield washers (19.7 percent); back-up lights (28.9 percent); directional signals (96.9 percent) and V-8 engine (63.7 percent). On Jan. 10, 1956, the new Fury ran the Flying Mile at Daytona Beach, Fla., and hit a speed of 124.01 mph. The Fury was timed at 9.6 seconds for 0-to-60 mph and 17 seconds for the quarter-mile.

"Suddenly, It's 1960!" This was Plymouth's slogan for 1957, and the new Plymouth was all-new with no resemblence to the past. The venerable 1940 chassis was completely gone, and the corporation replaced it with the totally new "Torsion-Aire" torsion bar suspension that made the Plymouth out-handle all its competition. The year 1955 had been Chevrolet's moment in the sun, but 1957 was Plymouth's. Ford outsold Chevrolet's dated styling in 1957, and Plymouth made them both hurry to catch up. Some Chevrolet dealers actually report hiding parts of the 1957 Chevrolet in the showroom by parking the cars against walls so customers would not see how badly they compared to the '57 Plymouths across the street.

The Plymouth was longer, lower, wider, and had all the second wave Forward Look elements that had finally come completely into their own. The headlights had deep but delicate brows, and there was a series of vertical slots under the front bumper. The fins swept high above the rear fenders, but the car looked light and delicate enough to fly. Everything on the road suddenly looked old. The taillights were solid vertical bars on the ends of the fins that fit the end of the very naturally, and round back-up lights sat right below the upright taillights.

Inside, a space age pod fronted the driver, and the three-speed TorqueFlite push-buttons occupied the left-hand end of the dash. Look closely at the chrome centerpiece on '57 trunk lids. It is a stylized version of the traditional Mayflower ship.

The Plymouth was all new from the ground up, but they were plagued with quality-control problems and quickly harmed Chrysler as much as they helped.

The beautiful new 1957 Plymouth Fury two-door hardtop marked the full flowering of the Exner-team's Forward Look.
W. P. Chrysler Museum

PLAZA/DELUXE SUBURBAN — (6-CYLINDER/V-8) — SERIES KP30/KP31-1: Plaza was the low-priced line. The Deluxe Suburban was part of a separate station wagon series, but had Plaza trim. Identification features included model nameplates on rear fenders, untrimmed body sides, small hubcaps, painted roof gutter rails, and V-shaped front fender tip emblems on V-8 models. Tapered "Sport Tone" side moldings were available at extra cost. Standard equipment included single speed windshield wipers, left-hand sun visor, dual horns, and five tubeless tires.

PLYMOUTH I.D. NUMBERS: The serial number plate was located on the left door post. Serial number started with P30-1 = Plaza six; P30-2 = Savoy six; and P30-3 = Belvedere six; P31-1 = Plaza V-8; P31-2 = Savoy V-8; and P31-3 = Belvedere V-8 and Fury, followed by sequential production numbers starting at 1001 at each factory. Factory codes: M=Detroit, Mich.; LA=Los Angeles, Calif.; E=Evansville, Ind.; SL=San Leandro, Calif.; ws (new) NJ=Newark, N.J. These codes do not appear in serial number. Six-cylinder engine numbers were near the front upper left of block between cylinders one and two and V-8 numbers were on top of the block, near the front, between cylinder heads. The engine number resembled serial number, but may not match. Engine numbers should not be used for identification. Serial numbers at each factory changed as follows: Six: (M) 14280001-14410539; (E) 20860001-20891720; (LA) 25215001-25222883 and (NJ) 28100001-28103737. V-8: (M) 1683001-16392956; (E) 22330001-22450693; (LA) 26595001-26643618 and (NJ) 28525001-28534683. Fury V-8: (M) 16083001-16392956. Engine numbers were: (Six) P30-1001 to P30-177184; (V-8) P31-1001 to P31-492995 and (Fury V-8) FP31-1001 to FP31-492995. Furys were assembled only at the Detroit factory.

Plaza Series/Deluxe Suburban

Series Number	Body/Style Number	Body Type & Seating	Factory Price	Shipping Weight	Production Total
KP30/KP31-1	N/A	4-dr Sedan-6P	$2,030/$2,130	3,260/3,405 lbs.	70,248
KP30/KP31-1	N/A	2-dr Club Sedan-6P	$1,984/$2,084	3,160/3,330 lbs.	49,137
KP30/KP31-1	N/A	2-dr Business Coupe-3P	$1,874/$1,974	3,155/3,315 lbs.	2,874
KP30/KP31-1	N/A	2-dr Deluxe Suburban-6P	$2,305/$2,405	3,555/3,685 lbs.	20,111
KP30/KP31-1	N/A	4-dr Taxi Special-6P	$2,174/$2,274	3,410/3,515 lbs.	N/A

NOTE 1: *Data above slash for six/below slash for V-8.*

SAVOY/CUSTOM SUBURBAN — (6-CYLINDER/V-8) — SERIES KP30/KP31-2: Savoys and Custom Suburbans shared the same general level of trim and appointments. They were Plymouth's mid-priced lines and had the same basic design changes as Plazas. The number of standard equipment and decorative items was one step up the scale. The Savoy had all features of the lower priced car plus air foam seat cushions, armrests, horn-blowing ring, dual sun visors, and a single horizontal side molding running from behind the headlights to just above the back-up lights. Dual, tapering "Sport Tone" molding treatments were an option available at extra cost. Savoy block lettering was placed on the side of fins on passenger cars, while the comparable Suburban had double nameplates attached at mid-fin height. They read "Custom" in script and "Suburban" in block letters. The Suburbans had slightly different rear fenders than other models and also came with contrasting Sport Tone finish, as an option.

Everything was new and eye catching inside the 1957 Plymouth as well.

Tom Glatch

Savoy Series/Custom Suburban

Series Number	Body/Style Number	Body Type & Seating	Factory Price	Shipping Weight	Production Total
KP30/KP31-2	N/A	4-dr Sedan-6P	$2,169/$2,269	3,265/3,415 lbs.	53,093
KP30/KP31-2	N/A	4-dr Sport Sedan-6P	$2,292/$2,392	3,375/3,480 lbs.	7,601
KP30/KP31-2	N/A	2-dr Club Sedan-6P	$2,122/$2,222	3,190/3,335 lbs.	55,590
KP30/KP31-2	N/A	2-dr Hardtop Coupe-6P	$2,204/$2,304	3,260/3,410 lbs.	31,373
KP30/KP31-2	N/A	4-dr Custom Suburban-6P	$2,469/$2,569	3,665/3,840 lbs.	40,227
KP30/KP31-2	N/A	4-dr Custom Suburban-9P	$2,624/$2,724	N/A/N/A	9,357
KP30/KP31-2	N/A	2-dr Custom Suburban	$2,415/$2,515	3,580/3,755 lbs.	11,196

NOTE 1: *Data above slash for six/below slash for V-8.*

BELVEDERE/SPORT SUBURBAN/FURY — (6-CYLINDER/V-8) — SERIES KP30/KP31-3: The Belvedere group represented the top Plymouth line. The Sport Suburban was the comparably equipped station wagon, and the Fury was a special high-performance model that had many standard extras. Belvederes had single side moldings as standard equipment and tapering dual side moldings, with Sport Tone contrast panels as a slight extra cost option. Belvedere block letters were positioned at the middle sides of the rear tailfins, just above the moldings. Standard equipment included all items found on Savoys plus full wheel covers, rear quarter stone shields, electric clock, lockable glovebox, and cigarette lighter. The Sport Suburban had a special thick pillar roof treatment which was also used on four-door Custom Suburbans, upright spare tire, and rear-facing third seat. Model nameplates appeared at mid-fin level above the rear tip of the horizontal side moldings or optional dual Sport Tone moldings. The Fury came only as a two-door hardtop with Fury rear fender nameplates Sand Dune White finish with gold anodized aluminum Sport Tone trim inserts, upswept front bumper end extensions, safety padded dash, padded sun visors, foam seat, front and rear, special clock, back-up lights, directional signals, dual outside rearview mirrors, and a 290-hp V-8. The new three-speed TorqueFlite automatic transmission was offered only in the Belvedere and Fury lines.

Belvedere Series/Sport Suburban/Fury

Series Number	Body/Style Number	Body Type & Seating	Factory Price	Shipping Weight	Production Total
KP30/KP31-3	N/A	4-dr Sedan-6P	$2,285/$2,385	3,270/3,475 lbs.	10,414
KP30/KP31-3	N/A	4-dr Sport Sedan-6P	$2,394/$2,494	3,350/3,505 lbs.	37,446
KP30/KP31-3	N/A	2-dr Club Sedan-6P	$2,239/$2,339	3,235/3,340 lbs.	55,590
KP30/KP31-3	N/A	2-dr Hardtop Coupe-6P	$2,324/$2,424	3,280/3,415 lbs.	67,268
KP31-3	N/A	2-dr Convertible-6P	$2,613	3,585 lbs.	9,866
KP30/KP31-3	N/A	4-dr Sport Suburban-6P	$2,597/$2,697	3,655/3,840 lbs.	15,444
KP30/KP31-3	N/A	4-dr Sport Suburban-9P	$2,752/$2,852	N/A/N/A	7,988
Fury Sub-series					
KP31-3	N/A	2-dr Hardtop Coupe-6P	$2,900	3,595 lbs.	7,438

NOTE 1: *Data above slash for six/below slash for V-8.*

NOTE 2: *Belvedere convertible came only with V-8 power.*

Engines:

SIX: Inline. L-head. Cast iron block. Displacement: 230.2 cid. Bore and stroke: 3.25 x 4.625 inches. Compression ratio: 8.0:1. Brake hp: 132 at 3600 rpm. Four main bearings. Solid valve lifters. Carburetor: Carter Type BBS one-barrel Model 2567S.

V-8: Overhead valve. Cast iron block. Displacement: 276.1 cid. Bore and stroke: 3.75 x 3.125 inches. Compression ratio: 8.0:1. Brake hp: 197 at 4400 rpm. Five main bearings. Hydraulic valve lifters. Carburetor: Carter Type BBD two-barrel Model 2407S. NOTE: The Deluxe Suburban used the 299.6 cid "301" V-8 as standard equipment.

FURY V-8: Overhead valve. Cast iron block. Displacement: 299.6 cid. Bore and stroke: 3.906 x 3.125 inches. Compression ratio: 8.5:1. Brake hp: 235 at 4400 rpm. Five main bearings. Solid valve lifters. Carburetor: Carter Type WCFB four-barrel Model 2631S.

OPTIONAL V-8: Overhead valve. Cast iron block. Displacement: 299.6 cid. Bore and stroke: 3.906 x 3.125 inches. Compression ratio: 8.5:1. Brake hp: 215 at 9700 rpm. Five main bearings. Solid valve lifters. Carburetor: Carter Type BBD two-barrel Model 2512S. Note: This engine is normally referred to as the 301 V-8, although its actual displacement was 299.6 cid. It was standard in all 1957 Suburbans.

OPTIONAL FURY V-8: Overhead valve. Cast iron block. Displacement: 317.6 cid. Bore and stroke: 3.906 x 3.312 inches. Compression ratio: 9.25:1. Brake hp: 290 at 5400 rpm. Five main bearings. Solid valve lifters. Carburetor: Two Carter Type WCFB four-barrel Model 2631S.

CHASSIS FEATURES: Wheelbase: (all passenger cars) 118 inches; (all Suburbans) 122 inches. Overall length: (Fury) 206.1 inches; (all other passenger cars) 204.6 inches; (all station wagons) 208.6 inches. Front tread: (all models) 60-29/32 inches. Rear tread: (all models) 59-39/64 inches. Tires: (Fury and nine-passenger Suburbans) 8.00 x 14; (all other models) 7.50 x 14.

OPTIONS: Power brakes ($38). Power steering ($84). Air conditioning ($446). Power windows ($102). Two-Way power seat ($48). Push-button transistor radio with antenna ($73). Search Tune transistor radio with antenna ($106). Search Tune transistor radio with antenna and Hi-Fi ($187). Rear seat speaker ($12). Heater and defroster ($69). White sidewall tires, exchange ($33). Disc wheel covers on Plaza or Savoy ($18). "Sport Tone" two-tone paint ($20). "Sport Tone" on Suburbans ($24). Tinted Solex glass ($32). Back-up lights ($8). Suburban back-up lights ($10). Front and rear bumper guards ($34). Variable speed windshield wipers ($6). Windshield washer ($12). Electric clock on Plaza and Savoy ($14). Padded dashboard and sun visors ($24). Undercoating and hood panel ($13).

POWERTRAIN OPTIONS: Oil filter ($6). Three-speed manual transmission was standard. Overdrive transmission ($108). PowerFlite two-speed automatic transmission ($180). TorqueFlite three-speed automatic transmission was optional with V-8 engines only ($220). Dual exhaust was optional with V-8 engines only ($19.80). V-8 229.6 cid/215 hp two-barrel engine. V-8 299.6 cid/235 hp four-barrel engine. V-8 317.6 cid/290 hp dual four-barrel engine ($320). Four-barrel carburetor ($39). Positive traction rear axle ($50). Available rear axle gear ratios: (standard) 3.53:1; (overdrive) 3.90:1; (automatic) 3.54:1 or 3.35:1.

HISTORICAL FOOTNOTES: The 1957 Plymouths were introduced Oct. 25, 1956, and the Fury appeared in dealer showrooms on Dec. 18, 1956. Model year production peaked at 762,231 units. Calendar year sales of 655,526 cars were recorded. J. P. Mansfield was the chief executive officer this year. Plymouth retained the third rank in American auto sales. A unique station wagon prototype called the Cabana was built this year. It was based on the experimental Plainsman show car, but failed to reach the production stage. The Savoy Sport Sedan (four-door hardtop) was a mid-year addition to the 1957 line introduced in March of the calendar year. The famous "Suddenly It's 1960" theme was used to promote the 1957 Plymouths. The Fury was re-introduced in January as a midyear high-performance model. With the 318-cid/290-hp engine it could do 0-to-60 mph in 8.6 seconds and cover the quarter-mile in 16.5 seconds.

The 1958 Plymouth changed very little from 1957. Styling revisions for the year included a new, horizontal bar grille below the front bumper, fin-like front fender top ornaments on Belvederes and Savoys, new taillights, redesigned side trim treatments and quad headlights on all models. The taillights and backup lights reversed from 1957 which put the white, bar-like backup light on the end of the fin and the round, red taillight below them. Some collectors call these taillights the "lollipops."

The 1958 Plymouth Belvedere two-door hardtop as seen at an All-Mopar event.

Tom Collins

PLAZA/DELUXE SUBURBAN — (6-CYLINDER/V-8) — SERIES LP1/LP2-L: The Plaza group again represented the base Plymouth model range. The Deluxe Suburban was the counterpart station wagon. Anodized aluminum Sport Tone moldings and inserts were now optional on Belvederes and Sport Suburbans. Plazas and Deluxe Suburbans could be identified by their respective rear fender nameplates. Normal side trim consisted of a straight sweep spear molding extending from the rear bumper to nearly across the front door. A molding arrangement forming a bullet-shaped side body cove with contrasting finish was optional at slight extra cost. Deluxe Suburbans had the same features as Plaza models, except for the rear fender-side nameplates. Basic equipment on the low-priced Plymouths included directional signals, quad headlights, single-speed electric windshield wipers, left-hand sun visor, dual horns, five tubeless tires. Gold V-shaped emblems at the center of the grille were used to identify models with V-8 power.

PLYMOUTH I.D. NUMBERS: The serial number plate was located on the left door post. Six-cylinder engine numbers were on the front upper left side of block between cylinders one and two; V-8 engine numbers on were on a flat surface, front top of block, between cylinder heads. The engine numbers resembled serial numbers, but may not match. Engine numbers should not be used for identification. Vehicle Identification Number: first symbol: L=1958; second symbol: P=Plymouth. The third symbol designated type of engine, as follows: 1=six-cylinder; 2=V-8. The fourth symbol designated the assembly plant as follows: Detroit, Mich. (no code used); Los Angeles=L; Evansville, Ind.=E and Delaware=N. The following group of symbols was the sequential unit production number, with series in mixed production, according to factory and engine type. Body/Style Numbers were not used, but a new method of coding trim levels shows up in the charts below. This code used the first three symbols of the serial number, followed by a letter that indicated the level of price and/or trim. These letters were "L" for low; "M" for medium; "H" for high end and "P" for premium. Serial numbers for 1958 models were as follows: (Six) LP1L-1001 to LP1L-6444; LP1N-1001 to LP1N-18176; LP1E-1001 to LP1E-23101 and LP1-1001 to LP1-66871. (V-8) LP2L-1001 to LP2L-39675; LP2N-1001 to LP2N-36506; LP2E-1001 to LP2E-84801 and LP2-1001 to LP2-140484. Engine numbers for 1958 sixes were LP6-1001 and up or LP230-100001 and up (after March 26,1958). Engine numbers for V-8s were LP8-1001 and up.

There were noticeable trim changes in the 1958 Plymouth including the taillights.

Tom Collins

Plaza Series/Deluxe Suburban

Series Number	Body/Style Number	Body Type & Seating	Factory Price	Shipping Weight	Production Total
LP½-L	N/A	4-dr Sedan-6P	$2,134/$2,242	3,255/3,415 lbs.	54,194
LP½-L	N/A	2-dr Club Sedan-6P	$2,083/$2,190	3,190/3,315 lbs.	39,062
LP½-L	N/A	2-dr Business Coupe-3P	$1,993/$2,101	3,170/3,320 lbs.	1,472
LP½-L	N/A	4-dr Deluxe Suburban-6P	$2,451/$2,558	3,580/3,740 lbs.	15,625
LP½-L	N/A	2-dr Deluxe Suburban-6P	$2,397/$2,504	3,475/3,645 lbs.	15,535

NOTE 1: *Data above slash for six/below slash for V-8.*

Savoy Series/Custom Suburban

Series Number	Body/Style Number	Body Type & Seating	Factory Price	Shipping Weight	Production Total
LP½-M	N/A	4-dr Sedan-6P	$2,270/$2,378	3,220/3,400 lbs.	67,933
LP½-M	N/A	4-dr Hardtop Sedan-6P	$2,365/$2,472	3,310/3,475 lbs.	5,060
LP½-M	N/A	2-dr Club Sedan-6P	$2,219/$2,327	3,220/3,360 lbs.	17,624
LP½-M	N/A	2-dr Hardtop Coupe-6P	$2,294/$2,401	3,240/3,400 lbs.	19,500
LP½-M	N/A	4-dr Custom Suburban-6P	$2,572/$2,680	3,575/3,755 lbs.	38,707
LP½-M	N/A	4-dr Custom Suburban-9P	$2,712/$2,820	3,685/3,840 lbs.	17,158
LP½-M	N/A	2-dr Custom Suburban-6P	$2,518/$2,626	3,570/3,690 lbs.	5,925

NOTE 1: *Data above slash for six/below slash for V-8.*

Quad headlights replaced the larger parking lights up front and Plymouth reversed the tall taillight/small backup light arrangement on the 1958 version.

John Lee

A beautiful 1958 Plymouth Belvedere two-door hardtop appears brand new. John Lee

The 1958 Belvedere convertible was an example of the best in Forward Look styling.
John Lee

BELVEDERE/SPORT SUBURBAN/FURY — (6-CYLINDER/V-8) — SERIES LP1/LP2-H: Belvedere represented the top full-line Plymouth series. The Sport Suburban was the comparable station wagon. The Fury was a Belvedere sub-series containing only the special high-performance sport coupe. Nameplates on the rear fender identified each particular car. The standard type of Belvedere side trim was a single, full-length horizontal molding of slightly distinctive design. Running with a slight downward slant, it moved from headlamp level towards the back fender. About a foot ahead of the taillights, the molding angled up towards the top of the fin. The optional Sport Tone package added a lower molding. It ran from above the back bumper and tapered towards the upper molding at the front fender tip. The area inside the moldings was then finished with contrasting colors, usually matching the roof. Belvederes and Sport Suburbans had all Savoy features plus full wheel covers, rear fender stone shields, electric clock, lockable glovebox, cigar lighter, and front fender top ornaments. The Fury was a limited-edition Buckskin beige two-door hardtop with Fury rear fender nameplates, Sport Tone moldings with gold anodized aluminum inserts, bumper wing guards, padded interior, front and rear foam seats, back-up lights, dual outside rearview mirrors, and special Dual Fury or Golden Commando V-8.

Belvedere Series/Sport Suburban/Fury

Series Number	Body/Style Number	Body Type & Seating	Factory Price	Shipping Weight	Production Total
LP½-H	N/A	4-dr Sedan-6P	$2,404/$2,512	3,255/3,430 lbs.	49,124
LP½-H	N/A	4-dr Hardtop-6P	$2,493/$2,600	3,330/3,520 lbs.	18,194
LP½-H	N/A	2-dr Club Sedan-6P	$2,354/$2,461	3,240/3,370 lbs.	4,229
LP½-H	N/A	2-dr Hardtop Coupe-6P	$2,422/$2,529	3,250/3,410 lbs.	36,043
LP2-H	N/A	2-dr Convertible-6P	$2,727	3,545 lbs.	9,941
LP½-H	N/A	4-dr Sport Suburban-6P	$2,725/$2,833	3,615/3,745 lbs.	10,785
LP½-H	N/A	4-dr Sport Suburban-9P	$2,865/$2,973	3,685/3,830 lbs.	12,385
Fury Sub-series					
LP2-H	N/A	2-dr HT Cpe-6P	$3,032	3,510 lbs.	5,303

NOTE 1: *Belvedere convertible came only with V-8 power.*

Engines:

SIX: Inline. L-head. Cast iron block. Displacement: 230.2 cid. Bore and stroke: 3.25 x 4.625 inches. Compression ratio: 8.0:1. Brake hp: 132 at 3600 rpm. Four main bearings. Solid valve lifters. Carburetor: Carter Type BBS one-barrel Model 2567S.

V-8: Overhead valve. Cast iron block. Displacement: 317.6 cid. Bore and stroke: 3.906 x 3.312 inches. Compression ratio: 9.0:1. Brake hp: 225 at 4400 rpm. Five main bearings. Solid valve lifters. Carburetor: Carter Type BBS two-barrel Model 2644S.

FURY V-8: Overhead valve. Cast iron block. Displacement: 317.6 cid. Bore and stroke: 3.906 x 3.312 inches. Compression ratio: 9.25:1. Brake hp: 290 at 5200 rpm. Five main bearings. Solid valve lifters. Carburetor: Two Carter WCFB four-barrel Model 2631S.

OPTIONAL GOLDEN COMMANDO V-8: Overhead valve. Cast iron block. Displacement: 350 cid. Bore and stroke: 4.062 x 3.375 inches. Compression ratio: 10.0:1. Brake hp: 305 at 5000 rpm. Five main bearings. Hydraulic valve lifters. Carburetor: two Carter four-barrel Model 2631S. (An electronic fuel injection option rated at 315 hp was short-lived.)

CHASSIS FEATURES: All passenger cars: 118 inches; all Suburbans 122 inches. Overall length: (Fury) 206 inches; all other passenger cars 204.6 inches and all Suburbans 213.1 inches. Front tread: (all models) 60-29/32 inches. Rear tread: (all models) 59-39/64 inches. Tires: (Fury and nine-passenger Suburban) 8.00 x 14-inch; (all other models) 7.50 x 14-inch.

OPTIONS: Power brakes ($38). Power steering ($77). Air conditioning ($446). Power windows ($102). Two-Way power seat ($48). Push-button transistor radio ($73). Search Tuner transistor radio ($106). Search Tuner transistor radio with HI-FI ($187). Rear seat speaker ($12). Heater and defroster ($69). Four-ply white sidewall tires, exchange ($33). Disc wheel covers, Plaza and Savoy ($18). "Sport-Tone" finish, passenger cars ($20). "Sport-Tone" finish, Suburbans ($24). Solex tinted glass ($32). Back-up lamps, passenger car ($8). Back-up lamps, Suburban ($10). Front and rear outer bumper guards ($34). Air Foam seat ($9). Variable-speed electric windshield wipers ($6). Windshield washers ($12). Electric clock on Plaza and Savoy ($14). Padded panel and sun visors ($24). Undercoating and fiberglass hood pad ($13). Sure-Grip. Three-speed manual transmission was standard. Overdrive transmission ($108). PowerFlite automatic transmission with all but Golden Commando V-8 ($180). TorqueFlite automatic transmission with V-8 only ($220). 318 cid/225 hp two-barrel Fury V-8 "Fury" engine ($107). 318 cid/250 hp four-barrel Fury Super-Pak ($146). V-8 318 cid/290 hp dual four-barrel "Dual Fury" engine. V-8 350 cid/305 hp "Golden Commando" engine ($324). V-8 350 cid/315 hp EFI engine ($500). Four-barrel carburetor ($39). Fuel injection ($500). Dual exhaust with V-8 engine only ($19.80). Oil filter ($6). Available rear axle gear ratios: 3.54:1; 3.73:1; 2.93:1; 3.15:1; 3.31:1; 3.90:1; 4.10:1.

HISTORICAL FOOTNOTES: The 1958 Plymouths were introduced Oct. 16, 1957, and the Fury appeared in dealer showrooms at the same time. Model year production peaked at 443,799 units. Calendar year sales of 367,296 cars were recorded. The term "Power Pack" applied to cars having a four-barrel carburetor installed as optional equipment. The "Dual Fury" V-8 came with two Carter WCFB-type four-barrel carburetors, 9.25:1 compression and 290 hp at 5200 rpm. The electronic fuel-injected (EFI) engine utilized a Bendix electronic fuel-injection system. All EFI equipped cars were Furys, which were first built with the "Dual Fury" induction setup and were then converted to EFI on a special assembly line in the De Soto factory in Detroit. Cars with this option were later recalled so that most, if not all, could be re-converted to the "Dual Fury" configuration. Plymouth retained its number three sales rank for the industry as a whole, with a 30.6 percent market share. Furys equipped with the wedge head 350 cid/305 hp big-block V-8 were capable of 0-to-60 mph in 7.7 seconds and could run the quarter-mile in 16.1 seconds.

To upgrade its image for 1959, Plymouth discarded the Plaza name and shuffled its series designations one notch. The Plaza became the Savoy; the Savoy the Belvedere, and the Belvedere the Fury. The special high-performance range, formerly known as the Fury, was now the Sport Fury series and had one new model, a two-door convertible. General styling features included, a twin section anodized aluminum egg-crate grille, new "double-barrel" front fenders, longer, outward canted rear "Airfoil" tailfins, oval-shaped "Ovalight Cluster" horizontal taillights and flatter, more sweeping rear deck contours. Several Plymouths also had the "Bubble-Canopy" windshield, "Dart-Spoke" full wheel covers and the "Sport Deck" featuring the memorable faux spare tire cover.

All Chrysler Corporation cars had a facelift in 1959 but Plymouth's seemed milder than some of the larger offerings.

John Lee

There is something new and something old in the '59 Plymouth logo according to Plymouth Bulletin #199. The Mayflower ship is sailing forward—the only time that view was ever used. And the rocket-shaped spear is pointing upward. It would be a long-time Plymouth logo into the future.

SAVOY/DELUXE SUBURBAN — (6-CYLINDER/V-8) — SERIES MP1-L/MP2-L: The Savoy line was now the base series offering as standard equipment directional signals, dual headlights, single-speed electric windshield wipers, left-hand sun visor, dual horns, five tubeless tires. Identification features included Savoy rear fender nameplates, single side spears running from the front wheel opening to the back of the car, and small hubcaps. The Deluxe Suburbans (now available in two- or four-door styles) were the station wagon counterparts of Savoys. The two-door station wagons had thin, straight roof pillars, while the four-door models had a thicker C pillar and a "flattop" rear roof look. Dual side trim moldings, with aluminum fin-shaped inserts below the greenhouse area, were optional on low-priced Plymouths.

PLYMOUTH I.D. NUMBERS: The Vehicle Identification Number was located on the left front hinge pillar of Savoys and Belvederes and on the left side of the cowl, below the hood on Furys. Engine numbers were found at the front of the engine block on the left side of sixes and on the top center of the V-8 block. Vehicle numbers began with a four symbol prefix. The first symbol: M=1959. The second symbol designated the engine as follows: 1=six-cylinder and 2=V-8. The third symbol designated the series as follows: 3=Savoy; 5=Belvedere; 6=Fury; 7=Suburban; and 9=Sport Fury. The fourth symbol designated the manufacturing/assembly plant as follows: 1=Detroit; 2=Detroit (Dodge); 5=California; 6=Newark, Del.; 7=St. Louis, Mo. Then came the sequential unit production number with series mixed in production, according to engine and factory. Numbers began with 100001 and up at each factory. Ending serial numbers are not provided in standard reference sources. Body/Style Numbers were used this year and are shown in the second column of the specifications charts below.

Savoy Series/Deluxe Suburban

Series Number	Body/Style Number	Body Type & Seating	Factory Price	Shipping Weight	Production Total
MP½-L	41	4-dr Sedan-6P	$2,283/$2,402	3,275/3,425 lbs.	84,274
MP½-L	21	2-dr Club Sedan-6P	$2,232/$2,352	3,240/3,390 lbs.	46,979
MP1-L	22	2-dr Business Coupe-3P	$2,143	3,130 lbs.	1,051
MP½-L	45A	4-dr Deluxe Suburban-6P	$2,641/$2,761	3,625/3,725 lbs.	35,086
MP½-L	25	2-dr Deluxe Suburban-6P	$2,574/$2,694	3,560/3,690 lbs.	15,074

NOTE 1: *Data above slash for six/below slash for V-8.*

NOTE 2: *The Business Coupe came only as a six.*

BELVEDERE/CUSTOM SUBURBAN — (6-CYLINDER/V-8) — SERIES MP1-M/MP2-M: Belvederes and Custom Suburbans represented middle-of-the-line Plymouths for 1959. The side trim moldings on these cars began behind the front wheel opening, flaring into a fin-shaped, tapering dual molding. This arrangement ran from just ahead of the front door, to the extreme rear of the body. Belvedere or Custom Suburban model nameplates appeared near the tops of the fins. Equipment included at regular prices began with all items found on Savoys and added foam seat cushions; armrests; horn ring; and dual sun visors. A special silver anodized insert could be ordered for $18.60 to fill the area between the bodyside moldings. As in the past, the Belvedere convertible was offered only with V-8 power. Many new options appeared for Plymouths this year and several became standard equipment on Sport Furys. Included were swivel-type front seats and deck lid tire cover impressions. Due to growth of the station wagon market in the late-1950s, Plymouth again offered three types of Custom Suburbans this season. Six-passenger editions came in two- and four-door styles, while the latter model could also be had with a rear-facing third seat. The nine-passenger Custom Suburban and two-door Custom Suburban also came with V-8 power only.

A 1959 Plymouth Fury four-door hardtop was seen at the Iola Car Show grounds.

Tom Collins

Belvedere Series/Custom Suburban

Series Number	Body/Style Number	Body Type & Seating	Factory Price	Shipping Weight	Production Total
MP½-M	41	4-dr Sedan-6P	$2,440/$2,559	3,275/3,430 lbs.	67,980
MP½-M	43	4-dr Hardtop Sedan-6P	$2,525/$2,644	3,275/3,475 lbs.	5,713
MP½-M	21	2-dr Club Sedan-6P	$2,389/$2,509	3,225/3,395 lbs.	13,816
MP½-M	23	2-dr Hardtop Sport Coupe-6P	$2,461/$2,581	3,230/3,405 lbs.	23,469
MP2-M	27	2-dr Convertible-6P	$2,814	3,580 lbs.	5,063
MP½-M	45A	4-dr Custom Suburban-6P	$2,762/$2,881	3,625/3,730 lbs.	35,024
MP2-M	45B	4-dr Custom Suburban-9P	$2,991	3,775 lbs.	16,993
MP2-M	25	2-dr Custom Suburban-6P	$2,814	3,690 lbs.	1,852

NOTE 1: *Data above slash for six below slash for V-8.*

FURY/SPORT SUBURBAN — (V-8) — SERIES MP2-H: Furys and Sport Suburbans were marketed as higher-level offerings and came only with V-8 attachments. Standard features included all items mentioned for the Belvedere series plus disc wheel covers, rear quarter stone shields, Deluxe steering wheel with horn ring, electric clock, lockable glove compartment, and cigar lighter. Fury signature script was positioned high on the tailfins. Side chrome was of a dual molding type, which began as a single spear behind the headlamps, flared into a double level arrangement behind the front wheel opening and tapered to a point in front of the tail lamp wraparound edges. A single molding then continued around the rear body corner and fully across the rear deck lid overhang. A Plymouth signature in chrome was placed at the left-hand corner of the deck lid. The rear bumper ran straight across the car and wrapped around the body corners, with a center depression below the license plate holder. All 1959 Plymouths with V-8 power, including all Furys and Sport Suburbans, had small V-shaped emblems near the Plymouth signature on the rear deck lid.

"We doubt the Sport Fury will take a back seat to any of them in the final overall analysis based on performance, ride, handling, economy and workmanship. It's quite a package!"

Racer Brown, Hot Rod, November 1958

Sport/Fury Suburban

Series Number	Body/Style Number	Body Type & Seating	Factory Price	Shipping Weight	Production Total
MP2-H	41	4-dr Sedan-6P	$2,691	3,455 lbs.	30,149
MP2-H	43	4-dr Hardtop-6P	$2,771	3,505 lbs.	13,614
MP2-H	23	2-dr Hardtop Coupe-6P	$2,714	3,435 lbs.	21,494
MP2-H	45A	4-dr Sport Suburban-6P	$3,021	3,760 lbs.	7,224
MP2-H	45B	4-dr Sport Suburban-9P	$3,131	3,805 lbs.	9,549

SPORT FURY — (V-8) — SERIES MP2-P: The alphabetical suffixes appearing in Plymouth series codes were L for low-priced, M for mid-priced, H for high-priced, and P for premium-priced. In past years, the limited-edition Fury had been designated an H model and was actually a Belvedere. This season the Belvedere moved down a notch and the new top dog was the Sport Fury. Two body styles, sport coupe and convertible, were marketed only with V-8 power. They had several special identification features. For example, the upper branch of the dual side spears curved upward on the rear fenders, to repeat the general contour of the fins. The lower branch wrapped around the rear body corners and ran fully across the deck lid overhang. A silver anodized aluminum insert panel was standard and Fury signature script was placed inside the dual moldings at the rear. Positioned directly behind the moldings were large, colorful Forward Look medallions. Standard equipment for these cars included all Fury features plus swivel front seats, Sport deck lid tire cover stamping and custom, padded steering wheel. The "Golden Commando" wedge head V-8 with four-barrel carburetor and 305 hp was optional.

Sport Fury Series

Series Number	Body/Style Number	Body Type & Seating	Factory Price	Shipping Weight	Production Total
MP2-P	23	2-dr Hardtop Coupe-6P	$2,927	3,475 lbs.	17,867
MP2-P	27	2-dr Convertible-6P	$3,125	3,670 lbs.	5,990

Engines:

SAVOY/BELVEDERE SIX: Inline. L-head. Cast iron block. Displacement: 230.2 cid. Bore and stroke: 3.25 x 4.625 inches. Compression ratio: 8.0:1. Brake hp: 132 at 3600 rpm. Four main bearings. Solid valve lifters. Carburetor: Carter Type BBS one-barrel Model 2567S.

SAVOY/BELVEDERE/FURY/STATION WAGON V-8: Overhead valve. Cast iron block. Displacement: 317.6 cid. Bore and stroke: 3.906 x 3.312 inches. Compression ratio: 9.0:1. Brake hp: 230 at 4400 rpm. Five main bearings. Solid valve lifters. Carburetor: Carter Type BBD two-barrel Model 2824S.

SPORT FURY V-8: Overhead valve. Cast iron block. Displacement: 317.6 cid. Bore and stroke: 3.906 x 3.312 inches. Compression ratio: 9.0:1. Brake hp: 260 at 4400 rpm. Five main bearings. Solid valve lifters. Carburetor: Carter Type AFB four-barrel Model 2813S.

GOLDEN COMMANDO 395 V-8: Overhead valve. Cast iron block. Displacement: 360.8 cid. Bore and stroke: 4.12 x 3.38 inches. Compression ratio: 10.0:1. Brake hp: 305 at 4600 rpm. Five main bearings. Hydraulic valve lifters. Carburetor: Carter Type AFB four-barrel Model 2813S. (The "395" designation is based on this engine's output of 395 pound-feet of torque at 3000 rpm.)

CHASSIS FEATURES: Wheelbase: (all passenger cars) 118 inches; (all Suburbans) 122 inches. Overall length: (all passenger cars) 210 inches; (all Suburbans) 214.5 inches. Tires: (nine-passenger Suburban) 8.00 x 14-inch; (all other models) 7.50 x 14-inch.

OPTIONS: Power brakes ($36). Power steering ($63). Air conditioning ($372); for station wagons ($531). Push-button radio ($59). Rear seat speaker ($11). Dual rear antenna ($10). Fresh air heater and defroster ($58). Instant Air gas heater ($86). Tinted glass ($36). Windshield washer ($10). Rear window defogger ($19). Variable speed windshield wipers ($6). Headlight dimmer ($40). Contour floor mats, pair ($8). Regular floor mats, pair ($4). Two-Way power seat ($40). Power windows ($84). Swivel seat ($57). Constant-Level air suspension ($88). Power tailgate window, standard on nine-passenger Sport Suburban ($28). Padded dashboard ($12). Padded sun visor ($6). Padded steering wheel, standard Sport Fury ($12). Clear plastic seat covers ($30). Antifreeze ($6). Safety belts, each ($13). White sidewall tires ($28). Oversize tires, exchange ($13). Tutone paint ($15). Silver side moldings, standard Fury ($19). Station wagon storage compartment ($24). Bumper guards ($12). Front bumper guards ($10). Front bumper end guards ($16). Cigar lighter, standard Fury ($4). Wheel covers, standard Fury ($17). Rear foam seat cushion ($10). Tilt-type rearview mirror ($4). Automatic tilt mirror ($14). Left-hand remote control outside rearview mirror ($16). Dual mirrors, left-hand remote control ($23). Undercoating with hood pad ($13). Side view mirror ($6). Group 311: wheel covers, stone shields, electric clock and glovebox lock, standard Fury ($32). Group 312: back-up lights, windshield washer and variable speed wipers ($24). Group 313: right sun visor; front armrests and front foam cushion, standard Belvedere and Fury ($20). Three-speed manual transmission was standard. PowerFlite automatic transmission was optional with all but Golden Commando V-8 ($189). Overdrive transmission ($84). TorqueFlite automatic transmission ($227). V-8 318 cid/260 hp "Super Pack" engine ($32). V-8 360.8 cid/305 hp "Golden Commando" engine ($74). Four-barrel carburetor ($32). Oil filter ($10). Dual exhaust, V-8 only ($23). Available rear axle gear ratios (various).

HISTORICAL FOOTNOTES: The 1959 Plymouths were introduced in October 1958. Plymouth sales leaped 11.6 percent. Model year production peaked at 458,261 units. Calendar year sales of 413,204 cars were recorded. Plymouth again held third rank on industry sales charts, but Rambler was closing the gap. Plymouth's market share was a declining 13.19 percent. Fuel-injection was deleted from the power options list, but new extras included air suspension, swiveling seats for driver and passenger, the "Flite Sweep" rear deck lid with spare tire embossment; an electric headlight dimmer and a self-dimming illuminated rearview mirror. This was Plymouth's 30th anniversary and General Manager Harry E. Cheesbrough marked the production of the company's 11-millionth vehicle in 1959. The Golden Commando 395 engine, named for the fact that it developed 395 pound-feet of torque, was optional in all Plymouths except the Savoy business coupe. A Fury four-door hardtop was converted into the latest in a series of Chrysler turbine-engined cars and made a 576-mile "cross-country" reliability run. Well, it certainly didn't cross the country, but Chrysler's promotional copywriters described the endurance trial that way.

The 1959 Plymouth Sport Fury two-door hardtop reflects 1950s optimism as expressed in Virgil Exner-influenced styling.
Phil Hall Collection

1950-59 CHRYSLER PRICE GUIDE

Vehicle Condition Scale

1. **Excellent.** Restored to current maximum professional standards of quality in every area or perfect original with components operating and appearing as new. A 95-plus point show car that is not driven.

2. **Fine.** Well-restored or a combination of superior restoration and excellent original parts. An extremely well-maintained original vehicle showing minimal wear.

3. **Very good.** Completely operable original or older restoration. A good amateur restoration, or a combination of well-done restoration and good operable components or partially restored car with parts necessary to complete and/or valuable NOS parts.

4. **Good.** A driveable vehicle needing no work or only minor work to be functional. A deteriorated restoration or poor amateur restoration. All components may need restoration to be "excellent" but the car is useable "as is."

5. **Restorable.** Needs complete restoration of body, chassis, and interior. May or may not be running. Isn't weathered or stripped to the point of being useful only for parts.

6. **Parts car.** May or may not be running but is weathered, wrecked and/or stripped to the point of being useful primarily for parts.

Selected prices here are from the *2007 Collector Price Guide.*

CHRYSLER

1950 Royal Series, 6-cyl., 125.5" wb

	6	5	4	3	2	1
4d T&C Sta Wag	1,160	3,480	5,800	13,050	20,300	29,000
4d Sta Wag	1,240	3,720	6,200	13,950	21,700	31,000

1950 Windsor Series, 6-cyl., 125.5" wb

	6	5	4	3	2	1
2d Conv	1,200	3,600	6,000	13,500	21,000	30,000
2d HT	960	2,880	4,800	10,800	16,800	24,000

1950 Saratoga, 8-cyl., 131.5" wb

	6	5	4	3	2	1
2d Clb Cpe	800	2,400	4,000	9,000	14,000	20,000

1950 New Yorker, 8-cyl., 131.5" wb

	6	5	4	3	2	1
2d Conv	1,360	4,080	6,800	15,300	23,800	34,000
2d HT	1,120	3,360	5,600	12,600	19,600	28,000

1950 Town & Country, 8-cyl., 131.5" wb

	6	5	4	3	2	1
2d HT	2,240	6,720	11,200	25,200	39,200	56,000

1951-52 Windsor Series, 6-cyl., 125.5" wb

	6	5	4	3	2	1
2d Clb Cpe	800	2,400	4,000	9,000	14,000	20,000
4d T&C Sta Wag	1,160	3,480	5,800	13,050	20,300	29,000

1951-52 Windsor DeLuxe, 6-cyl., 125.5" wb

	6	5	4	3	2	1
2d Conv	1,120	3,360	5,600	12,600	19,600	28,000
2d HT	960	2,880	4,800	10,800	16,800	24,000

1951-52 Saratoga, V-8, 125.5" wb

	6	5	4	3	2	1
2d Conv (1952 only)	1,120	3,360	5,600	12,600	19,600	28,000
2d HT Nwpt (1952 only)	1,000	3,000	5,000	11,250	17,500	25,000
4d T&C Sta Wag (1951 only)	1,200	3,600	6,000	13,500	21,000	30,000

1951-52 Windsor or Saratoga, V-8, 125.5" wb

	6	5	4	3	2	1
4d Sed	820	2,460	4,100	9,230	14,350	20,500
4d T&C Sta Wag (1952 only)	1,120	3,360	5,600	12,600	19,600	28,000
4d Limo (1951 only)	900	2,700	4,500	10,130	15,750	22,500

1951-52 New Yorker, V-8, 131.5" wb

	6	5	4	3	2	1
2d Conv	1,240	3,720	6,200	13,950	21,700	31,000
2d HT	1,040	3,120	5,200	11,700	18,200	26,000
4d T&C Sta Wag (1951 only)	1,200	3,600	6,000	13,500	21,000	30,000

1953 Windsor Series, 6-cyl., 125.5" wb

	6	5	4	3	2	1
4d T&C Sta Wag	1,120	3,360	5,600	12,600	19,600	28,000

1953 Windsor DeLuxe Series, 6-cyl., 125.5" wb

	6	5	4	3	2	1
2d Conv	1,000	3,000	5,000	11,250	17,500	25,000
2d HT	920	2,760	4,600	10,350	16,100	23,000

1953 New Yorker, V-8, 125.5" wb

	6	5	4	3	2	1
2d HT	1,000	3,000	5,000	11,250	17,500	25,000
4d T&C Sta Wag	1,160	3,480	5,800	13,050	20,300	29,000

1953 New Yorker Deluxe, V-8, 125.5" wb

	6	5	4	3	2	1
2d Conv	1,200	3,600	6,000	13,500	21,000	30,000
2d HT	1,040	3,120	5,200	11,700	18,200	26,000

1954 Windsor DeLuxe Series, 6-cyl., 125.5" wb

	6	5	4	3	2	1
2d Conv	1,200	3,600	6,000	13,500	21,000	30,000
2d HT	1,040	3,120	5,200	11,700	18,200	26,000
4d T&C Sta Wag	1,040	3,120	5,200	11,700	18,200	26,000

1954 New Yorker Series, V-8, 125.5" wb

	6	5	4	3	2	1
2d HT	1,120	3,360	5,600	12,600	19,600	28,000
4d T&C Sta Wag	1,080	3,240	5,400	12,150	18,900	27,000

1954 New Yorker Series, V-8, 139.5" wb

	6	5	4	3	2	1
4d Sed	800	2,400	4,000	9,000	14,000	20,000

1954 New Yorker DeLuxe Series, V-8, 125.5" wb

	6	5	4	3	2	1
2d Conv	1,440	4,320	7,200	16,200	25,200	36,000
2d HT	1,160	3,480	5,800	13,050	20,300	29,000

1955 Windsor DeLuxe Series, V-8, 126" wb

	6	5	4	3	2	1
2d Conv	1,360	4,080	6,800	15,300	23,800	34,000
2d HT Newport	1,080	3,240	5,400	12,150	18,900	27,000
2d HT Nassau	1,040	3,120	5,200	11,700	18,200	26,000

1955 New Yorker Deluxe Series, V-8, 126" wb

	6	5	4	3	2	1
2d Conv	1,480	4,440	7,400	16,650	25,900	37,000
2d HT St. Regis	1,120	3,360	5,600	12,600	19,600	28,000
2d HT Newport	1,080	3,240	5,400	12,150	18,900	27,000
4d T&C Sta Wag	1,040	3,120	5,200	11,700	18,200	26,000

1955 300 Series, V-8, 126" wb

	6	5	4	3	2	1
2d Spt Cpe	2,080	6,240	10,400	23,400	36,400	52,000

1956 Windsor Series, V-8

	6	5	4	3	2	1
2d Conv	1,320	3,960	6,600	14,850	23,100	33,000
2d HT Newport	1,120	3,360	5,600	12,600	19,600	28,000
2d HT Nassau	1,080	3,240	5,400	12,150	18,900	27,000

1956 New Yorker Series, V-8

	6	5	4	3	2	1
2d Conv	1,440	4,320	7,200	16,200	25,200	36,000
2d HT St. Regis	1,200	3,600	6,000	13,500	21,000	30,000
2d HT Newport	1,160	3,480	5,800	13,050	20,300	29,000

1956 300 Letter Series "B", V-8

	6	5	4	3	2	1
2d HT	2,200	6,600	11,000	24,750	38,500	55,000

1957 Windsor Series, V-8

	6	5	4	3	2	1
2d HT	1,040	3,120	5,200	11,700	18,200	26,000

1957 Saratoga Series, V-8

	6	5	4	3	2	1
2d HT	1,120	3,360	5,600	12,600	19,600	28,000

1957 New Yorker Series, V-8

	6	5	4	3	2	1
2d Conv	1,440	4,320	7,200	16,200	25,200	36,000
2d HT	1,240	3,720	6,200	13,950	21,700	31,000

1957 300 Letter Series "C", V-8

	6	5	4	3	2	1
2d Conv	3,000	9,000	15,000	33,750	52,500	75,000
2d HT	2,280	6,840	11,400	25,650	39,900	57,000

1958 Windsor Series, V-8

	6	5	4	3	2	1
2d HT	1,000	3,000	5,000	11,250	17,500	25,000

1958 Saratoga Series, V-8

	6	5	4	3	2	1
2d HT	1,040	3,120	5,200	11,700	18,200	26,000

1958 New Yorker Series, V-8

	6	5	4	3	2	1
2d Conv	1,520	4,560	7,600	17,100	26,600	38,000
2d HT	1,120	3,360	5,600	12,600	19,600	28,000

1958 300 Letter Series "D"

	6	5	4	3	2	1
2d Conv	2,960	8,880	14,800	33,300	51,800	74,000
2d HT	2,240	6,720	11,200	25,200	39,200	56,000

NOTE: Add 40 percent for EFI.

1959 Windsor Series, V-8

	6	5	4	3	2	1
2d Conv	1,120	3,360	5,600	12,600	19,600	28,000
2d HT	920	2,760	4,600	10,350	16,100	23,000

1959 Saratoga Series, V-8

	6	5	4	3	2	1
2d HT	960	2,880	4,800	10,800	16,800	24,000

1959 New Yorker Series, V-8

	6	5	4	3	2	1
2d Conv	1,440	4,320	7,200	16,200	25,200	36,000
2d HT	1,040	3,120	5,200	11,700	18,200	26,000

1959 300 Letter Series "E", V-8

	6	5	4	3	2	1
2d Conv	2,920	8,760	14,600	32,850	51,100	73,000
2d HT	2,200	6,600	11,000	24,750	38,500	55,000

DE SOTO

1950 S-14 DeLuxe, 6-cyl.

	6	5	4	3	2	1
4d 8P Sed	720	2,160	3,600	8,100	12,600	18,000

1950 S-14 Custom, 6-cyl.

	6	5	4	3	2	1
2d Conv	1,160	3,480	5,800	13,050	20,300	29,000
2d HT Sptman	920	2,760	4,600	10,350	16,100	23,000
4d 6P Sta Wag	1,320	3,960	6,600	14,850	23,100	33,000

1951-52 DeLuxe, 6-cyl., 125.5" wb

	6	5	4	3	2	1
4d Sed	692	2,076	3,460	7,790	12,110	17,300
2d Clb Cpe	740	2,220	3,700	8,330	12,950	18,500

1951-52 Custom, 6-cyl., 125.5" wb

	6	5	4	3	2	1
2d HT Sptman	1,000	3,000	5,000	11,250	17,500	25,000
2d Conv	1,160	3,480	5,800	13,050	20,300	29,000
4d Sta Wag	920	2,760	4,600	10,350	16,100	23,000

1951-52 Custom, 6-cyl., 139.5" wb

	6	5	4	3	2	1
4d Sub	720	2,160	3,600	8,100	12,600	18,000

1951-52 Firedome, V-8, 125.5" wb (1952 only)

	6	5	4	3	2	1
2d HT Sptman	1,040	3,120	5,200	11,700	18,200	26,000
2d Conv	1,280	3,840	6,400	14,400	22,400	32,000
4d Sta Wag	920	2,760	4,600	10,350	16,100	23,000

1953-54 Powermaster Six, 6-cyl., 125.5" wb

	6	5	4	3	2	1
2d HT Sptman (1953 only)	920	2,760	4,600	10,350	16,100	23,000

1953-54 Firedome, V-8, 125.5" wb

	6	5	4	3	2	1
2d HT Sptman	1,040	3,120	5,200	11,700	18,200	26,000
2d Conv	1,280	3,840	6,400	14,400	22,400	32,000
4d Sta Wag	880	2,640	4,400	9,900	15,400	22,000

1955 Firedome, V-8

	6	5	4	3	2	1
2d HT Sptman	1,120	3,360	5,600	12,600	19,600	28,000
2d Conv	1,280	3,840	6,400	14,400	22,400	32,000
4d Sta Wag	1,080	3,240	5,400	12,150	18,900	27,000

1955 Fireflite, V-8

	6	5	4	3	2	1
2d HT Sptman	1,160	3,480	5,800	13,050	20,300	29,000
2d Conv	1,320	3,960	6,600	14,850	23,100	33,000

1956 Firedome, V-8

	6	5	4	3	2	1
2d HT Sev	1,040	3,120	5,200	11,700	18,200	26,000
2d HT Sptman	1,120	3,360	5,600	12,600	19,600	28,000
2d Conv	1,320	3,960	6,600	14,850	23,100	33,000

1956 Fireflite, V-8

	6	5	4	3	2	1
2d HT Sptman	1,160	3,480	5,800	13,050	20,300	29,000
2d Conv	1,360	4,080	6,800	15,300	23,800	34,000
2d Conv IPC	1,640	4,920	8,200	18,450	28,700	41,000

1956 Adventurer

	6	5	4	3	2	1
2d HT	1,200	3,600	6,000	13,500	21,000	30,000

1957 Firesweep, V-8, 122" wb

	6	5	4	3	2	1
2d HT Sptman	1,000	3,000	5,000	11,250	17,500	25,000

1957 Firedome, V-8, 126" wb

	6	5	4	3	2	1
2d HT Sptman	1,040	3,120	5,200	11,700	18,200	26,000
2d Conv	1,640	4,920	8,200	18,450	28,700	41,000

1957 Fireflite, V-8, 126" wb

	6	5	4	3	2	1
2d HT Sptman	1,080	3,240	5,400	12,150	18,900	27,000
2d Conv	1,880	5,640	9,400	21,150	32,900	47,000

1957 Fireflite Adventurer, 126" wb

	6	5	4	3	2	1
2d HT	1,520	4,560	7,600	17,100	26,600	38,000
2d Conv	2,600	7,800	13,000	29,250	45,500	65,000

1958 Firesweep, V-8

	6	5	4	3	2	1
2d HT Sptman	1,000	3,000	5,000	11,250	17,500	25,000
2d Conv	1,560	4,680	7,800	17,550	27,300	39,000

1958 Firedome, V-8

	6	5	4	3	2	1
2d HT Sptman	1,040	3,120	5,200	11,700	18,200	26,000
2d Conv	1,640	4,920	8,200	18,450	28,700	41,000

1958 Fireflite, V-8

	6	5	4	3	2	1
2d HT Sptman	1,080	3,240	5,400	12,150	18,900	27,000
2d Conv	1,880	5,640	9,400	21,150	32,900	47,000

1958 Adventurer, V-8

	6	5	4	3	2	1
2d HT	1,520	4,560	7,600	17,100	26,600	38,000
2d Conv	2,600	7,800	13,000	29,250	45,500	65,000

NOTE: With EFI, value inestimable.

1959 Firesweep, V-8

	6	5	4	3	2	1
2d HT Sptman	960	2,880	4,800	10,800	16,800	24,000
2d Conv	1,520	4,560	7,600	17,100	26,600	38,000

1959 Firedome, V-8

	6	5	4	3	2	1
2d HT Sptman	1,000	3,000	5,000	11,250	17,500	25,000
2d Conv	1,600	4,800	8,000	18,000	28,000	40,000

1959 Fireflite, V-8

	6	5	4	3	2	1
2d HT Sptman	1,040	3,120	5,200	11,700	18,200	26,000
2d Conv	1,840	5,520	9,200	20,700	32,200	46,000

1959 Adventurer, V-8

	6	5	4	3	2	1
2d HT	1,320	3,960	6,600	14,850	23,100	33,000
2d Conv	2,200	6,600	11,000	24,750	38,500	55,000

DODGE

1950 Series D33 Wayfarer, 6-cyl., 115" wb

	6	5	4	3	2	1
2d Rds	1,240	3,720	6,200	13,950	21,700	31,000

1950 Series D34 Coronet, 123.5" wb - 137.5" wb, (*)

	6	5	4	3	2	1
2d Conv	1,240	3,720	6,200	13,950	21,700	31,000
2d HT Dipl	840	2,520	4,200	9,450	14,700	21,000
4d Sta Wag	2,200	6,600	11,000	24,750	38,500	55,000

1951-52 Wayfarer Series D41, 6-cyl., 115" wb

	6	5	4	3	2	1
2d Rds (1951 only)	1,160	3,480	5,800	13,050	20,300	29,000

1951-52 Coronet Series D42, 6-cyl., 123.5" wb

	6	5	4	3	2	1
2d HT Dipl	920	2,760	4,600	10,350	16,100	23,000
2d Conv	1,160	3,480	5,800	13,050	20,300	29,000

1953 Series D44 Coronet, V-8, 119" wb

	6	5	4	3	2	1
4d Sed	680	2,040	3,400	7,650	11,900	17,000

1953 Series D48 Coronet, V-8, 119" wb - 114" wb, (*)

	6	5	4	3	2	1
2d HT Dipl	880	2,640	4,400	9,900	15,400	22,000
2d Conv	1,160	3,480	5,800	13,050	20,300	29,000

1954 Series D52 Coronet, 6-cyl., 114" wb

	6	5	4	3	2	1
4d 8P Sta Wag	800	2,400	4,000	9,000	14,000	20,000

1954 Series D50-2 Coronet, V-8, 119" wb

	6	5	4	3	2	1
4d Sed	692	2,076	3,460	7,790	12,110	17,300
2d Clb Cpe	700	2,100	3,500	7,880	12,250	17,500

1954 Series D53-2 Coronet, V-8, 114" wb

	6	5	4	3	2	1
4d 2S Sta Wag	780	2,340	3,900	8,780	13,650	19,500
4d 3S Sta Wag	820	2,460	4,100	9,230	14,350	20,500

1954 Series D50-3 Royal, V-8, 119" wb

	6	5	4	3	2	1
4d Sed	760	2,280	3,800	8,550	13,300	19,000
2d Clb Cpe	760	2,280	3,800	8,550	13,300	19,000

1954 Series D53-3 Royal, V-8, 114" wb

	6	5	4	3	2	1
2d HT	1,000	3,000	5,000	11,250	17,500	25,000
2d Conv	1,200	3,600	6,000	13,500	21,000	30,000
2d Pace Car Replica Conv	1,320	3,960	6,600	14,850	23,100	33,000

1955 Coronet, V-8, 120" wb

	6	5	4	3	2	1
2d HT	1,000	3,000	5,000	11,250	17,500	25,000
4d 8P Sta Wag	800	2,400	4,000	9,000	14,000	20,000

1955 Royal, V-8, 120" wb

	6	5	4	3	2	1
2d HT	1,040	3,120	5,200	11,700	18,200	26,000
4d 8P Sta Wag	840	2,520	4,200	9,450	14,700	21,000

1955 Custom Royal, V-8, 120" wb

	6	5	4	3	2	1
2d HT	1,080	3,240	5,400	12,150	18,900	27,000
2d Conv	1,360	4,080	6,800	15,300	23,800	34,000

NOTE: Add 10 percent for La-Femme.

1956 Coronet, V-8, 120" wb

	6	5	4	3	2	1
2d HT	960	2,880	4,800	10,800	16,800	24,000
2d Conv	1,520	4,560	7,600	17,100	26,600	38,000

1956 Royal, V-8, 120" wb

	6	5	4	3	2	1
2d HT	1,040	3,120	5,200	11,700	18,200	26,000
4d 8P Sta Wag	820	2,460	4,100	9,230	14,350	20,500

1956 Custom Royal, V-8, 120" wb

	6	5	4	3	2	1
2d HT	1,120	3,360	5,600	12,600	19,600	28,000
2d Conv	1,560	4,680	7,800	17,550	27,300	39,000

NOTE: Add 30 percent for D500 option. Add 10 percent for Golden Lancer, La Femme or Texan.

1957 Coronet, V-8, 122" wb

	6	5	4	3	2	1
2d HT	960	2,880	4,800	10,800	16,800	24,000

1957 Coronet Lancer

	6	5	4	3	2	1
2d Conv	1,520	4,560	7,600	17,100	26,600	38,000

DODGE cont.

1957 Royal, V-8, 122" wb

	6	5	4	3	2	1
2d HT	1,200	3,600	6,000	13,500	21,000	30,000

1957 Royal Lancer

	6	5	4	3	2	1
2d Conv	1,680	5,040	8,400	18,900	29,400	42,000

1957 Custom Royal, V-8, 122" wb

	6	5	4	3	2	1
2d HT	1,240	3,720	6,200	13,950	21,700	31,000
4d 9P Sta Wag	900	2,700	4,500	10,130	15,750	22,500

1957 Custom Royal Lancer

	6	5	4	3	2	1
2d Conv	1,800	5,400	9,000	20,250	31,500	45,000

NOTE: Add 30 percent for D500 option.

1958 Coronet, V-8, 122" wb

	6	5	4	3	2	1
2d HT	920	2,760	4,600	10,350	16,100	23,000
2d Conv	1,480	4,440	7,400	16,650	25,900	37,000

1958 Royal

	6	5	4	3	2	1
2d HT	1,040	3,120	5,200	11,700	18,200	26,000

1958 Custom Royal

	6	5	4	3	2	1
2d HT	1,040	3,120	5,200	11,700	18,200	26,000
2d Conv	1,760	5,280	8,800	19,800	30,800	44,000

NOTE: Add 30 percent for D500 option, 50 percent for E.F.I. and Super D500.

1959 Coronet, V-8

	6	5	4	3	2	1
2d HT	880	2,640	4,400	9,900	15,400	22,000
2d Conv	1,440	4,320	7,200	16,200	25,200	36,000

1959 Royal, V-8

	6	5	4	3	2	1
2d HT	920	2,760	4,600	10,350	16,100	23,000

1959 Custom Royal, V-8

	6	5	4	3	2	1
2d HT	960	2,880	4,800	10,800	16,800	24,000
2d Conv	1,720	5,160	8,600	19,350	30,100	43,000

1959 Sierra, V-8

	6	5	4	3	2	1
4d 9P Cus Wag	840	2,520	4,200	9,450	14,700	21,000

NOTE: Add 30 percent for D500 option.

The beauty of the 1954 Chrysler Corporation offerings in full color.

IMPERIAL

1950 Imperial, 8-cyl., 131.5" wb

	6	5	4	3	2	1
4d Sed	840	2,520	4,200	9,450	14,700	21,000

1950 Crown Imperial, 8-cyl., 145.5" wb

	6	5	4	3	2	1
4d Sed	880	2,640	4,400	9,900	15,400	22,000

1951-52 Imperial, V-8, 131.5" wb

	6	5	4	3	2	1
2d Conv (1951 only)	1,200	3,600	6,000	13,500	21,000	30,000
2d HT	1,080	3,240	5,400	12,150	18,900	27,000

1951-52 Crown Imperial, V-8, 145.5" wb

	6	5	4	3	2	1
4d Sed	880	2,640	4,400	9,900	15,400	22,000
4d Limo	1,000	3,000	5,000	11,250	17,500	25,000

1953 Custom Imperial Series, V-8, 133.5" wb

	6	5	4	3	2	1
4d Twn Limo	920	2,760	4,600	10,350	16,100	23,000

1953 Custom Imperial, V-8, 131.5" wb

	6	5	4	3	2	1
2d HT	1,240	3,720	6,200	13,950	21,700	31,000

1954 Custom Imperial, V-8, 133.5" wb

	6	5	4	3	2	1
4d Limo	1,000	3,000	5,000	11,250	17,500	25,000

1954 Custom Imperial, V-8, 131" wb

	6	5	4	3	2	1
2d HT Newport	1,240	3,720	6,200	13,950	21,700	31,000

1954 Crown Imperial, V-8, 145.5" wb

	6	5	4	3	2	1
4d Sed	940	2,820	4,700	10,580	16,450	23,500

1955 Imperial, V-8

	6	5	4	3	2	1
2d HT Newport	1,240	3,720	6,200	13,950	21,700	31,000

1955 Crown Imperial, V-8

	6	5	4	3	2	1
4d 8P Sed	1,000	3,000	5,000	11,250	17,500	25,000

1956 Imperial, V-8

	6	5	4	3	2	1
4d HT S Hamp	960	2,880	4,800	10,800	16,800	24,000
2d HT S Hamp	1,240	3,720	6,200	13,950	21,700	31,000

1956 Crown Imperial, V-8

	6	5	4	3	2	1
4d 8P Sed	1,040	3,120	5,200	11,700	18,200	26,000

1957 Imperial Custom, V-8

	6	5	4	3	2	1
2d HT S Hamp	1,160	3,480	5,800	13,050	20,300	29,000
4d HT S Hamp	1,040	3,120	5,200	11,700	18,200	26,000

1957 Imperial Crown, V-8

	6	5	4	3	2	1
2d Conv	1,600	4,800	8,000	18,000	28,000	40,000
2d HT S Hamp	1,200	3,600	6,000	13,500	21,000	30,000
4d HT S Hamp	1,080	3,240	5,400	12,150	18,900	27,000

1957 Imperial LeBaron, V-8

	6	5	4	3	2	1
4d Sed	1,040	3,120	5,200	11,700	18,200	26,000
4d HT S Hamp	1,120	3,360	5,600	12,600	19,600	28,000

1957 Crown Imperial Ghia, V-8

	6	5	4	3	2	1
4d 8P Limo	1,280	3,840	6,400	14,400	22,400	32,000

1958 Imperial Custom, V-8

	6	5	4	3	2	1
2d HT S Hamp	1,120	3,360	5,600	12,600	19,600	28,000
4d HT S Hamp	1,000	3,000	5,000	11,250	17,500	25,000

1958 Imperial Crown, V-8

	6	5	4	3	2	1
2d Conv	1,640	4,920	8,200	18,450	28,700	41,000
2d HT S Hamp	1,200	3,600	6,000	13,500	21,000	30,000
4d HT S Hamp	1,040	3,120	5,200	11,700	18,200	26,000

1958 Imperial LeBaron, V-8

	6	5	4	3	2	1
4d Sed	1,040	3,120	5,200	11,700	18,200	26,000
4d HT S Hamp	1,120	3,360	5,600	12,600	19,600	28,000

1958 Crown Imperial Ghia, V-8

	6	5	4	3	2	1
4d Limo	1,280	3,840	6,400	14,400	22,400	32,000

1959 Imperial Custom, V-8

	6	5	4	3	2	1
2d HT S Hamp	1,120	3,360	5,600	12,600	19,600	28,000

1959 Imperial Crown, V-8

	6	5	4	3	2	1
2d Conv	1,680	5,040	8,400	18,900	29,400	42,000
2d HT S Hamp	1,200	3,600	6,000	13,500	21,000	30,000

1959 Imperial LeBaron, V-8

	6	5	4	3	2	1
4d Sed	880	2,640	4,400	9,900	15,400	22,000
4d HT S Hamp	1,000	3,000	5,000	11,250	17,500	25,000

1959 Crown Imperial Ghia, V-8

	6	5	4	3	2	1
4d Limo	1,280	3,840	6,400	14,400	22,400	32,000

PLYMOUTH

1950 Special DeLuxe, 6-cyl., 118.5" wb

	6	5	4	3	2	1
2d Conv	1,000	3,000	5,000	11,250	17,500	25,000
4d Sta Wag	1,280	3,840	6,400	14,400	22,400	32,000

1951-52 P23 Cranbrook, 6-cyl., 118.5" wb

	6	5	4	3	2	1
2d HT	800	2,400	4,000	9,000	14,000	20,000
2d Conv	1,000	3,000	5,000	11,250	17,500	25,000

1953 P24-2 Cranbrook, 6-cyl., 114" wb

	6	5	4	3	2	1
2d HT	840	2,520	4,200	9,450	14,700	21,000
2d Conv	1,080	3,240	5,400	12,150	18,900	27,000

1954 P25-1 Plaza, 6-cyl., 114" wb

	6	5	4	3	2	1
4d Sed	512	1,536	2,560	5,760	8,960	12,800
2d Sta Wag	700	2,100	3,500	7,880	12,250	17,500

1954 P25-3 Belvedere, 6-cyl., 114" wb

	6	5	4	3	2	1
2d HT	920	2,760	4,600	10,350	16,100	23,000
2d Conv	1,120	3,360	5,600	12,600	19,600	28,000

1955 Belvedere, V-8, 115" wb

	6	5	4	3	2	1
2d HT	1,000	3,000	5,000	11,250	17,500	25,000
2d Conv	1,240	3,720	6,200	13,950	21,700	31,000

1956 Savoy, V-8, 115" wb

	6	5	4	3	2	1
2d HT	960	2,880	4,800	10,800	16,800	24,000

1956 Belvedere, V-8, 115" wb

	6	5	4	3	2	1
2d HT	1,120	3,360	5,600	12,600	19,600	28,000
2d Conv	1,320	3,960	6,600	14,850	23,100	33,000

1956 Suburban, V-8, 115" wb

	6	5	4	3	2	1
4d Spt Sta Wag	840	2,520	4,200	9,450	14,700	21,000

1956 Fury, V-8, (avail. as V-8 only)

	6	5	4	3	2	1
2d HT	1,400	4,200	7,000	15,750	24,500	35,000

1957-58 Savoy, V-8

	6	5	4	3	2	1
2d HT	920	2,760	4,600	10,350	16,100	23,000

1957-58 Belvedere, V-8, 118" wb

	6	5	4	3	2	1
2d HT	1,280	3,840	6,400	14,400	22,400	32,000

8-cyl. only)

	6	5	4	3	2	1
2d Conv	1,800	5,400	9,000	20,250	31,500	45,000

1957-58 Suburban, V-8, 122" wb

	6	5	4	3	2	1
4d Spt Sta Wag	920	2,760	4,600	10,350	16,100	23,000

1957-58 Fury, V-8, 118" wb

	6	5	4	3	2	1
2d HT	1,440	4,320	7,200	16,200	25,200	36,000

NOTE: Add 25 percent for 350 cid/305 hp V-8. Add 50 percent for Bendix EFI.

1959 Belvedere, V-8, 118" wb

	6	5	4	3	2	1
2d HT	880	2,640	4,400	9,900	15,400	22,000
2d Conv	1,400	4,200	7,000	15,750	24,500	35,000

1959 Fury, V-8, 118" wb

	6	5	4	3	2	1
2d HT	1,000	3,000	5,000	11,250	17,500	25,000

1959 Sport Fury, V-8, 118" wb

	6	5	4	3	2	1
2d HT	960	2,880	4,800	10,800	16,800	24,000
2d Conv	1,360	4,080	6,800	15,300	23,800	34,000

NOTE: Add 30 percent for Golden Commando V-8.

Bolster Your Collecting Knowledge with Insider Expertise!

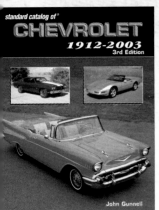

Standard Catalog of® Chevrolet 1912-2003

3rd Edition
by John Gunnell

America's best-selling automobile has come a long way, from the 1912 "Classic Six" – a large, five-passenger touring sedan. This user-friendly and comprehensive guide to every Chevrolet ever built between 1912 and 2003 delivers key facts, detailed photos and collector-market values.

Additional features include:
- Expanded VIN information and factory color scheme details
- Listings with equipment and technical specifications and production data

Softcover • 8-1/2 x 11 • 456 pages
1,000+ b&w photos • 8-page color section

Item# AV03 • $24.99

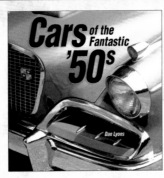

Cars of the Fantastic '50s

by Dan B. Lyons

Take a nostalgic trip back to the days of big bumpers, huge tail fins and chrome in this superb pictorial reference! Fifty of the best Ford, Chrysler, Chevy and independently manufactured cars are covered in technical and stunning photographic detail.

This must-have collector guide delivers:
- A unique picturesque journey through the era of automobile innovation
- Historic and performance details in an eye-catching package

Hardcover • 10-3/4x10-3/4• 192 pages
250+ color photos

Item# CF02 • $29.99

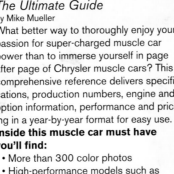

Chrysler Muscle Cars

The Ultimate Guide
by Mike Mueller

What better way to thoroughly enjoy your passion for super-charged muscle car power than to immerse yourself in page after page of Chrysler muscle cars? This comprehensive reference delivers specifications, production numbers, engine and option information, performance and pricing in a year-by-year format for easy use.

Inside this muscle car must have you'll find:
- More than 300 color photos
- High-performance models such as Super Bee, Charger, Challenger, Cuda and Dart

Softcover • 8-1/4 x 10-7/8 • 224 pages
300+ color photos

Item# CHYM • $24.99

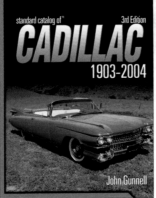

Standard Catalog of® Cadillac 1903-2004

3rd Edition
by John Gunnell

Feed your passion for Cadillac with the most comprehensive reference available – *Standard Catalog of® Cadillac*. From full-color photos to year-by-year breakdown of models, you'll find specifications, production figures, options, historical footnotes and evolution of this classic line of luxury vehicles.

This one-of-a-kind guide features:
- Coverage of every model of Caddy ever made
- More than 500 brilliant color photos for identifying and enjoying your favorite Cadillac

Softcover • 8-1/4 x 10-7/8 • 336 pages
500+ color photos

Item# AL03 • $27.99

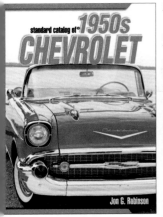

Standard Catalog of® 1950s Chevrolet

by Jon G. Robinson

There's nothing that compares to this era of innovation, and no other book on the market delivers the wealth of details like the Standard Catalog series. This book offers a perfect combination of technical and production details, rich nostalgia, and 300 stunning color photos.

In addition to the book's technical details, you'll discover:
- A full price guide to '50s Chevy cars to aid in any purchases or sales
- Drive Report features cover performance

Softcover • 8-1/4 x 10-7/8 • 224 pages
300+ color photos

Item# FTCHV • $24.99

Chrysler Muscle

Detroit's Mightiest Machines
by Bill Holder and Phil Kunz

Muscle cars radiate an attitude that's hip, youthful and bold – thanks in large part to the MOPAR marketing machine. Using eye-popping colors and entertaining cartoon mascots, the muscle car legacy was put into motion. This book chronicles the mystique surround Chrysler's muscle car family and looks at what mighty marketing did to create a legendary ride.

Inside this unique guide you'll find:
- More than 200 color photos of legendary MOPAR cars from the late 1960s and early 1970s
- Outrageous print advertising campaigns

Softcover • 8-1/4 x 10-7/8 • 160 pages
200+ color photos

Item# MOPAR • $24.99

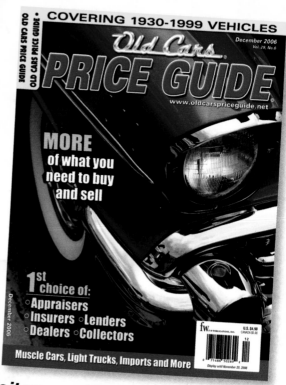